Empowering
Women

Empowering Women

Legal Rights and Economic Opportunities in Africa

Mary Hallward-Driemeier and Tazeen Hasan

A copublication of the Agence Française de Développement and the World Bank

ISBN (paper): 978-0-8213-9533-2
ISBN (electronic): 978-0-8213-9534-9
DOI: 10.1596/978-0-8213-9533-2

Cover photo: Dana Smillie, World Bank. *Cover design:* Debra Naylor, Naylor Design, Inc.

Library of Congress Cataloging-in-Publication Data
Hallward-Driemeier, Mary, 1966–
  Empowering women : legal rights and economic opportunities in Africa / by Mary Hallward-Driemeier and Tazeen Hasan.
    p. cm.
  Includes bibliographical references and index.
    ISBN 978-0-8213-9533-2 — ISBN 978-0-8213-9534-9 (electronic)
  1. Women—Africa—Economic conditions. 2. Women—Africa—Social conditions. 3. Women's rights—Africa. 4. Sex discrimination against women—Africa. I. Hasan, Tazeen. II. Title.
    HQ1787.H35 2012
    331.4096—dc23
                                                                            2012010863

Africa Development Forum Series

The **Africa Development Forum series** was created in 2009 to focus on issues of significant relevance to Sub-Saharan Africa's social and economic development. Its aim is both to record the state of the art on a specific topic and to contribute to ongoing local, regional, and global policy debates. It is designed specifically to provide practitioners, scholars, and students with the most up-to-date research results while highlighting the promise, challenges, and opportunities that exist on the continent.

The series is sponsored by the Agence Française de Développement and the World Bank. The manuscripts chosen for publication represent the highest quality in each institution and have been selected for their relevance to the development agenda. Working together with a shared sense of mission and interdisciplinary purpose, the two institutions are committed to a common search for new insights and new ways of analyzing the development realities of the Sub-Saharan Africa region.

Advisory Committee Members

Agence Française de Développement
Pierre Jacquet, Chief Economist
Robert Peccoud, Director of Research

World Bank
Shantayanan Devarajan, Chief Economist, Africa Region
Célestin Monga, Senior Adviser, Development Economics and Africa Region
Santiago Pombo-Bejarano, Editor-in-Chief, Office of the Publisher

Sub-Saharan Africa

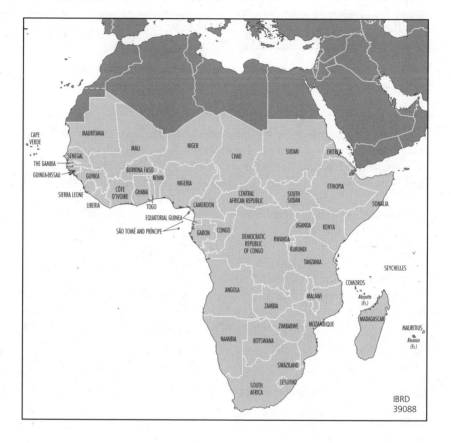

IBRD
39088

Titles in the Africa Development Forum Series

Contents

Boxes

Figures

Tables

Foreword

Expanding opportunities for women has intrinsic value. It is also instrumental in fostering development. Realizing the potential of all people is needed to ensure growth, productivity, and a vibrant society. *Empowering Women: Legal Rights and Economic Opportunities in Africa* brings new data and analysis to recommend how best to move this agenda forward.

Strengthening the incentives and abilities to pursue opportunities expands women's economic empowerment. Property rights are central in this process because they ensure that people can reap the benefits of their efforts. Policy makers shape property rights through laws and regulations, and the legal system supports their enforcement. Yet despite their importance, before the publication of this volume, no study had looked systematically across Sub-Saharan Africa to examine the impacts on women's economic empowerment.

Assessments of laws and regulations governing the business environment rarely examine whether they have different impacts on women and men. They fail to do so partly because they look at issues such as how to register property or enforce contracts, presuming that everyone can own property or enter into a contract. A major contribution of this book is to demonstrate that in many Sub-Saharan countries, economic rights for women and men are not equal. Areas of family law, inheritance law, and land law are not generally included in studies of business regulations. But it is precisely these areas of law that define legal capacity and the ability to own and control assets—and it is in these areas that explicit gender gaps are most likely.

To document the gender gaps in formal economic rights, the book draws on the Women's Legal and Economic Empowerment Database for Africa (Women–LEED–Africa). Covering all 47 countries in Sub-Saharan Africa, this new database provides detailed indicators and links to statutes, constitutions, and international conventions on issues of legal capacity, marital property, land ownership, and labor law. The book's recommendations focus not only on specific substantive changes to the law but also on ensuring that rights are enforced and the system of justice is made more accessible. The recommendations also target women, showing how a few key decisions—such as registering a marriage, choosing a marital property regime, titling assets and businesses, and writing wills—can have dramatic impacts on their rights to property.

The book illustrates the benefits of bringing law and economics together. For lawyers, it provides evidence on how laws and legal reforms can improve economic outcomes. Links to specific statutes and case law facilitate comparisons of de jure gender gaps in rights, and discussions of the de facto functioning of the legal system show how it can hamper women's access to justice. For economists, the book demonstrates that a broader set of laws beyond business regulations has direct gender impacts. The rich set of programs and approaches to expand access to the legal system the book discusses invite further research into their effectiveness in expanding women's access to credit, investment, and entrepreneurship.

This book provides compelling evidence that the areas of law it examines need to be addressed—in terms of substance, enforcement, awareness, and access—if economic opportunities for women in Sub-Saharan Africa are to continue to expand.

Ngozi Okonjo-Iweala
Coordinating Minister of Economy and
Minister of Finance for the Federal Republic of Nigeria

Preface

This book looks at the effect of legal and economic rights on women's economic opportunities. It focuses on entrepreneurship because women in Africa are active entrepreneurs, and the links between property rights and the ability to enter contracts in one's own name affect entrepreneurial activities.

The laws that are the focus of this book are not business laws and regulations, which are generally gender blind and presuppose that individuals can own property or enter into contracts. Instead, the book examines family, inheritance, and land laws, which often restrict these rights in ways that hurt women. This book surveys constitutions and statutes in all 47 countries in Sub-Saharan Africa to document where gender gaps in these laws impinge on women's legal capacity, property rights, or both. The results are introduced in a new database: the Women's Legal and Economic Empowerment Database for Africa (Women–LEED–Africa).

The book also looks at some labor law issues, such as restrictions on the types of industries or hours of work in which women may engage and provisions for equal pay for work of equal value. These laws affect women as employees and influence the attractiveness of wage employment versus entrepreneurship. They were also selected because they affect the choice of enterprise women may run. The equal pay for work of equal value provisions are also of interest as an indicator of the recognition of women's broader economic rights.

This book provides a series of indicators that show whether a country does or does not provide particular legal provisions. Several points are worth emphasizing in interpreting these indicators. First, the indicators are binary; there is no attempt to differentiate between small and large gender gaps. Second, the indicators are not used to generate an index or otherwise aggregate the indicators; no weights are given to differentiate the relative importance of different sets of laws. Third, the indicators reflect whether certain legal provisions are recognized in a country or not; because the link between the indicator and gender gaps is not always straightforward, care must be taken in making value judgments. Although some indicators reveal that women are treated equally or identify gender differences in treatment, others do not. For example, the database includes indicators on whether customary or religious law is recognized as a formal source of law. Although recognition of these sources of law can have implications for women's rights (as discussed in chapter 3), it does not necessarily imply that women's rights are stronger or weaker. Conversely, the inclusion of some protections for women's rights may reflect not the strong standing of women but rather the fact that gender equality is not seen as axiomatic and needs to be explicitly stated.

Chapter 1 argues for the importance of broadening the set of laws that need to be examined in order to determine how law affects women's economic opportunities. Chapters 2 and 3 focus on formal rights and how they have been upheld in court decisions. Chapter 4 examines the gap between laws on the books and practice on the ground. Chapter 5 looks at how both the substance of law and women's access to justice issues can be improved to expand women's ability to pursue economic opportunities.

Most assessments of the business climate for women overlook the areas of law this study examines. Policy makers need to focus more closely on closing these legal—and other—gaps in order to expand the economic opportunities for women in Sub-Saharan Africa.

A companion volume, *Enterprising Women: Expanding Opportunities in Africa* (forthcoming 2013), examines in more detail ways to improve women's ability to move into higher return activities. Drawing on the findings of this report, it finds a significant role for improving women's legal and economic rights.

Acknowledgments

This book was written with important contributions from colleagues at the World Bank. In addition to contributions to chapters 1, 2, and 4, Mark Blackden provided invaluable assistance by introducing the authors to key local partners, moderating workshops, and pushing the authors to broaden the scope of the work. Tazeen Hasan, Jane Kamangu, and Emilia Lobti collected the information on the formal legal economic rights of women in the region, assembling the *Legal and Economic Empowerment Database* (Women–LEED–Africa). They also brought together and distilled the lessons from case law that, together with the database, form the basis of the analysis in this book.

Insightful comments and suggestions were provided by participants in workshops in Addis Ababa, Cape Town, Dakar, Nairobi, and Washington DC, from Cameroon, the Democratic Republic of Congo, Ethiopia, The Gambia, Ghana, Kenya, Malawi, Mali, Nigeria, Rwanda, Senegal, South Africa, Sudan, Tanzania, and Uganda. Particular thanks are given to Mekonnen Firew Ayano, Reena Badiani, Elena Bardasi, Lisa Bhansali, Christina Biebesheimer, Rea Abada Chiongson, Aline Coudouel, Susan Deller Ross, Asli Demirgüç-Kunt, Deval Desai, Shanta Devarajan, Louise Fox, Anne Goldstein, Markus Goldstein, Sarah Iqbal, Sandra Joireman, Maureen Lewis, Waleed Malik, Andrew Mason, Nicholas Menzies, Ferenc Molnar, Ana Maria Munoz Boudet, Pierella Paci, Rita Ramalho, Ana Revenga, Bob Rijkers, Caroline Sage, Carolina Sanchez-Paramo, Sudhir Shetty, Sevi Simavi, and Vijay Tata for their comments and suggestions. The text benefited from the editorial services of Bruce Ross-Larson.

Financial support from the Dutch BNPP Trust Fund, and the World Bank's Gender Action Plan, the Africa Chief Economist Regional Studies Program, the Finance and Private Sector Development Chief Economist Office, and the Development Economics Department is gratefully acknowledged. The study was carried out under the overall guidance of Marilou Uy, director for Finance and Private Sector Development in Africa, and Shanta Devarajan, chief economist for the Africa Region.

About the Authors

Mary Hallward-Driemeier is a lead economist and adviser to the Chief Economist of the World Bank. Since joining the World Bank as a Young Professional in 1997, she has published articles on entrepreneurship, firm productivity, the impact of the investment climate on firm performance, the impact of financial crises, and determinants of foreign direct investment. She was the deputy director for *World Development Report 2005: A Better Investment Climate for Everyone*. Mary helped establish the World Bank's Enterprise Surveys Program, now covering more than 100,000 enterprises in 100 countries. She is also a founding member of the Microeconomics of Growth Network and is co-leading the Jobs Knowledge Platform. She received her MS in development economics from Oxford University as a Rhodes Scholar and her PhD in economics from the Massachusetts Institute of Technology.

Tazeen Hasan is a lawyer with expertise in finance and private sector development and justice and gender issues. She was the legal specialist on the team for *World Development Report 2012: Gender Equality and Development* and the MENA companion report, "Opening Doors: Gender Equality in the Middle East and North Africa." Prior to joining the World Bank Group, Tazeen practiced as a barrister in the United Kingdom for 10 years, specializing in civil and commercial law. While living in Kenya, she also worked on legal issues relating to the conflict in South Sudan; she is currently a trustee of the International Association for Digital Publications, a nongovernmental organization focusing on higher education in developing countries. Tazeen obtained a masters (LLM) in international law from the London School of Economics and a BA in law from Pembroke College, University of Oxford. She is a member of the London Bar.

Abbreviations

CEDAW	Convention on the Elimination of All Forms of Discrimination against Women
GDP	gross domestic product
ILO	International Labour Organization
Women–LEED–Africa	Women's Legal and Economic Empowerment Database for Africa

Overview

Most assessments of the business climate for women look at regulations, availability of credit, and similar features of the economy. They overlook the areas of the law this book examines: marriage, divorce, inheritance, land rights, and labor. But these are the laws that determine who has control over assets, thereby influencing the types of economic opportunities that are available. Men and women in Sub-Saharan Africa are all too often treated differently in all of these areas—almost always to the detriment of women. To expand economic opportunities for women—particularly opportunities for entrepreneurship, which is key to economic growth in the region—policy makers need to focus on closing these gaps.

Chapter 1: Law, Gender, and the Business Environment

Can individuals reap the rewards of their investments of time and resources? Are they restricted in their legal ability to make decisions that affect their economic activities? These are central questions for people in business everywhere. To answer them, one has to understand property rights and the ability of entrepreneurs to make economic decisions in their own name.

This book looks at the property rights and legal capacity of women, how and why they differ from those of men, and how these differences affect women's economic and entrepreneurial opportunities in Sub-Saharan Africa. It looks at the formal property and legal rights of women and men, examining constitutions, international agreements, statutes, and case law. It presents evidence of the practical challenges to exercising these rights and makes recommendations for strengthening women's economic rights—on the books and in practice.

Business regulations stipulate the procedures for registering property or businesses, enforcing contracts, and safeguarding investor or creditor rights. They would seem the natural starting point for a legal analysis. Such regulations rarely include gender-differentiated provisions. But seemingly gender-blind

1

regulations presuppose that the parties can enter into contracts, move freely, access forums of economic exchange, and own property or control assets in their own name. This is not always true for men and women equally.

A principal finding of this study is that other areas of the law, rarely addressed in analysis of the business environment, play a determining role in framing women's economic rights. Laws governing marriage, divorce, inheritance, land rights, and labor markets, rather than business regulations, determine whether women and men are equally able to make economic decisions in their own name or whether their ability to enter into contracts or own, administer, transfer, or inherit assets and property is restricted. It is precisely in these areas that gender differences, including outright discrimination, are most apparent.

Strengthening women's economic and legal rights is a good thing in and of itself. But it also has real effects—on women's investment, agricultural productivity, and labor force participation (box O.1).

Chapter 2: Women's Legal Rights across the Region

A new database, the *Women's Legal and Economic Empowerment Database for Africa* (Women–LEED–Africa), was created for this study. It documents which countries legally allow differential treatment between women and men and along which dimensions. The database covers all 47 Sub-Saharan countries and the 5 most important sources of law:

- *International treaties and conventions* provide legal protections that are binding on their signatories. The extent of their direct application domestically depends partly on whether the country is a "monist" or "dualist" state (treaties and conventions are directly applicable in monist states but need to be incorporated into domestic laws in dualist states).

- *Constitutions* are the highest source of law in a country. They lay out the guiding principles for legal rights. The database focuses on constitutional provisions for nondiscrimination based on gender and, as appropriate, provisions explicitly relating to promoting gender equality.

- The *statutes* examined include family and civil codes, marital property laws, inheritance laws, land laws, and labor laws. These areas, rather than being generic business regulations, determine who has legal capacity, who can own and dispose of property, and who has restricted labor opportunities.

- *Customary law* is recognized in constitutions, statutes, or both as a separate—and often equal—source of law in many Sub-Saharan countries. This recognition is sometimes restricted to certain areas. The database focuses on how customary law affects legal capacity, property rights, and inheritance.

- *Religious law* is recognized as a separate—and often equal—source of law in many countries. In some cases, it is recognized as the primary source of law; in others, it is recognized as the applicable source of law for members of a particular religion for certain issues. The database focuses on how religious law affects legal capacity, property rights, and inheritance.

The database includes seven "scoresheets." The scoresheets assess where each country stands with regard to international agreements and conventions; constitutional nondiscrimination and gender-equality provisions; recognition of customary and religious law; legal capacity; property rights, notably in marriage and inheritance; land laws; and labor laws.

Four key messages emerge from the database:

- All countries' constitutions recognize the principle of nondiscrimination. All but two countries have also signed international conventions prohibiting discriminating against women. But legal exceptions are widespread in constitutions and in statutes governing marital property, inheritance, land, and labor.

- Many of the discriminatory provisions apply not to women as women but to women as married women. In many countries, marriage changes the legal status and rights of women, conferring legal capacities and responsibilities on husbands and removing them from wives.

- The treatment of women's economic rights is not closely related to a country's income. Raising national income by itself is thus unlikely to improve women's legal and economic rights—more interventionist reforms will probably be needed.

- Gender gaps in economic rights reduce women's ability to grow a business and employ workers. The share of female employers is larger where women's economic rights are stronger (box O.2).

Constitutional Recognition of Nondiscrimination

All Sub-Saharan countries recognize the principle of nondiscrimination in constitutions, in the international conventions to which they are signatories, or both (figures O.1 and O.2).

The constitutional recognition of customary law is widespread—it applies in all common law countries and in almost half the civil law countries in Sub-Saharan Africa. Where constitutions do not recognize customary law, it is implicitly recognized in statutes, particularly statutes on marriage or inheritance. What varies across countries is the extent to which constraints are placed on customary law in upholding the principle of nondiscrimination (figure O.3).

BOX 0.1

How Do Property Rights Affect Economic Opportunities?

An extensive literature shows the importance of property rights for growth, investment, and government effectiveness. Aggregate cross-country data show a positive association between the quality of institutions or property rights and growth, though the exact causal mechanism can be hard to establish.

Many recent studies are microeconomic analyses, generally within a single country that has changed legal rights or that grants different rights to different groups. Examples of such changes are described below.

Strong Land Rights Can Promote Investment

Empirical work suggests that when women control a larger share of resources, agricultural productivity rises (Saito, Mekonnen, and Spurling 1994; Udry and others 1995; Quisumbing 1996; Besley and Ghatak 2009) and poverty falls (World Bank 2001). Insecure property rights to land have multiple ramifications for agriculture and how rural economic activity is organized. The risk that land will be expropriated deters investment. Insecure property rights also reduce borrowers' ability to pledge land as collateral, tightening credit constraints. Ill-defined property rights to land can inhibit land transactions—rentals or sales—preventing potential gains from trade (Aryeetey and Udry 2010).

Goldstein and Udry (2008) examine the effect of contested land rights on investment and productivity in agriculture in Akwapim, Ghana. They show that individuals who hold powerful positions in a local political hierarchy have more secure tenure rights—and therefore invest more in land fertility, leading to much higher output. The intensity of investments on different plots cultivated by a given individual corresponds to the individual's security of tenure over the plots.

Besley (1995) shows that individuals in Ghana vary their investment across plots depending on the security of their rights—and that property rights need to be understood as embedded in a broader social context.

Some evaluations have shown an increase in agricultural productivity and a (weak) increase in access to credit where formal titling programs are in place (see, for example, Pande and Udry 2005). The weak increase in access to credit has been attributed to two factors. First, creditors often have only weak rights to foreclose on land (Field and Torero 2008). Second, collateral is not the only constraint to accessing finance: a profitable idea and the ability to work in a reasonably hospitable investment climate are also needed (Besley and Ghatak 2009).

One of the challenges for women is that titling has too often been done under a single name, the male head of household. As a result, in some countries, such as

Kenya, land is overwhelmingly titled only in men's names. Ethiopia has tried to remedy this situation by mandating that land be titled jointly. Its effort has greatly increased women's ownership over land (Deininger and others 2008).

. . . And Increase Labor Supply

Field (2007) evaluates the impact of titling program in the slums of Peru. She finds little impact of titling on decisions to invest in the home or plot of land, but she does find an impact on labor supply, particularly for women. Holding title freed members of the household from having to remain on the plot to ensure a claim over it.

Changes in Inheritance Laws Alter the Incentive of Families to Invest in Their Daughters

Deininger, Goyal, and Nagarajan (2010) analyze the effect of changes to the Hindu Succession Act in some southern states of India that gave equal rights to girls and women in inheriting property. The new law, which raised the likelihood of their inheriting land (although it did not fully eliminate the gender difference), was associated with increased age at marriage for girls, higher educational attainment of girls, and increased household investments in daughters. Roy (2008) finds that the law also increased women's autonomy.

Changes in Family Law Can Strengthen Women's Economic Empowerment

As family law determines who controls assets in the family, changes in legislation can affect economic opportunities. Part of the effect may come from shifts in intra-household bargaining power, as illustrated by Gray (1998) and Stevenson and Wolfers (2006), who looked at changes in divorce laws in the United States. In U.S. states where women's bargaining position was strengthened, women were more likely to initiate a divorce, and domestic violence fell.

Ethiopia changed its family law in 2000, raising the minimum age of marriage for women, removing the ability of a husband to deny a wife permission to work outside the home, and requiring both spouses' consent in the administration of marital property. The reform, initially rolled out in selected regions and cities, now applies across the country. Using two nationally representative household surveys, one in 2000 just before the reform and one five years later, Hallward-Driemeier and Gajigo (2010) find a substantial shift in women's economic activities. In particular, women's participation in occupations that require work outside the home, full-time hours, and higher skills rose more where the reform had been enacted (controlling for time and location effects).

Source: Hallward-Driemeier, forthcoming 2013.

BOX O.2

Stronger Economic Rights, Greater Opportunities for Self-Employed Employers

Entrepreneurs include individuals who are self-employed and individuals who work for themselves and employ others. Increasing the share of employers among entrepreneurs is one important way to expand opportunities.

The gender pattern between the two types of entrepreneurship is striking. Women represent about 40 percent of the nonagricultural labor force in Sub-Saharan Africa, 50 percent of the self-employed, but only a little more than 25 percent of employers (box figure O.2.1). Factors that can help bridge this gap are thus important in helping women entrepreneurs in particular.

In cross-country patterns, the share of self-employed individuals in the nonagricultural labor force is inversely related to income: it is very high in low-income countries and declines as country income rises. The same pattern does not hold for employers: the share, which is small, changes little as country income rises (box figure O.2.2). Instead, the share of female employers depends on the extent of gender gaps in economic rights (box figure O.2.3). More men than women are employers, but the gap is smaller where rights are stronger. More women are employers where they have stronger rights to access, control assets, and can enter into contracts in their own name.

Figure BO.2.1 Women Are Active Entrepreneurs, Particularly in Lower-Income Countries, But Largely Self-Employed

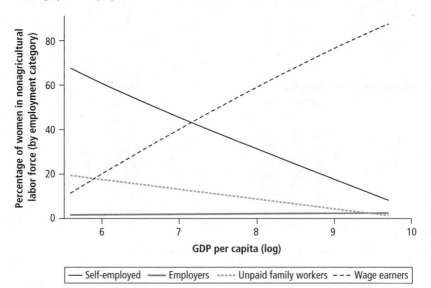

Source: Based on data from household and labor force surveys in low- and middle-income countries.

Figure BO.2.2 The Share of Female Employers Does Not Vary with National Income

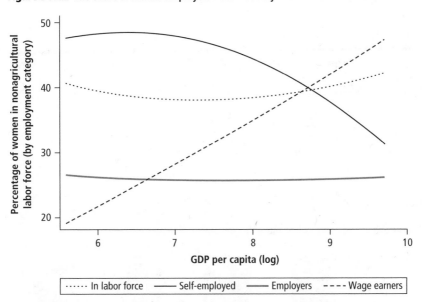

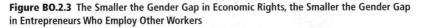

Source: Based on data from household and labor force surveys in low- and middle-income countries.
Note: GDP = gross domestic product.

Figure BO.2.3 The Smaller the Gender Gap in Economic Rights, the Smaller the Gender Gap in Entrepreneurs Who Employ Other Workers

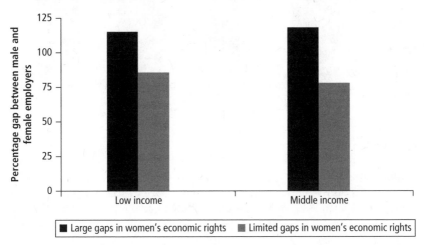

Source: Hallward-Driemeier, forthcoming 2013.
Note: The bars exceed 100 percent if men are more than twice as likely as women to be employers.

—*Continued*

BOX 0.2 *continued*

An important policy implication from these results is that simply relying on income will not be sufficient to close gender gaps among self-employed employers. Indeed, as chapter 2 demonstrates, gaps in economic rights in Sub-Saharan Africa are as prevalent in middle-income countries as in low-income countries. More needs to be done to address legal reforms to enable more women entrepreneurs to move into the ranks of employers.

The companion volume to this book, *Enterprising Women: Expanding Opportunities in Africa* (Hallward-Driemeier, forthcoming 2013), explores in more detail the ways in which gaps in economic rights affect the opportunities facing women entrepreneurs.

Figure 0.1 All Countries Recognize the Principle of Nondiscrimination

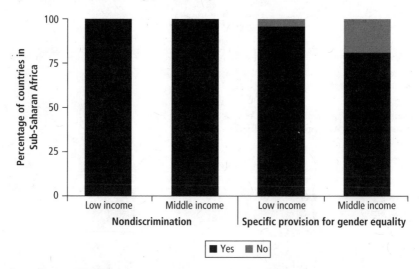

Source: Women–LEED–Africa.

Legal Capacity

Restrictions on women's legal capacity do not vary by income. They do vary by type of legal system; they are found largely in civil law countries (the two common law countries that do so are Sudan and Swaziland), where various laws stipulate the man as "head of household" (figure O.4). Merely looking at which countries include a "head of household" provision can be misleading,

Figure O.2 Most Countries Have Ratified International Conventions on Women's Rights

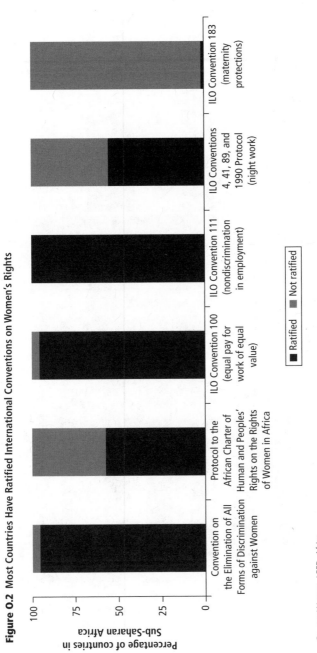

Source: Women–LEED–Africa.
Note: ILO = International Labour Organization.

Figure O.3 Some Countries Recognize Customary Law and Allow It to Discriminate against Women

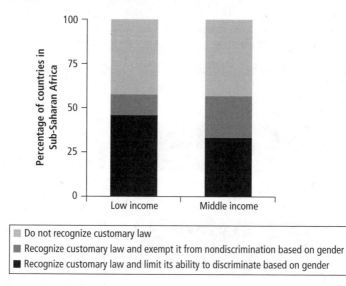

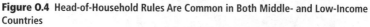

Source: Women–LEED–Africa.

Figure O.4 Head-of-Household Rules Are Common in Both Middle- and Low-Income Countries

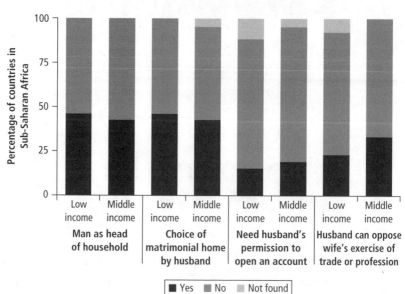

Source: Women–LEED–Africa.

however, for two reasons. First, some countries without such a provision have statutes that provide the same powers of husbands over their wives. Second, some countries that deem the man as head of household do so largely as a social distinction; explicit provisions in these countries indicate that husbands do not have power over the economic decisions of their wives. In short, a head of household provision is not a reliable indicator of who makes the economic decisions.

Husbands can have power over their wives' economic activities in three main ways. The right of the husband to choose the matrimonial home is the most common, followed by the ability to deny a wife permission to pursue a job or profession. The need to obtain a husband's signature to open a bank account is less common, at least in laws governing marriage (though many countries allow banks to require a husband's signature as part of their business practice).

Property Regime for Marriage

The type of property regime in marriage determines the ability of both spouses to own property during marriage and after its dissolution through death or divorce. These property rights determine spouses' access to and control of assets and other productive resources that can be used as collateral for loans or other business purposes.

Statutory, customary, and religious marriages are subject to various property regimes. The most common are community of property (including universal community of property), separate ownership of property, dowry, and customary law. The default marital regime that applies is regulated by the relevant family statute or code, which in turn depends on the type of union (statutory marriage, customary or religious marriage, or consensual union).

Inheritance Regime

Inheritance remains one of the main ways for women to acquire and control property (figure O.5). It is also one of the main areas in which property disputes arise. Constitutions, family and inheritance (succession), customary, and religious laws determine the legal framework for inheritance laws. Common law practices and judicial precedent, particularly in common law countries, also plays an important role in determining whether women, married and unmarried, can own and control property and thus their ability to use such assets in their business.

Land

Land is central to obtaining credit, especially in Africa's collateral-based banking systems. It is a key resource for enterprise development.

Land issues are also where many of the problems associated with multiple legal systems come to the fore. Some land laws explicitly give rights only to men,

Figure O.5 Different Types of Property Regimes Grant Women Very Different Rights to Inherit Marital Property

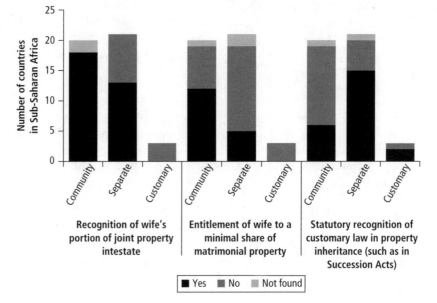

Source: Women–LEED–Africa.

some are gender neutral, and others recognize the rights of women to own land (figure O.6).

Where there is no will, intestate succession laws in several countries, including Ghana and Zambia, exclude customary land from the property a widow can inherit from her husband. Under customary rules of inheritance, such land usually passes to a male heir. This practice strips women of their right to inherit a great deal of land, as customary land represents the majority of land in many countries (81 percent in Zambia, 80 percent in Mozambique, 72 percent of all land in Malawi, and 60 percent in Swaziland) (Economic Commission for Africa 2003).

Labor

Women's labor rights in Sub-Saharan Africa are legally protected in countries' constitutions and labor laws as well as in the International Labour Organization conventions that states ratify. Labor laws affect employees directly. They can

Figure O.6 Only a Minority of Countries Protect Women's Land Rights

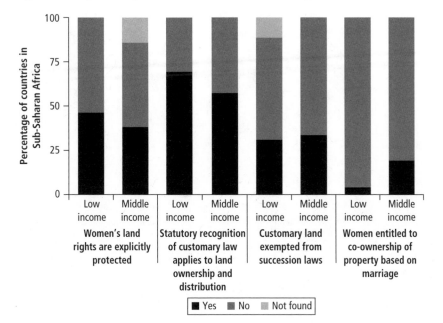

Source: Women–LEED–Africa.

also affect entrepreneurship by influencing the availability and attractiveness of wage employment.

The constitutions of 30 countries in the region go beyond a general clause on nondiscrimination to provide equal rights to work, equal pay, or both. Implementing the principle of nondiscrimination is critical to ensuring that these provisions are respected.

Many countries restrict the hours women can work or the type of work they can perform (figure O.7). Fifteen countries restrict the nature of the work woman can engage in; 20 more apply such restrictions only to pregnant women. Twenty-three countries restrict the hours all women can work; another 12 restrict the hours of pregnant women only. These restrictions—ostensibly intended to protect women—limit women's earning potential as wage workers. They may be one of the factors contributing to the fact that, outside agriculture, women in Sub-Saharan Africa are predominantly self-employed in informal and small enterprises.

Figure O.7 Many Countries Restrict the Type of Work Women Can Perform and Women's Hours

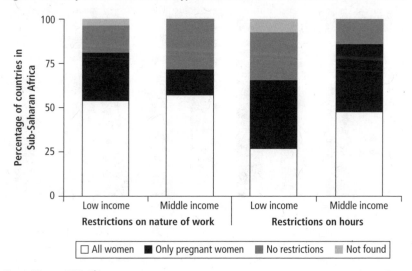

Source: Women–LEED–Africa.

Chapter 3: Legal Pluralism: Multiple Systems, Multiple Challenges

The coexistence of customary, statutory, and religious laws in all Sub-Saharan countries create two main challenges. First, the very existence of multiple systems of law and sources of jurisprudence provides opportunity for discrimination and bias—and raises questions as to which system prevails in which circumstances. Second, many core areas relevant to business, including property rights, are governed by conflicting, and sometimes contradictory, provisions in legal systems. Customary law is important because it touches the lives of most of the population in many parts of Africa. Religious law can also apply to substantial segments of the population and in some countries is the principle source of family and inheritance laws.

The issue is not unique to Africa: inconsistent and conflicting sources of law permeate every legal system in the world. To reduce uncertainty, a legal system has to have a clear hierarchy regarding which law prevails when a conflict arises. To reduce discrimination within a legal system, it is essential that the principle of nondiscrimination be regarded as paramount and that it supersedes conflicting provisions.

Chapter 3 examines the extent to which countries in the region define this hierarchy. It uses case law to illustrate how courts have interpreted cases at the intersections of different sources of law and conflicting provisions on the books. Case law is itself a formal source of law in common law systems and an integral part of the legal landscape, as judicial decision making and precedent can shape rights to property as much as any other source of law. Judicial precedent exists to a lesser degree in civil law systems. For this reason, this chapter gives more coverage to case law in a common law framework.

As the many case examples in this chapter illustrate, judicial interpretations vary across countries and even over time in the same country. Case law can help push for more progressive decisions by referring to constitutional principles of nondiscrimination or obligations under international conventions such as the Convention on the Elimination of all Forms of Discrimination against Women (CEDAW); by filling gaps in statutory law; and by supporting the evolution of customary law to reflect contemporary reality. However, judicial decision making can also entrench discriminatory principles. The chapter highlights the importance of passing clear legislation and effectively implementing it to reduce uncertainty in economic rights.

Chapter 4: Women's Rights in Practice: Constraints to Accessing Justice

Discriminatory laws are not the only source of gaps in women's economic rights—de facto constraints in accessing justice can also be an important source of discrimination. For this reason, the de jure indicators in the database may not always accurately reflect rights in practice. It is therefore instructive to examine the gaps between de jure rights and de facto practice.

Practical constraints—including lack of awareness, distance, cost, language, and bias—can shape the ability to exercise statutory economic rights, especially for women. When courts are located only in urban centers, conduct business only in European languages, and charge high fees, many women do not see them as a viable option. Few people in the region engage with the formal judicial system or even have much knowledge of the legal protections it affords. Particularly in parts of the region that are rural, have low income and education levels, and retain strong customary traditions, people rarely perceive the formal judicial system as relevant for securing their economic rights. Local elders or chiefs and customary practices are more likely to determine how disputes are resolved and property divided. Unless the formal system recognizes customary law, access to property by millions of women is resolved outside the protections afforded in constitutions and statutes.

Women face multiple constraints in accessing justice in the customary legal system, too. Even though customary law may be physically and culturally more accessible to them, their experience in customary institutions can differ greatly from that of men. Most customary courts are adjudicated by men and tend to favor men in their decision making. Because women have historically been excluded from adjudicating on matters of customary law, they cannot influence the law's evolution. Women may be unable to voice their grievances directly, having to rely instead on the male head of the family to even bring a grievance to the attention of the community's elders.

The challenge is thus to balance the best elements of formal customary law and informal traditional systems with expanded access to statutory protections where they offer greater rights to women.

Chapter 5: The Way Forward

Property rights and legal capacity shape a woman's ability to engage in economic activity. Discriminatory family, marital property, and inheritance laws, alongside formal legal restrictions on mobility, employment outside the home, and administration of personal assets, are barriers that states all too often condone. The customary and social norms from which these laws derive represent a still deeper challenge to reform. The study makes recommendations for reform at four levels.

Improving the Substance of Laws

The principle of nondiscrimination should cover all sources of law, including customary and religious law. Protection should specifically cover, rather than exclude, the important family and financial decisions that all people face.

Four areas of law stand out as ripe for reform:

- *Family law.* The legal recognition of nonmonetary contributions during a marriage in the division of property on divorce or death should be strengthened. Head-of-household and related provisions that diminish women's legal capacity and economic autonomy should be removed from family codes and other statutes.

- *Land law.* Mandatory joint titling should be encouraged in order to strengthen women's claims to land.

- *Labor and employment law.* Restrictions that limit the type of work women may engage in or the hours they may work should be removed.

- *Customary law.* Application of the nondiscrimination principle should be enhanced, especially for marital property, inheritance, and land. Policy makers should build on the strengths and accessibility of customary dispute-resolution mechanisms while offsetting areas of gender bias in the application of customary law.

Securing Existing Benefits

Five sets of measures are needed to enhance the administration of law and access to justice:

- strengthening the enforcement of laws
- expanding access to laws and legal decisions
- improving the transparency and accountability of the justice system
- making the system more hospitable to women
- removing practical constraints to accessing justice, by reducing costs and simplifying procedures and broadening the scope of legal services through mobile courts, paralegals, expansion of small claims courts, and alternative dispute resolution mechanisms

Empowering Women to Exercise Their Economic Rights

Women need to be aware of their legal protections and empowered to exercise them. Practical steps to facilitate their empowerment focus on a few key decisions: encouraging registration of marriages (including customary marriages), encouraging the use of prenuptial agreements and the writing of wills, choosing the marital property regime that best safeguards their access to property, registering marital property jointly, and registering their businesses in their own name.

Proceeding with Conviction—and Respect

In drafting new laws that are appropriate to a country's situation, reformers must consider the sociocultural context, thoroughly analyze the national legal framework, and build on the strengths of existing systems. They must focus not only on laws but also on education, acceptance, and enforcement. Changes in social norms take time—but without targeted reform, they are likely to take even longer.

References

Aryeetey, Ernest, and Christopher Udry. 2010. "Creating Property Rights: Land Banks in Ghana." *American Economic Review Papers and Proceedings* 100 (2): 130–34.

Besley, Timothy. 1995. "Property Rights and Investment Incentives: Theory and Evidence from Ghana." *Journal of Political Economy* 103 (5): 903–37.

Besley, Timothy, and Maitreesh Ghatak. 2009. "Property Rights and Economic Development." CEPR Discussion Paper 7234, Centre for Economic Policy Research, London.

Deininger, Klaus, Daniel A. Ali, Stein Holden, and Jaap Zevenbergen. 2008. "Rural Land Certification in Ethiopia: Process, Initial Impact, and Implications for Other African Countries." *World Development* 36 (10): 1786–812.

Deininger, Klaus, Aparajita Goyal, and Hari Nagarajan. 2010. "Inheritance Law Reform and Women's Access to Capital: Evidence from India's Hindu Succession Act." Policy Research Working Paper 5338, World Bank, Washington, DC.

Economic Commission for Africa. 2003. *Land Tenure Systems and Sustainable Development in Southern Africa*. Addis Ababa: Economic Commission for Africa. ECA/SA/EGM.Land/2003/2, Southern Africa Office, Lusaka, Zambia. http://www.uneca.org/eca_resources/publications/srdcs/land_tenure_systems_and_sustainable_development_in_southern_africa.pdf.

Field, Erica. 2007. "Entitled to Work: Urban Property Rights and the Labor Supply in Peru." *Quarterly Journal of Economics* 122: 1561–602.

Field, Erica, and Maximo Torero. 2008. "Do Property Titles Increase Credit Access Among the Urban Poor? Evidence from a Nationwide Titling Program." Working Paper, Department of Economics, Harvard University, Cambridge, MA.

Goldstein, Markus, and Christopher Udry. 2008. "The Profits of Power: Land Rights and Agricultural Investment in Ghana." *Journal of Political Economy* 116 (6): 981–1022.

Gray, Jeffrey S. 1998. "Divorce-Law Changes, Household Bargaining, and Married Women's Labor Supply." *American Economic Review* 88 (3): 628–42.

Hallward-Driemeier, Mary. Forthcoming 2013. *Enterprising Women: Expanding Opportunities in Africa*. Washington DC: World Bank.

Hallward-Driemeier, Mary, and Ousman Gajigo. 2010. "Strengthening Economic Rights and Women's Occupational Choice: The Impact of Reforming Ethiopia's Family Law." Development Economics, World Bank, Washington, DC.

Hallward-Driemeier, Mary, Tazeen Hasan, Jane Kamangu, Emilia Lobti, and Mark Blackden. 2011. *Women's Legal and Economic Empowerment Database* (Women–LEED–Africa), Development Economics, World Bank, Washington, DC.

Pande, Rohini, and Christopher Udry. 2005. "Institutions and Development: A View from Below." Economic Growth Center Discussion Paper 928, Yale University, New Haven, CT.

Quisumbing, Agnes. 1996. "Male-Female Differences in Agricultural Productivity: Methodological Issues and Empirical Evidence." *World Development* 24 (10): 1579–95.

Roy, Sanchari. 2008. "Female Empowerment through Inheritance Rights: Evidence from India." STICERD Working Paper, London School of Economics, London.

Saito, Katerine A., Hailu Mekonnen, and Daphne Spurling. 1994. "Raising Productivity of Women Farmers in Sub-Saharan Africa." Discussion Paper 230, World Bank, Washington, DC.

Stevenson, Betsey, and Justin Wolfers. 2006. "Bargaining in the Shadow of the Law: Divorce Laws and Family Distress." *Quarterly Journal of Economics* 121 (1): 267–88.

Udry, Christopher, John Hoddinott, Harold Alderman, and Lawrence Haddad. 1995. "Gender Differentials in Farm Productivity: Implications for Household Efficiency and Agricultural Policy." *Food Policy* 20 (5): 407–23.

Women–LEED–Africa (Women's Legal and Economic Empowerment Database), http://documents.worldbank.org/query?title=Women+LEED+Africa+Database developed by Mary Hallward-Driemeier, Tazeen Hasan, Jane Kamangu, Emila Lobti, and Mark Blackden. Development Economics, World Bank.

World Bank. 2001. "Engendering Development: Through Gender Equality in Rights, Resources and Voice." Policy Research Report, World Bank, Washington, DC.

Chapter 1

Law, Gender, and the Business Environment

Can individuals reap the rewards of their investments of time and resources? Are they restricted in their legal ability to make decisions that affect their economic activities? These questions are central for people in business everywhere. To answer them, one has to address property rights and the ability of people in business to make economic decisions in their own name.[1] The strength of these rights determines the incentives to invest and to put time and energy into a business, the ability to control collateral to obtain credit, and the types of risks that people are able and willing to take.

This study addresses how the system of legal rights and access to justice affects the strength of women's economic rights and how and why they differ from those of men. The focus is the areas relevant to entrepreneurs.[2]

Securing equality of women's economic rights has intrinsic value. Securing economic rights for all—so that both women and men can fully participate in the economy—has important instrumental benefits, too.

Business regulations stipulate the procedures for registering property or businesses, enforcing contracts, and safeguarding investor or creditor rights. With the exception of some labor laws, business regulations rarely have gender-differentiated provisions. This does not mean that women have the same economic rights as men, however.

A critical finding of this study is that other areas of the law, usually not addressed in analyses of the business environment, play a determining role in framing gender differences in economic rights. These areas include family laws governing marriage and divorce, inheritance laws, and land laws. It is these laws, more than business regulations, that determine whether women and men can make economic decisions in their own name and own, administer, transfer, and inherit assets and property. It is precisely in these areas that gender differences, including outright discrimination, are most apparent.

Two other factors are also important. First, these areas are the ones most commonly subject to overlapping legal systems in Sub-Saharan Africa. Many constitutions and statutes explicitly recognize the areas of marriage, inheritance, and rights over land as domains where formal, customary, or religious law applies. Second, they are the areas that are often exempt from nondiscrimination provisions.

This study provides an overview of a new legal database of indicators of gender equality for all 47 countries in Sub-Saharan Africa. Built for this study, the Women's Legal and Economic Empowerment Database for Africa (Women–LEED–Africa) measures formal (de jure) provisions of property rights and legal capacity as protected in constitutions, international agreements, and statutes. It shows where nondiscrimination based on gender is provided (box 1.1) and where statutes provide different powers over economic decisions to husbands and wives. It also addresses ways in which inheritance and land law provisions treat men and women differently. The aim is to provide an overview of how and why the economic rights protected in family, inheritance, and land laws affect women's economic opportunities.

Structure of the Book

The rest of this chapter discusses the reasons for looking at legal economic rights and the relevant dimensions to be examined. It shows that differences in property rights and legal capacity have a substantial impact on economic

---

BOX 1.1

Defining "Discrimination"

The vast majority of countries have ratified the Convention on the Elimination of All Forms of Discrimination against Women (CEDAW), adopted by the United Nations General Assembly in 1979. It has become the primary international vehicle for monitoring and advocating for nondiscrimination against women.

The convention defines discrimination against women as "any distinction, exclusion or restriction made on the basis of sex which has the effect or purpose of impairing or nullifying the recognition, enjoyment or exercise by women, irrespective of their marital status, on a basis of equality of men and women, of human rights and fundamental freedoms in the political, economic, social, cultural, civil or any other field." This definition covers both direct discrimination, in which explicit differences are made on the basis of gender, and indirect discrimination, in which laws are gender neutral on their face but not in their outcomes. The focus in this study is largely on direct discrimination, but references to indirect discrimination (such as land titling that provides for a single owner on the title) are also made and should be kept in mind.

Source: http://www.un.org/womenwatch/daw/cedaw/cedaw.htm.

opportunities, including rates of investment, labor force participation, and the shift of the composition of entrepreneurs from the self-employed to employers.

Chapter 2 describes Women–LEED–Africa, which lists indicators of gender differences in economic rights on the books. It briefly discusses the issues the indicators capture and describes some cross-country patterns.

Chapters 3–5 look more closely at the implications of these gender gaps in legal rights. Chapter 3 analyzes how the presence of multiple sources of law can undermine women's economic rights, particularly if the constitutional principle of nondiscrimination is not binding on all sources—as in the case of customary law, for example. The chapter examines the role and importance of customary law and how it intersects with statutory law. It uses case law to address how contradictions between (and within) constitutions and statutes, as well as between statutory and customary law, undermine the principles of nondiscrimination.

Chapter 4 examines how women experience these rights in practice, by addressing shortcomings of legal systems and the administration of justice. It provides a de facto counterpoint to the de jure principles articulated earlier. It also addresses additional practical challenges that can make it difficult for women to access justice.

A more interventionist agenda is needed to secure women's full legal and economic rights. Chapter 5 concludes by making recommendations for tackling legal and regulatory obstacles while building on the positive developments that help define women's legal status.

Importance of Economic Rights in Business Incentives

Two key dimensions of economic rights are property rights and contract rights. Since the time of Adam Smith, the protection of property rights has been seen as essential to capital accumulation and ultimately to economic growth and poverty reduction. The protection of property rights can be understood not only in the narrow sense of rights to own land but also more broadly to include the ownership and control of assets. Stronger property rights increase confidence that one can benefit from working and investing. With certain risks reduced, the range of activities that can be profitable expands (World Bank 2004).

For businesses to flourish, their owners or managers need to invest, hire employees, purchase materials, and sell goods or services. Most of these steps involve commitments over time and with different groups of people. They involve trust. If business dealings depend exclusively on trust, however, the circle of people with whom entrepreneurs can engage is limited. With formal rules underlying agreements, including how to redress breaches in trust, commerce can expand. Entrepreneurs no longer need to rely on reputation and family or community links to redress potential wrongs: formal mechanisms can enforce property rights.[3]

The enforceability of contracts in the formal system allows for greater special-ization. Entrepreneurs do not need to perform all the activities in their business: they can subcontract or purchase some of them from other firms. This specializa-tion can raise efficiency dramatically, further expanding market size. It can also lengthen commitments, making more investments attractive and encouraging parties to extend credit to finance them. By setting transparent and enforceable rules, the law facilitates transactions between third parties (North 1990).

Stronger property rights encourage people to invest their resources and protect their investments. The opposite is also true: failure to protect property rights limits opportunities. Hernando de Soto (1989) has been outspoken in calling for greater protection of the property rights of poor people, arguing that giving them title to their plots of land could be a critical step in strengthening their ability to escape poverty. His work highlights that property rights are not uniform and that failure to protect them for everyone in society can be costly. Particularly where property is titled to individuals, it is important that women receive title, too.

Yet even if formal property rights are not a panacea, informal systems of pro-tecting rights can still be insufficient. Informal networks or communal property rights can provide some measure of de facto security. But they can lead to even greater disparities for women if they are not equal members of these networks or communities.

Given the centrality of economic rights to business, differences in property rights between men and women—in either their content or the ways in which they are safeguarded in practice—are likely to have substantial effects on the opportunities facing entrepreneurs of both genders. This study strengthens the instrumental argument for closing gender gaps by examining how doing so improves economic opportunities for women. Ensuring equal property rights for women is particularly important in Sub-Saharan Africa given the high rates of entrepreneurship (box 1.2).

Extent of Legal Protection of Women's Economic Rights

Formal law ultimately defines formal economic rights in an economy. Much of the content of such rights can be found in international law, constitutions, and statutes.[4] But for the law to be reliable, the legal system itself must be effective. The strength of formal economic rights is thus determined by both the content of formal laws and the effectiveness with which the formal legal system oper-ates. Ambiguity in defining or enforcing these rights limits the use of property, raises the costs of exchange, and can cause uncertainty after any contract.[5]

Practical constraints and customs can also shape the ability to exercise for-mal economic rights. For this reason, the de jure indicators presented here do not capture the whole picture and may not always be an accurate reflection of de facto rights (as discussed in chapter 5).

Much of the population in Sub-Saharan Africa does not engage with the formal legal system—or even has much knowledge of the legal protections it affords. Particularly in areas that are emerging from conflict or remain fragile, have lower incomes and education, are rural, or retain strong customary traditions (or a combination of these elements), people do not see the formal system as relevant for securing economic rights. Local elders or chiefs and customary practices are more likely to determine how disputes are resolved or property divided.[6]

The law is not the only factor that influences whether a person becomes an entrepreneur or how an enterprise performs. Many others—including the skills of the entrepreneur; the access to assets, technology, infrastructure, and markets; and the extent of competition—are also important. Women and men may differ in how they spend their time. They may also have different interests and abilities in undertaking economic activities at different points in their lives. Changing the law to protect equal economic rights between women and men is not likely to bring about equal access to economic opportunities for women and men—but differential legal protections will make such equality virtually impossible.

Formal rules reflect what should happen if the legal system is functioning well. The incentives and protections the rules provide thus need to be examined. Particularly as countries develop, the importance and reliance on the formal legal system grows. The strength of de jure rights also provides a measure of the potential to use the law to address discriminatory practices or behavior. And if formal laws do not provide safeguards, an important avenue of redress is closed.

This study shows that even de jure rights are ambiguous and inconsistent, undermining the equality of economic rights for women. The proposed recommendations (chapter 5) involve legal reforms to address these issues. Beyond that, more needs to be done to build awareness of women's legal rights and develop women's capacity to exercise these rights. The many practical challenges of helping women access the legal protections in the formal system must also be overcome.

Main Areas of the Law for Women In Business

The most obvious starting point in an analysis of legal regimes is laws directly governing business. The legal requirements for registering a business—and laws and regulations governing licensing, contract enforcement, banking, bankruptcy, labor, taxation, dispute resolution, and trade—are all natural candidates. All are important for entrepreneurs (as shown, for example, in the World Bank's *Doing Business* reports).

BOX 1.2

Importance of Property Rights for Economic Opportunity

High rates of labor force participation in agriculture and entrepreneurship reinforce the importance of property rights and legal capacity in shaping economic opportunities for large segments of the population. Box figure 1.2.1 shows the sectors in which economically active men and women work in the world's developing regions. It indicates that Sub-Saharan Africa has the largest share of the population active in agriculture as well as the highest rates of entrepreneurship (box figure 1.2.2), a reflection of both high labor force participation rates (stemming from the acute need for income) and

Figure B1.2.1 Types of Employment of Men and Women, by World Region

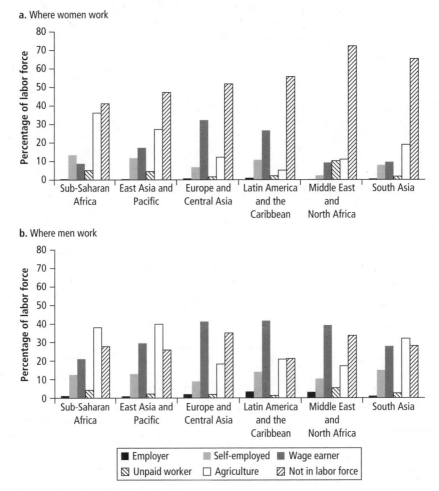

a. Where women work

b. Where men work

Source: Hallward-Driemeier, forthcoming 2013.
Note: Figures are for most recent year available.

Figure B1.2.2 Percentage of Labor Force That Is Self-Employed and Employs Other Workers, by Gender and Region

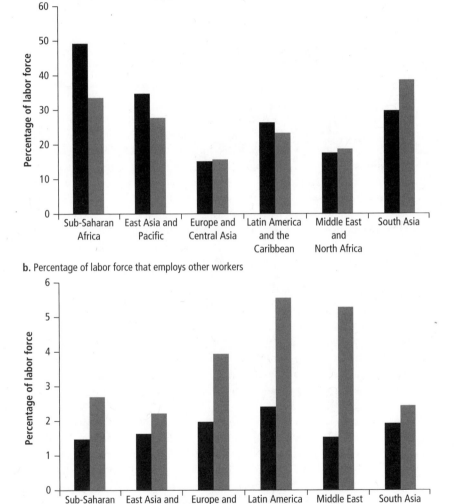

a. Percentage of labor force that is self-employed

b. Percentage of labor force that employs other workers

■ Women   ■ Men

Source: Hallward-Driemeier, forthcoming 2013.
Note: Figures exclude agriculture.

—Continued

BOX 1.2 *continued*

the relative scarcity of wage employment in the region. These trends are true for both women and men.

With two-thirds of the region's population in rural areas, land rights are thus critical in determining income opportunities in Sub-Saharan Africa. Women's rights to their assets and income are central to their ability and incentive to operate and expand their businesses. As many people work in rural areas and informally, customary law and traditional forms of justice, rather than the formal legal system, may be more relevant.

The letters of these laws seldom combine to spell out "gender discrimination." Indeed, with the exception of some labor laws, almost all of these laws are gender blind. But the impact in practice may not be gender neutral. Gender-blind business regulations presuppose that the parties can enter into contracts, move freely, access forums of economic exchange, and own property or control assets in their own name.[7] This is not always equally true for men and women.

Constitutional and statutory provisions do not treat women as a homogeneous group. In some cases, they treat men and women differently based purely on gender. In other cases, they recognize a gender difference upon marriage: it is most often upon marriage that women's legal capacity and the strength of their property rights weaken. The impact of "marriage" on women's rights is not necessarily restricted to the marriage itself—in many cases rights vary even after a marriage has ended because of divorce or the death of a spouse. An analysis of de jure rights must thus consider both gender and marital status.

The areas of the law that touch on roles within families thus play a determining role in women's and men's economic rights. These areas include family, inheritance, land, and labor laws, the provisions of which are sometimes shaped by the principles in the country's constitution or in international treaties the government has ratified.[8]

A country's overarching legal principles are laid forth in its constitution or in international agreements, which guide how the legal system should function and identifies the values it strives to protect. Of particular importance for women is the recognition of nondiscrimination based on gender. In assessing the applicability of this principle, one must look at whether formal customary law or statutory law prevails in the key areas of family, inheritance, land, and labor laws or whether they are given formal exemption from the constitutional principle of nondiscrimination.

Most assessments of the business environment do not consider family law, even though it is central in defining whether women can participate in business as equals. Family law is important to women entrepreneurs both for the subject matter it covers and for how it treats women and men. On the subject matter, it is the body of law that defines the legal capacity of family members. Without full legal capacity, one cannot enter into contracts or litigate independently. Family law also defines who can control, own, or transfer assets. It can also affect the mobility and freedom of association of different individuals. It is central in defining the legal capacity and property rights of family members, as well as the incentives and ability to run a business. In its treatment of women and men, family law is the area that most often allows differences by gender—in constitutions, statutes, or both. As chapter 2 shows, family law, rather than business law, is generally the area in which women's economic rights differ most from men's.

Inheritance laws, too, can differ on the basis of gender. For example, a widow may have only user rights during her lifetime to her deceased husband's immovable property (which can cease on remarriage), whereas a widower may have full rights to sell or otherwise deal with or bequeath property he inherits from his deceased wife.

Land laws may also treat women's rights differently from men's. Because ownership of land can be important for the site of a business or for collateral, this area, which can explicitly restrict women's rights, warrants particular attention.

Among business regulations, labor laws are the most likely to include restrictions by gender. They are often limited to certain industries, particular hours of work, or activities during pregnancy. Many are well intentioned, keeping women's safety in mind, but they can still narrow opportunities and deny women choices. This area is not subject to customary law or exemptions from nondiscrimination.

Nature of the Legal System

Legal systems differ across Sub-Saharan Africa. Most follow either a common law or civil law system, but many are hybrids of the two, making simple classification difficult.[9] Analysis must consider the systems' features in assessing the strength of women's economic rights and what is required to strengthen formal rights. Some of the features reflect historical (including colonial) experience; others reflect characteristics of the system itself. Precedent, the ability of individuals to have standing to challenge the constitutionality of statutes, the fundamental unit of the justice system, and "domestication" of international conventions all play roles. Each feature is examined below.

Precedent
The role of precedent in a legal system has implications for assessing the strength of rights on the books and how these rights may be changed. When courts actively look to precedents in guiding decisions (primarily in common law systems), precedents can have a substantial impact.[10] Analyzing the strength of a statute or provision in isolation may therefore be misleading.

One example concerns how "silence" is interpreted. If rights are extended to certain groups (such as religious or ethnic groups), does the principle apply to other groups (such as women), even if that group is not explicitly identified? In a general provision of nondiscrimination, can the principle be interpreted to imply nondiscrimination on the basis of gender?

Another example relates to the interpretation of a "fair distribution of assets between spouses," which could be seen as an even division or as one based entirely on relative monetary contributions to acquiring the assets. In many countries, in such instances judges' rulings fill the interpretive gap in the statutes, binding future decisions on the same subject. (See, for example, the Echaria case in Kenya, described in chapter 3.)

The fact that judges have issued widely differing interpretations of similarly worded statutes, even in the same country (as discussed in chapter 3), signals a note of caution regarding the importance of precedents in some countries. Precedents can be overruled. Some of the different interpretations can reflect changes in the composition of judges in a court over time or evolutions in legal philosophy or even a lack of access to earlier decisions. It is also true that some judges are not above being influenced illicitly in their decisions.

Although shifting precedents can make it harder to measure the impact of a specific provision, they can also open another avenue for helping change how provisions are applied. In every country, legislation can change the content of the law. But where precedent plays a larger role, activists can help push for more favorable rulings. Precedents can, however, also be set in ways that restrict women's rights further—and overturning them can make it harder to secure future rulings that are more favorable to women. It is not that a greater role for precedents inherently favors or disfavors women; it is that assessing how well economic rights are protected in practice needs to consider precedents.

The role of precedents is not incorporated into the database. Instead, a section in chapter 3 examines the role of precedents and how changing interpretations affect the way de jure rights are applied in practice. The database classifies de jure economic rights based solely on the language of the provisions, in order to ensure that the analysis interprets the same language the same way across countries, to avoid having to address countries in which the applicable case law could not be found, and to prevent a country's classification from changing with a new ruling on the same provision.

Standing

Countries provide different rules on who has standing to challenge statutes or regulations. It is beyond the scope of this study to look at all the provisions of administrative law. Instead, the focus is on the ability of individuals to challenge the constitutionality of statutes. In most of the common law systems and about half of the civil law countries, individual parties affected by a statute can challenge a statute.[11] This provision broadens the way in which statutes and legal precedents are set. Women who show that they are sufficiently disadvantaged by a statute because of gender can bring a suit challenging that statute and appealing to the principle of nondiscrimination. In some civil law countries, though, only the executive or a majority of the legislature can challenge the constitutionality of statutes, leaving only a political channel for trying to change statutes and the ways in which they are applied.

Fundamental Unit

The individual is generally the fundamental unit in formal legal systems. Individuals are seen as endowed with certain rights as individuals, which are the same for women and men.

Some statutes and codes emphasize the household as the fundamental unit, placing less emphasis on safeguarding the individual rights of its members. One example is a head of household statute that give rights over the household to a single person, the male head. Such a statute reduces women's rights within the household. In other cases, rights embedded in households can favor women, as they do in communal property regimes. Larger community units, extended families, and villages are also considered in the recognition of customary law.

Domestication of International Conventions

Most civil law countries are "monist" (as opposed to "dualist") states: they do not need any formal parliamentary procedure to domesticate the international conventions they have ratified for them to apply in their national territories. The act of ratifying the international convention constitutes incorporation into national law. Ratified international conventions can be directly applied by a judge, and directly invoked by citizens, just as if they were national law.

Most common law countries, by contrast, are dualist states: international law has to be legislatively incorporated into national law.[12] If a state accepts a treaty but does not adapt its national law to conform to the treaty or does not create a national law explicitly incorporating the treaty, it violates international law. One cannot claim that the treaty has become part of national law, citizens cannot rely on it, and judges cannot apply it. Citizens of common law systems may be able to bring declaratory proceedings to state that the executive is obligated to "domesticate" international law, but they cannot force the executive to implement international law. Because subsequent national law can also override earlier national law enacting international agreements, national legislation has to be constantly screened for its conformity with international law principles.

In a dualist state, the domestication process can be delayed, with fewer mechanisms for enforcement. But if laws are changed and brought into line with a convention, women's rights are likely to be all the more strongly protected, as gender inequalities will have been addressed directly. In monist states, laws not conforming to the international convention may well stay on the books.[13]

Impact of Rights on Economic Opportunities

The literature on the importance of property rights to growth, government effectiveness, and investment is extensive.[14] Aggregate cross-country data show a positive association between the quality of institutions or property rights and growth, though the causal relationship is hard to establish. Omitted variables could account for both the quality of institutions and growth. There may also be reverse causation.

Finding appropriate instruments to resolve these issues is difficult (see Acemoglu, Johnson, and Robinson 2001; Johnson, McMillan, and Woodruff 2002; Glaeser and others 2004; Rodrik, Subramanian, and Trebbi 2004; Acemoglu and Johnson 2005). Much of the recent literature instead focuses on microeconomic analyses, generally in a single country that has either changed legal rights or grants differential rights to various groups. This section presents examples of both approaches.

Strength of Land Rights

Empirical work suggests that increasing the resources controlled by women raises agricultural productivity (Saito, Mekonnen, and Spurling 1994; Udry and others 1995; Quisumbing 1996; Besley and Ghatak 2009) and helps reduce poverty (World Bank 2001). Insecure property rights to land have multiple ramifications for agriculture and the organization of rural economic activity. They deter investment and can reduce borrowers' ability to pledge land as collateral, thereby tightening credit constraints. Ill-defined property rights to land can inhibit land transactions (rentals or sales), causing potential gains from trade to be forgone (Aryeetey and Udry 2010).

Box 1.3 illustrates this phenomenon in customary land rights by examining the effect of contested land rights on investment and productivity in agriculture in Akwapim, Ghana. It suggests that property rights must be understood as embedded in a broader social context. People who hold powerful positions in the local political hierarchy in Ghana have more secure tenure rights. As a consequence, they invest more in land fertility and have substantially higher output. The intensity of investments on different plots cultivated by a given individual corresponds to that individual's security of tenure over those plots. People in Ghana also vary their investment across plots based on the security of their rights to the plot (Besley 1995).

Many countries have introduced formal titling programs.[15] Some evaluations of titling have documented an increase in agricultural productivity but only weak growth in access to credit (Pande and Udry 2005). The lack of a substantial

BOX 1.3

Women and Land in Ghana: Precarious Rights, Lower Yields

Complex and overlapping rights to land in Akwapim, Ghana, are associated with barriers to investment in land fertility. People who are not central to the networks of social and political power in these villages cannot be confident of maintaining their rights to land while it is fallow. As a result, they allow their land to lie fallow for a shorter than optimal period, and their farm productivity falls correspondingly.

This pattern has a strong gender dimension, because women are rarely in positions of sufficient political power to be confident of their land rights. They thus fallow their plots less often than their husbands and achieve much lower yields.

Source: Goldstein and Udry 2008.

---

effect on access to credit may be attributable to two factors. First, creditors often have only weak rights to foreclose on land titles (Field and Torero 2008). Second, the availability of collateral is not necessarily the only constraint to accessing finance. A profitable idea and the ability to work in a reasonably hospitable investment climate are also needed. Thus, expanding access to property that may be pledged as collateral is important, but potentially only one of the steps required to expand economic opportunities (Besley and Ghatak 2009).

A seminal study evaluating the impact of a titling program was carried out in the slums of Peru (Field 2007). Being granted a title had little impact on decisions to invest in the home or plot of land, but it did affect labor supply, particularly for women. Securing the title freed members of the household from having to remain on the plot to ensure claim over it.

Empowering Women Economically through Changes in Family Law

Because family law can determine legal capacity and the control of assets within the family, changes in the law are likely to affect economic opportunities. Changes in outcomes come partly from shifts in intrahousehold bargaining power, as evidence from the United States reveals (box 1.4).

Ethiopia, for example, changed its family law in 2000, raising the minimum age of marriage for women, removing the ability of the husband to deny permission for the wife to work outside the home, and requiring both spouses' consent in administering marital property. The reform was initially rolled out in three of Ethiopia's nine regions and in two chartered cities. Two nationally representative household surveys—one in 2000 just before the reform and one five years later—allow for a difference-in-difference estimation of the reform's impact. Five years later, women's economic activities had shifted significantly.

BOX 1.4

Changing the Balance of Intrahousehold Power in the United States

Divorce laws in the United States vary across states. These differences in law and varia-tions in times of reform help isolate the impact of the legal change on the outcomes of interest. In particular, changes in divorce laws that shifted the likely division of property following divorce provide an opportunity to investigate the impact of marital property regimes on rates of divorce, women's labor supply, and even domestic violence.

Gray (1998) finds that the introduction of unilateral divorce laws led to an increase in women's labor supply when it increased the bargaining power of women. Steven-son and Wolfers (2006) examine the effects of unilateral divorce laws on household bargaining position. They find that such laws significantly reduced domestic violence because they not only led to the dissolution of violent marriages but also helped lower the prevalence of violence within existing marriages. In effect, by reducing the cost of divorce, exit threats became credible. Focusing on only the rates of divorce would underestimate the impact of the introduction of unilateral divorce because the divorce law likely changed bargaining positions in existing marriages, too.

In particular, women's relative participation in occupations that require work outside the home, full-time work, and higher skills rose more where the reform had been enacted, after controlling for time and location effects (Hallward-Driemeier and Gajigo 2010).

In 1994, two states in India, Karnataka and Maharashtra, changed their inheritance laws, altering the incentive of families to invest in their daughters. Deininger, Goyal, and Nagarajan (2010) analyze the effect of the changes to the Hindu Succession Act, which gave equal rights to both genders in inheriting property. They find that the new law increased families' investment in their daughters. The new provisions increased the chances of women inheriting land (although they did not fully eliminate the gender difference), lifted the marriage age of girls, and raised girls' educational attainment. Their results are consistent with those of Roy (2008), who finds that the same changes had a significant effect on women's autonomy.

Among patterns that are evident across countries, particularly interesting is the impact of stronger property rights on entrepreneurship and opportunities in entrepreneurship. One of the most important ways to expand opportunities is to enable more entrepreneurs to move from self-employment to the ranks of employers. Closing gender gaps in economic rights is an important way to do so (box 1.5).

BOX 1.5

Stronger Economic Rights, Greater Opportunities for Self-Employed Employers

Entrepreneurs include individuals who are self-employed and individuals who work for themselves and employ others. Increasing the share of employers among entrepreneurs is one important way to expand opportunities.

The gender pattern between the two types of entrepreneurship is striking. Women represent about 40 percent of the nonagricultural labor force in Sub-Saharan Africa, 50 percent of the self-employed, but only a little more than 25 percent of employers (box figure 1.5.1). Factors that can help bridge this gap are thus important in helping women entrepreneurs in particular.

In cross-country patterns, the share of self-employed individuals in the nonagricultural labor force is inversely related to income: it is very high in low-income countries and declines as country income rises. The same pattern does not hold for employers: the share, which is small, changes little as country income rises (box figure 1.5.2). Instead, the share of female employers depends on the extent of gender gaps in economic rights (box figure 1.5.3). More men than women are employers, but the gap is smaller where rights are stronger. More women are employers where they have stronger rights to access, control assets, and can enter into contracts in their own name.

Figure B1.5.1 Women Are Active Entrepreneurs, Particularly in Lower-Income Countries, But Largely Self-Employed

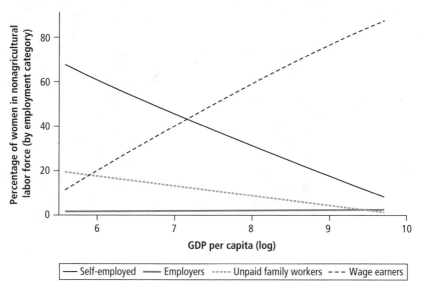

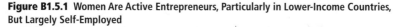

Source: Based on data from household and labor force surveys in low- and middle-income countries.
Note: GDP = gross domestic product.

—*Continued*

BOX 1.5 *continued*

Figure B1.5.2 The Share of Female Employers Does Not Vary with National Income

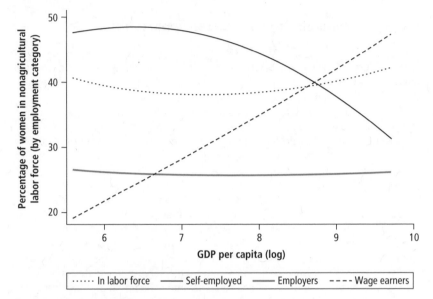

Source: Based on data from household and labor force surveys in low- and middle-income countries.
Note: GDP = gross domestic product.

Figure B1.5.3 The Smaller the Gender Gap in Economic Rights, the Smaller the Gender Gap in Entrepreneurs Who Employ Other Workers

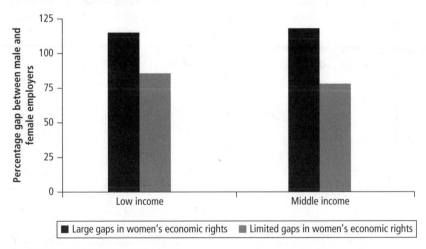

Source: Hallward-Driemeier, forthcoming 2013.
Note: The bars exceed 100 percent if men are more than twice as likely as women to be employers.

—Continued

An important policy implication from these results is that simply relying on income will not be sufficient to close gender gaps among self-employed employers. Indeed, as chapter 2 demonstrates, gaps in economic rights in Sub-Saharan Africa are as prevalent in middle-income countries as in low-income countries. More needs to be done to address legal reforms to enable more women entrepreneurs to move into the ranks of employers.

The companion volume to this book, *Enterprising Women: Expanding Opportunities in Africa* (Hallward-Driemeier, forthcoming 2013), explores in more detail the ways in which gaps in economic rights affect the opportunities facing women entrepreneurs.)

Conclusion

The areas of law that bring a gender dimension to property rights and legal capacity are largely in family, inheritance, and land laws, areas that few policy makers look at when considering how to improve the investment climate for women. Their effect on who can access and control assets or enter into contracts is central in determining the ability and incentives of individuals to run a business. Labor laws can also shape entrepreneurial activities, indirectly, through the relative attractiveness of employment, and potentially directly, by restricting the types of activities that women entrepreneurs can perform. Analyses of variations in legal rights across countries and of legal reforms over time illustrate how reforms in family, inheritance, and land laws can strengthen the ability of women to pursue economic opportunities.

Notes
1. Other rights, such as civil or political rights, can certainly matter. The focus here is on issues that most directly affect the ability to engage in business, primarily from a gender perspective.
2. The implications for women employees enter in a few places, too, such as discussions of labor laws and equal pay for work of equal value provisions. However, as the emphasis here is on entrepreneurship, the coverage of labor laws is restricted to laws that affect the choice of enterprise (industry, hours of operation) that women could run. Equal pay for equal work indicators can affect the relative attractiveness of entrepreneurship. Here they are taken largely as a summary indicator of the recognition of women's economic rights more broadly.
3. See Haldar and Stiglitz (2008) for a more nuanced discussion of social capital. It is not that informal networks cannot fund investments or facilitate transactions, it is that they are likely to be more limited in scope if they need to be relationship based. Well-connected individuals would no doubt be better positioned to receive funding through networks than through rule-based systems (though it is unclear which system leads to a more efficient allocation of resources).

4. Additional sources of formal rules and laws (such as executive orders, administrative law, and binding statements of policy) are not considered here. They do not seem to play a substantial role in issues of marital property or inheritance. They may have important effects on land. Given the challenge of finding even the relevant statutes, it was beyond the scope of this study to collect all the relevant additional sources of rules.

5. One school of thought argues that ambiguity is inherent in the definition of any property right. See especially Kennedy (1981, 2002).

6. Whether the formal system is seen as a legitimate form of justice can be a significant issue discouraging the use of courts to settle disputes in some areas; see Chopra (2008, 2009) for detailed examination in Kenya.

7. Women may also be more time constrained and limited in their ability to travel to government offices, have less information about the procedures needed, or be viewed as softer targets for harassment by officials.

8. Other sources of law, such as criminal or welfare laws, may also affect women's economic opportunities. They are beyond the scope of this study.

9. Cameroon, for example, formally recognizes both systems. Rwanda is switching from civil to common law as it seeks to join the East African Community, and countries in southern Africa have hybrid systems.

10. In civil law countries, the role of judges is more strictly to apply the relevant codes, not to interpret them or analyze a case in the context of broader precedents.

11. Thresholds to show "harm" vary across countries. Countries also differ in terms of whether such harm needs to be "direct" or "indirect." In theory, if the threshold is set high enough, it can restrict the ability of individual parties to bring suits.

12. Kenya is the most recent example of a common law country shifting from a dualist to a monist approach to international conventions under the terms of its new 2010 constitution.

13. This point should not be overstated. In Europe, for example, both monist and dualist countries overhaul their laws at about the same pace.

14. Pande and Udry (2005) provide a review of the literature, focusing on microeconomic analyses. Besley and Ghatak (2009) provide a synthesizing theoretical framework of the relationship of property rights and economic outcomes (particularly investment) and also discuss the existing evidence of the importance of property rights.

15. A challenge for women is that property is often titled under a single name—the male head of household (see box 5.2 in chapter 5).

References

Acemoglu, Daron, and Simon Johnson. 2005. "Unbundling Institutions." *Journal of Political Economy* 113 (5): 949–95.

Acemoglu, Daron, Simon Johnson, and James A. Robinson. 2001. "The Colonial Origins of Comparative Development: An Empirical Investigation." *American Economic Review* 91 (5): 1369–401.

Aryeetey, Ernest, and Christopher Udry. 2010. "Creating Property Rights: Land Banks in Ghana." *American Economic Review Papers and Proceedings* 100 (2): 130–34.

Besley, Timothy. 1995. "Property Rights and Investment Incentives: Theory and Evidence from Ghana." *Journal of Political Economy* 103 (5): 903–37.

Besley, Timothy, and Maitreesh Ghatak. 2009. "Property Rights and Economic Development." CEPR Discussion Paper 7234, Centre for Economic Policy Research, London.

Chopra, Tanja. 2008. *Building Informal Justice in Northern Kenya.* Nairobi: Legal Resources Foundation Trust.

———. 2009. "Justice Versus Peace in Northern Kenya." Justice and Development Working Paper Series 2 (1), World Bank, Nairobi.

Deininger, Klaus, Aparajita Goyal, and Hari Nagarajan. 2010. "Inheritance Law Reform and Women's Access to Capital: Evidence from India's Hindu Succession Act." Policy Research Working Paper 5338, World Bank, Washington, DC.

De Soto, Hernando. 1989. *The Other Path: The Invisible Revolution in the Third World.* New York: Harper Collins.

Field, Erica. 2007. "Entitled to Work: Urban Property Rights and the Labor Supply in Peru." *Quarterly Journal of Economics* 122: 1561–602.

Field, Erica, and Maximo Torero. 2008. "Do Property Titles Increase Credit Access Among the Urban Poor? Evidence from a Nationwide Titling Program." Working Paper, Department of Economics, Harvard University, Cambridge, MA.

Glaeser, Edward L., Rafael La Porta, Florencio Lopez-de-Silanes, and Andrei Shleifer. 2004. "Do Institutions Cause Growth?" *Journal of Economic Growth* 9 (3): 271–303.

Goldstein, Markus, and Christopher Udry. 2008. "The Profits of Power: Land Rights and Agricultural Investment in Ghana." *Journal of Political Economy* 116 (6): 981–1022.

Gray, Jeffrey S. 1998. "Divorce-Law Changes, Household Bargaining, and Married Women's Labor Supply." *American Economic Review* 88 (3): 628–42.

Haldar, Antara, and Joseph Stiglitz. 2008. "The Dialectics of Law and Development: Analyzing Formality and Informality." Paper prepared for the China Task Force of the Initiative for Policy Dialogue, New York, June.

Hallward-Driemeier, Mary. Forthcoming 2013. *Enterprising Women: Expanding Opportunities in Africa.* Washington, DC: World Bank.

Hallward-Driemeier, Mary, and Ousman Gajigo. 2010. "Strengthening Economic Rights and Women's Occupational Choice: The Impact of Reforming Ethiopia's Family Law." Development Economics, World Bank, Washington, DC.

Johnson, Simon, John McMillan, and Christopher Woodruff. 2002. "Property Rights and Finance." *American Economic Review* 92 (5): 1335–56.

Kennedy, Duncan. 1981. "Cost-Benefit Analysis of Entitlement Problems: A Critique." *Stanford Law Review* 33 (3): 387–445.

———. 2002. "The Critique of Rights in Critical Legal Studies." In *Left Legalism/Left Critique,* ed. Wendy Brown and Janet Halley, 178–228. Durham, NC: Duke University Press.

North, Douglass C. 1990. *Institutions, Institutional Change and Economic Performance.* Cambridge: Cambridge University Press.

Pande, Rohini, and Christopher Udry. 2005. "Institutions and Development: A View from Below." Economic Growth Center Discussion Paper 928, Yale University, New Haven, CT.

Quisumbing, Agnes. 1996. "Male-Female Differences in Agricultural Productivity: Methodological Issues and Empirical Evidence." *World Development* 24 (10): 1579–95.

Rodrik, Dani, Arvind Subramanian, and Francesco Trebbi. 2004. "Institutions Rule: The Primacy of Institutions Over Geography and Integration in Economic Development." *Journal of Economic Growth* 9 (2): 131–65.

Roy, Sanchari. 2008. "Female Empowerment through Inheritance Rights: Evidence from India." STICERD Working Paper, London School of Economics, London.

Saito, K. A., H. Mekonnen, and D. Spurling. 1994. "Raising Productivity of Women Farmers in Sub-Saharan Africa." Discussion Paper 230, World Bank, Washington, DC.

Stevenson, Betsey, and Justin Wolfers. 2006. "Bargaining in the Shadow of the Law: Divorce Laws and Family Distress." *Quarterly Journal of Economics* 121 (1): 267–88.

Udry, Christopher, John Hoddinott, Harold Alderman, and Lawrence Haddad. 1995. "Gender Differentials in Farm Productivity: Implications for Household Efficiency and Agricultural Policy." *Food Policy* 20 (5): 407–23.

World Bank. 2001. "Engendering Development: Through Gender Equality in Rights, Resources and Voice." Policy Research Report, World Bank, Washington, DC.

———. 2004. *World Development Report 2005: A Better Investment Climate for Everyone.* Washington, DC: World Bank.

Chapter 2

Women's Legal Rights across the Region

This chapter documents the differences in the de jure economic rights of women and men, using indicators of women's legal rights according to the official sources of law in each country.[1] The database documents which countries legally allow differential treatment of women and men in areas that most directly affect their ability to pursue economic opportunities. It focuses on areas that have first-order effects on existing and potential businesspeople: property rights (land and assets), legal capacity, and restrictions in labor laws.

The Women–LEED–Africa Database

The Women's Legal and Economic Empowerment Database for Africa (Women–LEED–Africa) database covers five important sources of law:

- *International treaties and conventions* provide legal protections that are binding on their signatories. The extent of their direct application domestically depends partly on whether the country is a monist or dualist state (see chapter 1).

- *Constitutions* are the highest source of law in a country. They lay out the guiding principles for legal rights. The database focuses on provisions for nondiscrimination based on gender and, as appropriate, provisions explicitly relating to promoting gender equality.

- The *statutes* examined include family and civil codes, marital property laws, inheritance laws, land laws, and labor laws. These areas, rather than generic business regulations, determine who has legal capacity, who can own and dispose of property, and who has restricted labor opportunities.

- *Customary law* is recognized in constitutions, statutes, or both as a separate—and often equal—source of law in many Sub-Saharan countries. This recognition is sometimes restricted to certain areas. The database focuses on how customary law affects legal capacity, property rights, and inheritance.[2]

- *Religious law* is recognized as a separate—and often equal—source of law in many countries. In some cases, it is recognized as the primary source of law; in others, it is recognized as the applicable source of law for members of a particular religion, for certain prescribed issues, or both. The database focuses on how religious or personal law affects legal capacity, property rights, and inheritance.

Structure of the Database

The database has two components. The legal records database lists the records of the relevant provisions from the sources identified above. It also provides summary indicators on seven scoresheets, described below, to show whether women and men are treated equally in a range of areas, by country. The database does not assess how extensive the differences are; the scoresheets, presented in appendix A, categorize countries simply as having or not having each indicator; countries cannot therefore be ranked by indicator (ranking was not the purpose).[3] The correspondence between the sources of law and the scoresheets is not one-to-one, because not all customary and religious laws are codified. Scoresheet 2 indicates whether these sources are officially recognized.[4]

Some care is needed in interpreting the indicators. First, not all indicators report direct discrimination, and indicators that appear gender neutral on their face may imply indirect discrimination. For example, indicators regarding the recognition of customary law do not on their face indicate discrimination or nondiscrimination. The content of customary law is not necessarily known, and elements of customary law can be advantageous to women. However, in countries whose constitutions recognize customary law and exempt it from nondiscrimination, women's rights do not have the same protection as men's.

Second, the fact that a country has a particular statute safeguarding women's rights may not necessarily be a positive sign. Inclusion of a gender-specific right could be a sign that women do not otherwise enjoy the right.

Scoresheets 1–3 primarily document a country's recognition of different sources of law that could affect protection of nondiscrimination on the basis of gender. These sources include the following:

- International treaties and conventions, including the Convention on the Elimination of All Forms of Discrimination against Women, the Protocol to the African Charter on Human and Peoples' Rights on the Rights of Women in Africa, and International Labour Organization (ILO) conventions on gender equality in labor
- Constitutional protections against nondiscrimination on the basis of gender and gender inequality
- Customary and religious laws and whether their recognition stems from provisions in the constitution or statutes and whether they are explicitly exempt from constitutional provisions for gender nondiscrimination.

Scoresheets 4–7 document whether the economic rights of men and women are the same in legal capacity, property rights (including marital property and inheritance), land, and labor. These four scoresheets provide indicators mainly of statutes, but they also record when customary or religious laws are recognized as the prevailing source of law in these areas.

The following seven subsections introduce the scoresheets. They discuss the main issues they aim to capture, list the indicators, and provide some overview figures.

Countries are grouped based on four characteristics: income level (the World Bank's definition of low-income and middle-income countries, based on gross domestic product [GDP] per capita levels); primary legal system (civil law and common law)[5]; default marital property regime; and strength of the rule of law. Much of the focus is on income, because there is an interest in knowing whether the process of development itself can help close gender gaps.[6]

Data collection was challenging. Data came from online sources for some countries. The U.S. Library of Congress was particularly important for laws unavailable online. Some systems of laws (such as information on the status of ratification of international instruments, constitutions, and labor laws) are well covered, and information is readily available. In contrast, information gaps on the recognition of customary law and family and land laws were wide, and no prior systematic attempts had been made to develop a comprehensive database for the whole region.

"Not found" is recorded to distinguish countries in which information was unavailable from countries in which a provision is known not to apply. In addition, many customary laws are rarely codified, making it especially difficult to determine precisely what these laws say and assess their possible impact.

Compilation of the database benefited from several concurrent initiatives, including the Gender Law Library and its accompanying *Women, Business, and the Law* publication (see appendix B) and the International Finance Corporation's Women in Business Program, which addresses the gender dimensions of investment climate reform (Simavi, Manuel, and Blackden 2010).

Principal Findings from the Database

Three key messages emerge from the database:

- All countries recognize the principle of nondiscrimination in their constitutions, in the treaties they have signed, or both. Even where nondiscrimination is recognized as a guiding principle of law, however, legal exceptions are widespread—sometimes even in constitutions themselves, some of which exempt customary law from the principle of nondiscrimination. And many countries still discriminate in their statutes.

- Many discriminatory provisions apply not to women as women but to women as married women. From a legal standpoint, marriage changes the status and rights of women, sometimes radically, often conferring legal capacities and responsibilities on husbands and removing them from wives.

This change applies particularly to property regimes and rights during and after marriage and to rules affecting women's economic capacity and decision making in marriage.

- The treatment of women's economic rights is not closely correlated with a country's income. Raising national income by itself is therefore unlikely to improve women's legal and economic rights. More interventionist reforms will probably be needed.

Scoresheet 1: Ratification of International Treaties and Conventions

Issues Captured

The indicators in scoresheet 1 report whether countries have ratified the highest-profile international agreements that aim to provide for nondiscrimination based on gender. A distinction needs to be made between signing and ratifying a treaty. Signing signals the intent of the president or prime minister to adhere to the treaty. But until it is ratified by the legislature, a treaty does not have the force of law.

The primary global convention is the Convention on the Elimination of All Forms of Discrimination against Women (CEDAW) (box 2.1; see box 1.1 in chapter 1 for its definition of discrimination). Sub-Saharan Africa has its own equivalent instrument, the Protocol to the African Charter on Human and Peoples' Rights on the Rights of Women in Africa (box 2.2).

On the more targeted issues related to labor, ILO conventions set out international standards governing employment and working conditions. The database covers four key conventions. The scoresheet also records whether ratified international conventions have the force of law domestically.[7]

Indicators

Scoresheet 1 includes the following indicators:

- Whether a country has ratified CEDAW
- Whether a country has ratified the Protocol to the African Charter on Human and Peoples' Rights on the Rights of Women in Africa
- Whether a country has ratified the following ILO conventions:
  - C100 Equal Remuneration Convention, 1951, which obligates state parties to guarantee equal remuneration for men and women for work of equal value through national laws or regulations
  - C111 Discrimination (Employment and Occupation) Convention, 1958, which requires states to guarantee equality of opportunity and treatment in employment and occupation, with a view to eliminating discrimination in that area

BOX 2.1

The Convention on the Elimination of All Forms of Discrimination against Women

The Convention on the Elimination of all forms of Discrimination against Women (CEDAW)—adopted in 1979 by the United Nations General Assembly—defined what constitutes discrimination against women and set up an agenda for national action to end it. It is often described as an international bill of rights for women. By ratifying the convention, countries commit to ending discrimination against women in all forms. Ratification represents a commitment to the following actions:

- Abolishment of all discriminatory laws and adoption of appropriate laws prohibiting discrimination against women in order to incorporate the principle of equality between men and women in their legal systems
- Establishment of tribunals and other public institutions to ensure the effective protection of women against discrimination
- Elimination of all acts of discrimination against women by persons, organizations, and enterprises

Article 11 lays out protections in employment, including gender equality in the right to work, the choice of profession, equal pay, and rights to social protections. Article 14 addresses the challenges of women in rural areas for income opportunities and for sharing the benefits of rural development. Articles 15 and 16 set out areas that fall under family law. Article 15 mandates the same personal rights for husband and wife, including the right to choose a family name, a profession, and an occupation. Article 16 mandates the same rights for both spouses with respect to the ownership, acquisition, management, administration, enjoyment, and disposition of property, whether free of charge or for a consideration.

Source: CEDAW (http://www.un.org/womenwatch/daw/cedaw/cedaw.htm).

    ◦ C171 Night Work Convention, 1990, which requires states to address the labor rights of women in regard to night work, particularly during pregnancy and after childbirth

    ◦ C183 Maternity Protection Convention, 2000, which reinforces labor rights for pregnant and breastfeeding women

- Whether the ratified international convention has the force of law domestically (that is, whether it is a monist or dualist state).

Patterns across Countries

All but 2 of the 47 countries (Somalia and Sudan) have ratified CEDAW.[8] As virtually all the civil law countries are monist, the provisions in CEDAW have

BOX 2.2

The Protocol to the African Charter on Human and Peoples' Rights on the Rights of Women in Africa

The Protocol to the African Charter on Human and Peoples' Rights on the Rights of Women in Africa requires African governments to eliminate all forms of discrimination and violence against women in Africa and to promote women's equality. It also commits African governments to include these fundamental principles in their national constitutions and other legislative instruments, if they have not already done so, and to ensure their effective implementation. It requires states to eliminate all forms of discrimination against women through legislative, institutional, and other measures and enjoins states to eliminate practices based on the idea of inferiority of either gender, stereotyped roles for men and women, or other harmful cultural and traditional practices. It also obligates states to integrate a gender perspective in their policy decisions, legislation, development plans, and activities and to ensure women's overall well-being.

More specifically, the protocol requires states to guarantee women's property rights during marriage and after its dissolution through death or divorce. States are obliged to guarantee women's labor rights, including equality in remuneration, the right to choose a profession, and protection when pregnant. The protocol also requires states to ensure that women can access credit.

The protocol was adopted July 11, 2003, at the second summit of the African Union in Maputo, Mozambique. It came into force November 25, 2005, 30 days after ratification by 15 countries. As of January 1, 2011, 46 countries had signed the protocol and 28 had ratified it.

Source: http://www.africa-union.org/root/au/Documents/Treaties/treaties.htm.

the force of law domestically. All of the common law countries in Sub-Saharan Africa except Sudan have ratified CEDAW (figure 2.1), but as CEDAW reports indicate, the process of domestication is incomplete in several countries.[9] More than half the countries have ratified the Protocol to the African Charter on Human and Peoples' Rights on the Rights of Women in Africa, with a higher proportion among common law countries.

All countries except Liberia and Somalia are signatories to ILO Convention 100 (on equal pay for work of equal value), and all countries are signatories to Convention 111 (on the equal right to work). Twenty-six countries are signatories to ILO Conventions 4, 41, and 89, which restrict night work for all women in certain industries, and Madagascar has ratified the 1990 Protocol to Convention 89, which obliges states to provide alternatives to night work for women during pregnancy and childbirth.[10] Only Ethiopia has ratified Convention 183 (on maternity protection).

Figure 2.1 Most Countries Have Ratified International Conventions on Women's Rights

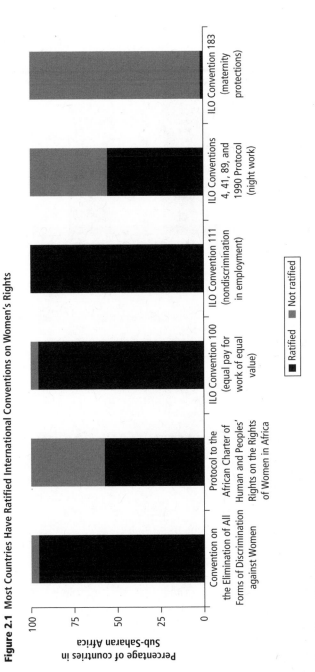

Source: Women–LEED–Africa.
Note: ILO = International Labour Organization.

Figure 2.2 For Most Civil Law Countries and a Quarter of Common Law Countries, Being a Monist State Automatically Gives International Conventions the Force of Law Domestically

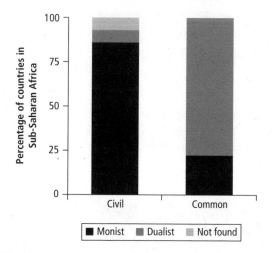

Source: Women–LEED–Africa.
Note: In a monist state, a ratified international convention has the force of law domestically; in a dualist state, domestic laws need to be reviewed and, if necessary, amended to comply with the ratified convention.

Most civil law countries and a quarter of common law countries are monist states (figure 2.2). For the majority of common law countries and two civil law countries, however, domestication is still required.

Scoresheet 2: Gender Provisions in Constitutions

Issues Captured

Scoresheet 2 examines whether constitutions include a clause on nondiscrimination or equality before the law. As constitutions provide the guiding principles for the legal system, the extent to which they provide for nondiscrimination based on gender is critical for women's economic rights.

Such a nondiscrimination clause does not mean that all statutes comply with it. Indeed, the importance of subsequent scoresheets is to discover the rate of noncompliance. For example, Cameroon still gives men the right to administer all marital property without the consent of their wives, and Swaziland's statutes recognize women as legal minors. Strengthening the constitution is an important first step, but ensuring that it prevails over statutes is critical to give it force.

An even stronger provision is one enshrining the principal of gender equality. This provision implies a higher standard. It not only bans discrimination, it also provides grounds for positive action to address gender equality.

The database captures whether a constitution includes a safeguard on individual property ownership, a general right to ownership for all citizens implicitly providing women (as well as men) with the right to own property. It also records whether the constitution explicitly guarantees women the right to own property. A provision mandating equal rights to own property reinforces the fact that women's ownership rights are equal to those of men—although it also can raise questions as to why such a gender-specific provision is necessary.

The database records whether countries recognize the principle of the equal right to work and the right to equal pay, reinforcing the standards in ILO Conventions 100 and 111. It also records whether individuals can directly appeal to the constitution to challenge a law or legal code. At issue is whether individuals, and not just the executive branch, have "standing" to challenge the constitutionality of a statute. The thresholds for showing standing—that is, demonstrating that a plaintiff has been adversely affected by a statute and showing the extent of harm in order to establish that he or she is entitled to bring a legal challenge—vary by country; if set high enough, they can choke off this avenue of redress.[11] The indicator records provisions in the constitution as well as statutory provisions (if they exist). Although a political process is usually available to engage with legislators to change laws, giving individuals standing to challenge the constitutionality of statutes provides them with another judicial avenue for overturning legislation.

Indicators

Scoresheet 2 includes the following indicators:

- Whether there is constitutional recognition of nondiscrimination based on gender, marital status, or both
- Whether there is constitutional provision for gender equality
- Whether there is constitutional guarantee of ownership of property
- Whether there is constitutional guarantee of women's right to own property or explicit guarantee of gender equality in ownership of property
- Whether there is constitutional protection for the equal right to work and the right to equal pay
- Whether individuals or only the executive branch can challenge the constitutionality of statutes

Patterns across Countries

The constitutions of every country in the region mention nondiscrimination based on gender or equality before the law. Many constitutions also contain the stronger provision of gender equality (figure 2.3). This provision is particularly common in low-income countries: four of the five countries that do not have a gender equality clause are middle-income countries (Botswana, Cape Verde, Ghana, and Mauritius). Liberia is the one low-income country without this

Figure 2.3 All Countries Recognize the Principle of Nondiscrimination

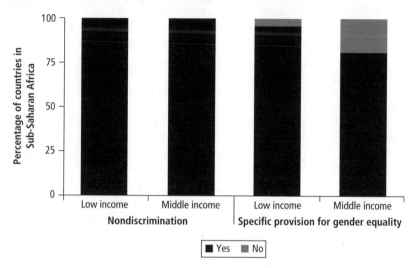

Source: Women–LEED–Africa.

provision. But this provision does not lead to fewer sources of gaps in women's economic rights: 22 countries with head-of-household statutes (statutes that give husbands rights to wives' property or economic activities) also have gender equality as a constitutional principle. Only Cape Verde has head-of-household provisions but no gender equality provision.[12]

Almost 80 percent of countries provide general protection of rights to property ownership (figure 2.4). Eight countries (Ethiopia, Guinea-Bissau, Kenya, Liberia, Malawi, Senegal, Swaziland, and Zimbabwe) go farther, explicitly providing that women have a right to own property. This explicit recognition could indicate stronger protection of women's property rights. Alternatively, the need for the law could reflect women's weaker status. Swaziland is the only middle-income country to have this provision, but it also keeps on the books a Deeds Registry Act that forbids married women from owning land in their own name—a reminder of the importance of both examining legal statutes and reviewing the statutes behind progressive principles in new constitutions to ensure consistent application of the law.[13] The constitutions of 31 of the 47 countries recognize the equal right to work and to equal pay for work of equal value, reinforcing the principle of ILO Conventions 100 and 111.

In terms of having standing to challenge the constitutionality of statutes, there is little variation by income (figure 2.5). There are closer ties to the type of legal system. Common law countries allow individuals to challenge the constitutionality of statutes. In contrast, in almost a third of civil law countries, only

Figure 2.4 Constitutions Recognizing Property Ownership, Equal Right to Work, and Right to Equal Pay

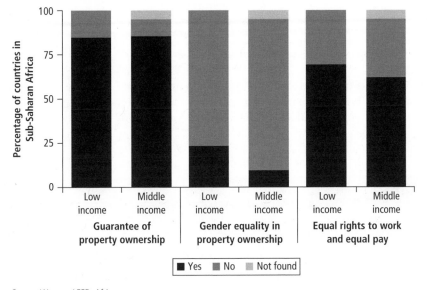

Source: Women–LEED–Africa.

Figure 2.5 Standing to Challenge the Constitutionality of Statutes Varies across Countries

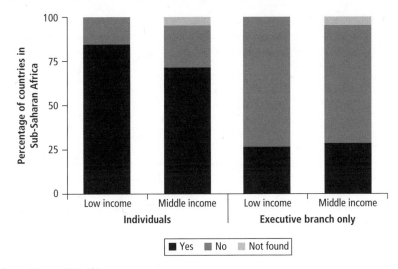

Source: Women–LEED–Africa.

the executive branch can file such challenges. (This indicator is based solely on provisions in the constitution, not on statutes, which may also give individuals the right to challenge the constitutionality of laws.)

Scoresheet 3: Recognition of Customary and Religious Law

Many Sub-Saharan African countries have multiple sources of law, as discussed in chapter 3. Customary law, religious law, or both are recognized as formal—and often equal—sources of law in many constitutions and some statutes. Indeed, customary law has a central place in African countries' legal systems (box 2.3)—often to the detriment of women.

BOX 2.3

The Central Place of Customary Law in Africa

Since independence, the legal systems in Africa have adopted three main approaches to customary law.

- English-speaking countries have retained much of the dual legal structures created during colonial rule while attempting to reform and adapt customary law to notions of British law.
- French- and Portuguese-speaking countries have pursued an integrationist course by trying to absorb customary law into the general law, codifying elements of customary law in statutes.
- Some countries, such as Ethiopia, have adopted measures to abolish particular aspects of customary law through legislation.

No African country proscribes or totally disregards customary law. It continues to be recognized and enforced, to different degrees depending on the jurisdiction. Many countries' constitutions and statutes recognize customary law as a major source of law, to be determined and applied in legal proceedings when it is raised by the parties.

Customary law can be defined in various ways. Nhlapo (1995, p. 53) defines it as "a customs based system whose legitimacy lies largely in its claims to a direct link with the past and with tradition." Henrysson and Joireman (2009) define it as a body of rules governing personal status, communal resources, and local organization.

Three characteristics of customary law make it difficult to determine what women's economic rights are: it is rarely codified; it is not uniform across communities, with differences stemming from language, proximity, origin, history, social structure, and economy; and it is dynamic, with rules evolving to reflect changing social and economic conditions.

Although the content of customary law differs from that of religious law, the laws share several features. Neither is always codified (though some countries have codified religious law, making it easier to determine its content), and the laws generally apply only to certain issues, subpopulations, or localities (religious law is more likely to be applied uniformly across the country to the relevant subpopulation). Some countries recognize religious law as a type of customary law. Other countries recognize it as the law of the land. Scoresheet 3 presents indicators in three areas: customary law in constitutions, religious law in constitutions, and customary and religious law in statutes. The indicators examine whether constitutions or statutes formally recognize customary or religious law as a source of law and whether the law is bound by (or exempted from) the provision of nondiscrimination.

Customary law is influenced by many sources, including Christian and Islamic values, central government administrative policy, pronouncements of superior courts of record, customary court records (where available), and district council and chiefdom bylaws (Kane, Oloka-Onyango, and Tejan-Cole 2005; Joireman 2008). It is binding on its members, and its rules include local sanctions for breaching them, making it all the more important to consider its role in determining women's rights locally.

Some countries' constitutions recognize customary law as a source of law; many countries' statutes, marriage laws, and inheritance practices recognize customary law. Several countries have recognized customary courts formally; some other countries allow them to operate parallel to the formal system. Togo Ordinance No. 78-35 of 1978, for example, sets out areas in which customary law is applicable, such as the capacity to contract, marry, divorce, and inherit.

Before colonization, customary law was the principal source of law in Africa. The colonists introduced their own laws and courts, creating a dual system in which Western-type courts presided over by expatriate magistrates and judges had jurisdiction in specific areas of criminal and civil matters. In colonies such as Botswana, Ghana, Malawi, Nigeria, South Africa, and Zimbabwe, customary courts were established, headed by traditional chiefs or local elders. During the colonial era, these courts, which remain in place today, had jurisdiction only over Africans and mainly applied local customary law.

Creating customary courts did not do away with precolonial traditional adjudication systems. The statutory customary courts only formalized and entrenched selected aspects of these systems that suited the purposes of the colonial administrations. Though generally not officially recognized, these traditional systems continued to be used by the parties as they wished. In countries such as Kenya and Tanzania, specific customary courts were not created. The formal judicial system adjudicated over customary law, with informal customary courts operating in villages.

Source: Kuruk 2002.

Customary Law in Constitutions

Issues captured.   The recognition of customary law and the consequent overlapping sources of law complicate the analysis of women's de jure economic rights. As customary law does not always hold nondiscrimination based on gender as one of its core values, recognizing it as a source of law can lead to differential treatment of women and men. Moreover, many countries' constitutions explicitly exempt customary law from the principle of nondiscrimination.

Customary law is not inherently discriminatory. The content of customary law varies, geographically and temporally (the general lack of codification of the law makes it hard to capture in the database). The findings from scoresheet 3 (on customary law and customary marriages and inheritance practices) are not that such law and practices are discriminatory but that they could be. And if they are, there is often little recourse.

Indicators.   Scoresheet 3 includes the following indicators:

- Whether the constitution allows for discrimination based on customary law only to the extent that such law is consistent with other higher principles and explicitly recognizes nondiscrimination as a higher principle
- Whether the constitution recognizes customary law and explicitly allows for gender discrimination in areas where customary law prevails
- Whether the constitution is silent on customary law

Patterns across countries.   Only about half of the 47 countries' constitutions formally recognize customary law as a source of law (figure 2.6). Patterns are similar in low- and middle-income countries.

When countries do not recognize customary law in their constitutions, they do so implicitly in statutes, particularly for marriage or inheritance (discussed below). What varies across countries is the extent to which they place constraints on customary law in upholding nondiscrimination.

Among countries that formally recognize customary law in their constitutions, a third exempt it from the nondiscrimination provision. The proportion is higher among middle-income than low-income countries. As most countries recognize customary law in marriage, property, and inheritance, such exemption strikes at the heart of women's ability to control assets and pursue economic opportunities.

The recognition of customary law and its formal exemption from provisions of nondiscrimination can set up potential contradictions in the constitution itself. Five countries—The Gambia, Lesotho, Sierra Leone, Zambia, and Zimbabwe—recognize gender equality (not just nondiscrimination) as a constitutional principle but exempt customary law from nondiscrimination. Zimbabwe

Figure 2.6 Some Countries Recognize Customary Law and Allow It to Discriminate against Women

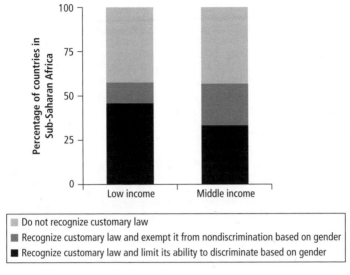

Source: Women–LEED–Africa.

also recognizes women's right to own property but recognizes customary law as prevailing in many property-related matters.

Legal tradition is more closely correlated with the treatment of customary law than is a country's income (figure 2.7). The constitutions of all but two common law countries recognize customary law as a source of law, whereas only a third of civil law countries do so.

Religious Law in Constitutions

Issues captured. Religious laws, such as Islamic Sharia (box 2.4) and Hindu personal laws, form part of Sub-Saharan Africa's many legal systems.[14] As with customary law, some constitutions and statutes recognize religious laws, to varying degrees. Although Christianity does not have a specific law relating to personal law per se, its influence can still be seen in many constitutional provisions and statutes.

In many countries, Sharia laws are not codified and are thus left open to misinterpretation, lack of observance, and conflicting decisions. Ignorance and misconceptions can also lead to injustice, especially where basic rights accorded

Figure 2.7 Constitutions Recognizing Customary Law, by Type of Legal Tradition

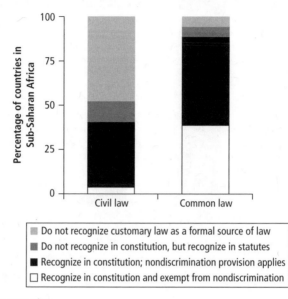

Source: Women–LEED–Africa.

under Sharia are not observed. But codifying Sharia can "freeze" the law and deprive it of flexibility.

Sharia law places obligations on parties. But as in all systems of laws, the existence of obligations does not ensure their enforcement. De facto practice can leave widows in a vulnerable position if the family refuses to support them or denies them their share of inheritance. Divorced women are also left potentially vulnerable, with limited rights to maintenance and lack of family support. In the Mossi Muslim communities of Burkina Faso and some Muslim communities of Senegal, for example, the birth family relinquishes responsibility for women once they are married. Moreover, patrilineal Mossi customs override Muslim norms of daughters' rights to inherit land. At most, daughters are given temporary user rights to their father's lands (Platteau and others 2000).

In recognizing religious law, only five low-income countries (Ethiopia, The Gambia, Kenya, Malawi, and Uganda) and two middle-income countries (Botswana and South Africa) place any limits on whether it can discriminate. (The indicator reflects only whether religious law is explicitly recognized as a source of law in some areas or for some populations.) Even countries that require that customary law be subject to nondiscrimination provisions do not always require that religious law be so (see figure 2.10).

BOX 2.4

How Does Sharia Treat Women's Property?

The provisions of Sharia vary by region, by historical and political context, and by the customary traditions of the community. In Mauritania and Sudan, Sharia is constitutionally recognized as the prevailing source of law; in Somalia it can rank above the constitution. It is recognized as a personal law by the constitution of Nigeria and is applicable to the Muslim population in some states in the country's north. In Kenya and Uganda, the constitution recognizes Sharia provisions on personal status, marriage, divorce, and inheritance. Both countries have established religious (*kadhi*) courts, which adjudicate on matters such as marriage and personal status where all parties are Muslim. State courts in Tanzania can refer to Sharia in personal disputes in which all parties are Muslim.

In countries where a large proportion of the population is Muslim, such as Chad, Comoros, Mali, Mauritania, Mauritius, and Senegal, religion has a greater impact on statutory laws. Senegal's family code is largely ignored in rural areas but is used in cases that make it to urban courts. Between 1974 and 1985, all but 452 of 4,607 judgments arising from inheritance cases were decided according to Sharia (Sowsidibe 1994). In Mali, which has no civil code governing inheritance, cases are usually decided based on the traditional or religious law that applies to the deceased (Wing 2009).

Many provisions of Sharia protect women's rights to property. All women—married and unmarried—are entitled to own property in their own right (Diara and Monimart 2006); to work outside the home; and to keep any income or profits they derive from their personal property, which they can deal with as they wish. Sharia accords women full legal capacity to enter into civil transactions. It also has a bilateral inheritance system under which both men and women inherit. *Mirath* (inheritance laws under Sharia) allows for inheritance by the female relatives of the deceased, including the mother, sisters, wives, and daughters. A widow is entitled to remain in the marital home and be maintained there for a year after her husband's death.

Where there are sons and daughters, the daughters' share of the inheritance is generally half the brothers', which is potentially discriminatory. The historical reason for this tradition, however, was that male family members were usually under an obligation to support the family's female members. When these social obligations are eroded and society's expectations change, injustice can set in.

Sharia laws are not a fixed code; their interpretation varies according to different historical schools of jurisprudence and social, geographic, and cultural contexts. Schools of jurisprudence differ regarding who is able to negotiate the marriage contract, for example. One school that historically empowered women as their own negotiators emerged from a cosmopolitan multiethnic environment rather than from a more traditional tribal society. Lack of awareness, cultural reluctance, and absence of political will to refer to provisions of Sharia that promote parity may result in failure to apply them in practice.

Indicators. Scoresheet 3 includes the following indicators:

- Whether the constitution recognizes religious law only to the extent that such law is consistent with the bill of rights and whether it explicitly recognizes nondiscrimination as a higher principle
- Whether the constitution recognizes religious law and does not place limits on the law on discrimination based on gender

Patterns across countries. A third of Sub-Saharan countries officially recognize religious law as prevailing for some proportion of the population, in certain areas of the law, or both. Almost half of these countries do not limit religious law from potentially discriminating on the basis of gender (figure 2.8).

Customary and Religious Law in Statutes

Issues covered. The indicators in this subsection focus on statutes that explicitly recognize customary law as a source of law. Statutes recognizing certain customary or religious practices as official are discussed under scoresheet 5.

Indicators. Scoresheet 3 includes the following indicators:

- Explicit recognition of customary law as a source of law (judicature acts, for example, which define jurisdiction of each layer of court within a legal system and the applicable sources of law).

Figure 2.8 Constitutions Recognizing Religious Law

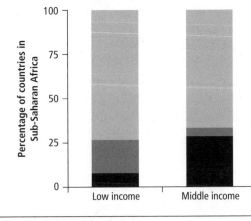

Source: Women–LEED–Africa.

- Statutory limits on customary law. In general, the nondiscrimination bar is lower in statutes, which may be able to discriminate as long as they pass the repugnancy test and do not undermine the status of women.[15] Interpretations of both conditions can be based on traditional gender roles (discussed in chapter 4).
- Recognition of religious law as a source of law.
- Statutory limits on religious law.
- Recognition of customary or religious courts.

Patterns across countries for customary law.   More than half of Sub-Saharan countries recognize customary law as an independent source of law in statutes (figure 2.9). In half of these countries, the application of customary law can be limited by statute (the most common means is the repugnancy test). Under the repugnancy test, customary law can still be discriminatory, but the differential treatment should not be repugnant or contrary to natural justice.

Zambia, which explicitly exempts customary law from nondiscrimination provisions in the constitution, calls for the repugnancy test in its Judicature Act. Botswana, Ghana, and Zimbabwe also exempt customary law from nondiscrimination, but they do not have a repugnancy test provision in their Judicature Acts. Tanzania does not have a repugnancy test provision in its Judicature Act, although it does require that customary law be consistent with the nondiscrimination clause in its Constitution.

Figure 2.9 Countries with Statutes Recognizing Customary Law as a Source of Law

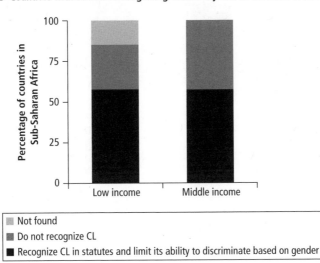

Source: Women–LEED–Africa.
Note: CL = customary law.

Patterns across countries for religious law.   Low-income countries are more likely than higher-income countries to recognize religious law. Of those that do, more than half do not explicitly limit its ability to discriminate based on gender (figure 2.10).

The likelihood that a country recognizes customary law, religious law, or both can be analyzed along three dimensions: income, legal tradition, and rule of law (as determined by the World Governance Indicators, a measure of the strength of courts and the application and enforcement of laws based on many sources). Low-income countries are more likely than middle- income countries to recognize customary and religious law. They are also more likely to do so in their statutes than in their constitutions. This pattern is less a reflection of their income, however, than of differences in legal tradition: common law countries are more likely to recognize customary and religious law in their constitutions, figure 2.11 indicates.

All but one common law country recognizes customary or religious law, with half providing constitutional exemption from nondiscrimination. Among civil law countries, less than 15 percent include this exemption. Half the civil law countries recognize customary and religious law in statutes rather than the constitution; only five countries remain silent on both potential sources of law.

Countries reveal no clear relationship in treatment of customary and religious laws based on the rule of law.[16] Countries in the top third (with the strongest legal institutions) are the most likely to exempt customary law from

Figure 2.10 Countries with Statutes Recognizing Religious Law as a Source of Law

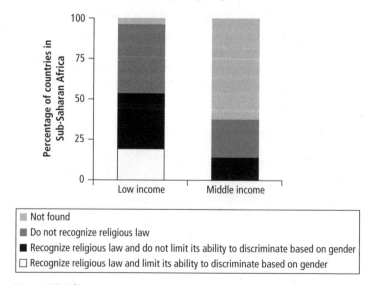

Source: Women–LEED–Africa.

Figure 2.11 Treatment of Customary and Religious Law, by Income, Legal Tradition, and Rule of Law

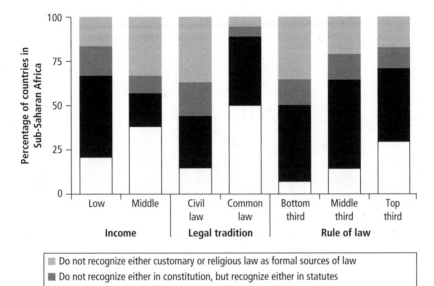

Source: Women–LEED–Africa.

nondiscrimination provisions, and countries in the middle third are least likely to do so. Countries with the weakest legal institutions are least likely to recognize customary or religious law as a source of law, in statutes or the constitution.

In recognizing customary or religious laws in statutes, few countries explicitly limit their ability to discriminate against women. Rather, the customary and religious laws of all countries are limited by the repugnancy test, and appeals can be made to the broader principles of the constitution.

Many countries' statutes recognize the function of customary and religious courts (figure 2.12). These courts strengthen the institutional role of customary or religious law. As chapter 4 discusses, customary and religious courts can be more accessible than the formal judicial system. However, judicial oversight of proceedings is generally weaker in customary and religious courts than in civil courts—and to the extent that there are inconsistencies between statutory rights and rights in customary or religious law, it is worth looking closely at which forum is more likely to be advantageous to whom in particular disputes. Across countries, formal customary courts are more common than religious courts, and both customary and religious courts are more prevalent in lower-income countries.

Figure 2.12 Statutory Recognition of Customary and Religious Courts

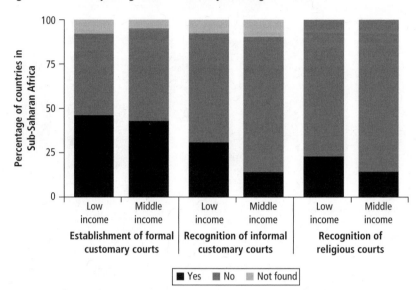

Source: Women–LEED–Africa.

Scoresheet 4: Legal Capacity

Issues Captured

Scoresheet 4 draws largely on family and marriage laws or codes. Only one country (Swaziland) explicitly grants women minority legal status (despite its constitutional provision that all laws be subject to the principle of nondiscrimination based on gender). In other countries, women's ability to run their own businesses is potentially affected by four factors: head-of-household laws; husbands' right to select the marital domicile; the need to obtain their husband's permission to enter contracts, open bank accounts, or obtain loans; and the need to obtain their husband's permission to work outside the home.

Head-of-household laws.   The most common area in which women's legal capacity is limited is head-of-household statutes. Head-of-household laws are a colonial heritage that remains mainly in former French colonies. Although removed in France in the 1960s and 1970s, they remain in the civil and family codes of some of the civil law countries in Sub-Saharan Africa. These laws establish the husband as the head of household and can give him the right to control decisions and marital property.

Only one common law country (Sudan) maintains statutory recognition of the husband as the head of household. Some legal hybrid countries used to have marital powers acts that granted husbands similar powers, based on the earlier Roman-Dutch tradition, but over the last 15 years, every legal hybrid African country except Swaziland has repealed these laws. Botswana has repealed these laws for civil marriages although not for customary marriages (box 2.5). Regardless of the statutes, the concept behind head-of-household laws has been influential in customary practices—and is still reflected in the application of customary law in many places.

Head-of-household provisions do not carry the same legal implications in all countries. Some countries without such provisions still have statutes that provide for the same powers of husbands over their wives as found in marital powers acts. In other countries, the man is acknowledged as the head of the household as a social distinction, but provisions in the law explicitly state that husbands do not have power over the economic decisions of their wives.

Head-of-household rules pose particular challenges where the husband is a migrant worker and the woman is left in charge of the household. In these cases, women may be legally constrained in many of their activities. In some cases, women have to apply for a court order to seek the transfer of marital powers— an extremely expensive and difficult process for most women.

BOX 2.5

Head-of-Household Laws in Common Law Countries

The abolition of marital power in South Africa (Matrimonial Property Act 88 of 1984), Namibia (Married Person Equality Act 1996 Act 1 of 1996), Botswana (Abolition of Marital Power Act 34 of 2004), and Lesotho (Legal Capacity of Married Persons Act 9 of 2006) has led to better protection of property rights for women in marriage. However, in Botswana, the abolition of marital power applies only to civil marriages of women of European descent; for the rest of the population, customary law prevails unless spouses specifically opt for a community of property regime at the time of marriage.

The restrictions removed in the four countries include the wife's ability to enter into contracts, register immovable property in her name, and litigate and administer joint property. Namibia provides that the domicile of a married woman shall not by virtue only of the marriage be considered the same as that of her husband, but shall be ascertained by reference to the same factors as apply in the case of any other individual capable of acquiring a domicile of choice. Women are also allowed to make decisions without interference from husbands, which is important for entrepreneurship.

Source: Kamangu 2009.

Husbands' rights to select the marital domicile.   If a business is run out of the home or where clients are located nearby, changing residence can have a significant impact on business. For example, a dressmaker can develop a clientele in her neighborhood. If her husband decides to move the household to another village or area of the city, she would have to build up her client base from scratch. This can happen in Benin, the Democratic Republic of Congo, Rwanda, and other countries that give the husband sole authority to choose the marital home. It can also happen under customary law. In Botswana, for example, the Abolition of Marital Power (2004), which entered force in 2005, applies only to civil marriages, not to customary or religious marriages. Thus, the husband still determines the wife's domicile on marriage in the vast majority of marriages (Republic of Botswana 2008).

Need to obtain husband's permission to enter contracts, open bank accounts, and obtain loans.   Banking and business laws tend to be gender blind, but in the Democratic Republic of Congo, Gabon, Mali, Niger, and Togo, a woman needs her husband's permission to open a bank account, deposit or withdraw any money made available to her by the husband, and even deposit or withdraw her own money. These laws hamper women's ability to do business.

Need to obtain husband's permission to work outside the home.   In Burundi, Cameroon, the Democratic Republic of Congo, the Republic of Congo, Côte d'Ivoire, Gabon, Guinea, Mali, Mauritania, Niger, Rwanda, and Togo, women have the right to exercise a profession or trade—but the husband has the right to oppose her activities if he deems them to be against the family's interest. In some countries, the law does not delimit what the family interest is, giving the husband discretion to decide. In Guinea, a wife can challenge her husband's opposition and continue to take on professional commitments and make contracts with third parties as long as the third party is aware of the husband's opposition (Article 329 of the Civil Code of Guinea). The husband's opposition is one more legal hurdle for the woman—and likely a costly one.

Indicators

Scoresheet 4 includes the following indicators:

- Recognition of husband as head of household
- Husband's ability to decide on marital domicile
- Need for husband's permission to open a bank account
- Husband's ability to deny wife permission to pursue a trade or profession or to work outside the home

Figure 2.13 Head-of-Household Rules Are Common in Both Middle- and Low-Income Countries

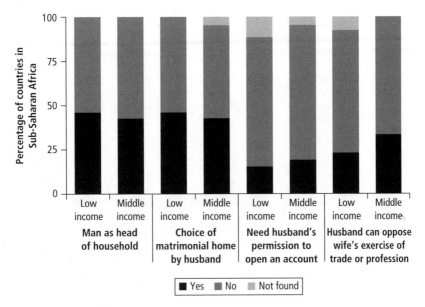

Source: Women–LEED–Africa.

Patterns across Countries

The prevalence of restrictions on women's legal capacity is not significantly different by country income (figure 2.13). It is more prominent in civil law countries,
where 18 of the 29 have head-of-household statutes. In common law countries,
only 3 of 18 do, with Swaziland recording all 4 head-of-household rules discussed
here and Sudan 3 of 4.

The right of the husband to choose the marital home is the most common way in
which men are given economic say over their wives' decisions, though the ability to
deny permission to pursue a job or profession is also common. The need to obtain a
husband's signature to open a bank account appears less common, but the database
captures only where this practice is required in marital statutes; many countries
allow banks to require a husband's signature as part of their business practice.

The rule of law shows a wider range of patterns than country income.
Countries are divided into three equal groups based (on the World Governance Indicators for Africa. Restrictions on a wife's legal capacity are less
common in the top third (countries with the strongest rule of law), particularly on the choice of the home and the ability to work outside the home
(figure 2.14). In the eight countries in which the quality of the rule of law
is above the global average (Botswana, Cape Verde, Lesotho, Mauritius,

Figure 2.14 Head-of-Household Rules Are More Common in Countries with Weaker Rule of Law

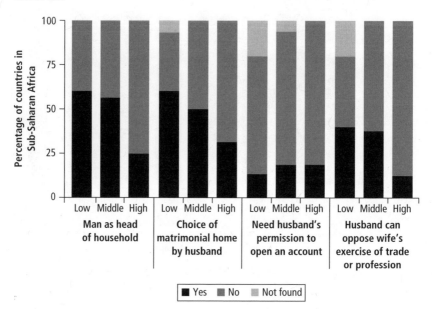

Source: Women–LEED–Africa.

Namibia, Rwanda, Seychelles, and South Africa), only Lesotho gives husbands the right to refuse their wives permission to work outside the home, and only Botswana and Cape Verde require a husband's signature before a wife can open a bank account.

Scoresheet 5: Marriage and Property

This section looks at gender differences in the ability to own, control, and inherit property following marriage. Default marital property regimes make a crucial difference, because they determine whether spouses communally hold property acquired during marriage (and sometimes even before) or each spouse holds such property separately. The default may be overridden, however.

Scoresheet 5 records the effect of the default regime on control of property in marriage, as well as on the division of property on divorce or the husband's death. It also indicates where statutes deviate from the patterns associated with either common or civil law patterns. The section covers four issues: default property regimes in marriage, women's property rights in marriage, the division of marital property on divorce, and the division of marital property on inheritance.

Default Property Regimes in Marriage

Issues captured.   The type of property regime largely determines a woman's ability to own property during marriage and on its dissolution through divorce or the death of the husband. These property rights determine married women's control over assets that can be used as collateral in applying for a loan or used in a business, as well as the incentive to accumulate additional assets or expand a business. The share of assets a woman is entitled to when a marriage ends can be critical in determining whether and what type of business she can run.

Default marital property regimes vary across countries. They are regulated by family code or statute, reflecting the type of marriage contract (customary, polygamous, or monogamous). They come into play if the spouses make no declaration or agreement on the regime before getting married (box 2.6).

The most common default property regimes are community ownership of property (including universal community of property), separate ownership of property, and customary law (table 2.1). These categories are generally mutually exclusive. Family codes or statutes may provide various options that the parties to a marriage can select, usually by a written declaration before or at the time of the marriage or after marriage by a postnuptial agreement. The default regime is the property regime that will apply unless another is actively selected. Only one regime may apply.

Community ownership of property (also known as community of property).   All property acquired during marriage is owned equally by husband and wife, except for property inherited or given as a gift to a spouse (unless the giver specifies that the property goes to both spouses). Personal property (property a spouse owned before getting married) is not joint marital property. Universal community of property is similar to this regime but also includes property owned by either spouse before marriage.

A community of property regime offers women a better chance of maintaining their property rights on dissolution of marriage than separate ownership regimes because it entitles them to a portion, generally half, of the property without having to make proof of contribution. Not having to prove contribution is vital, because millions of women in Africa contribute to marital property through nonmonetized activities, such as performing household chores and working in subsistence agriculture.

Even when community of property is the default regime, it may not always apply, particularly in polygamous marriages, where the default is separate ownership. Separate property in a polygamous marriage protects a wife from having her property divided among other wives, but it also limits a wife's access to assets acquired during marriage.

Separate ownership of property (also known as separate property).   Parties to a marriage generally retain control over property they owned before the marriage and any property they acquired during the marriage. Property such as a marital

BOX 2.6

Alternatives to Default Marital Property Regimes: Prenuptial and Postnuptial Contracts

In many civil law countries (such as Benin, Madagascar, Mauritania, and Senegal) and common law countries (such as Botswana, Ethiopia, Namibia, Nigeria,[a] Kenya, South Africa, and Swaziland), parties to a marriage can select or vary the marital regime by signing prenuptial contracts. (In some countries, spouses can also vary the marital regime during the marriage, through a postnuptial agreement.) In pre- and postnuptial agreements contracts, the spouses agree on how property will be owned in marriage and distributed on separation. The laws of most countries demand that prenuptial agreements be made in front of a notary before or on the day of marriage. Such contracts give room for the parties to determine their property (and other rights), allowing them to add whatever clause they see fit before the marriage. Without such an agreement, the default regime comes into play.

Prenuptial agreements can be advantageous for women, but few African women use them, because they lack knowledge of the law or are reluctant to jeopardize their relationship by proposing one. Many women may own limited property and do not see the value in making such an arrangement. Where bargaining power between the spouses is unequal, prenuptial and postnuptial agreements can deprive women of their rights under a statutory regime.

Prenuptial agreements can cover more than just assets. In Mauritania, for example, Article 28 of the Personal Status of Persons Code 2001 provides that "in a marriage contract, the wife can stipulate that, the husband should not get married to another wife, should not prohibit her from continuing her studies, should not prohibit her from working, should not be absent for a certain period of time, and any other conditions not contrary to the finality of the marriage contract." Article 29 states that "the partial or total breach of the above conditions by the husband will lead to judicial dissolution of the marriage initiated by the wife and an assistance of consolation, the amount which will be determined by the judge."

Source: Kamangu 2009.
[a] Nigeria does not offer the option of a community of property regime, but it recognizes prenuptial and postnuptial agreements under Section 72(2) of the Matrimonial Causes Act (1990) of Nigeria.

---

home can be jointly owned by the spouses, but both have to make an express agreement specifying so, such as registering the title in both their names.

One might expect this regime to protect women, because it allows them to own and manage their property separately, an advantage particularly for women in business, who then can use a title to property to access credit. In fact, a woman's rights may not be protected where her contribution is in the home or in a family business

Table 2.1 Main Features of Default Marital Property Regimes

Type of property	Definition	Administration of property within marriage	Division of property on divorce	Inheritance of marital property by wife on intestate death of husband
Default regimes				
Community of property	Property acquired during marriage is owned jointly by husband and wife (except gifts or inheritance earmarked for either spouse).	Consent of both husband and wife is required on joint assets (not on separate property).	Joint assets acquired during marriage (excluding separate property, such as gifts or bequests) are divided 50–50.	Wife keeps separate property acquired before marriage and inherits 50 percent of joint property acquired during marriage. The other 50 percent and husband's separate property are part of husband's estate and may (or may not) go to wife.
Separate property	Each spouse acquires and owns property as individual.	Each spouse administers his or her own property.	Each spouse receives 100 percent of his or her own property. No presumption is made that a spouse is entitled to any of the property of the other spouse unless he or she can show that financial contributions were made.	No presumption is made that a wife is entitled to any of her husband's property.
Separate property, with recognition of nonmonetary contributions	Each spouses acquires and owns property as individuals.	Each spouse administers his or her own property.	A spouse may be entitled to some of the other spouse's separate property; the share is determined by the monetary contribution to the purchase and maintenance of the property and on nonmonetary contributions (with this share determined by statute, country case law, or both and generally limited to less than 50 percent).	No uniform approach is made to wife's share of husband's property on his death; nonmonetary contributions are not necessarily considered for inheritance; statutory benchmarks are generally less than 50 percent and can be 0.
Universal community of property	Property acquired before and during marriage is owned jointly by husband and wife.	Consent of both husband and wife is required.	There is 50–50 division of all joint assets, regardless of when acquired.	Wife inherits 50 percent of joint property (regardless of when it was acquired). Other 50 percent is part of husband's estate and may (or may not) go to wife.
Traditional regimes				
Dowry	Groom's family pays dowry to bride.	Dowry is wife's property, but husband administers it.	Wife keeps dowry.	Wife keeps dowry.
Bride price	Groom's family pays bride price to bride's family.	Bride price belongs to bride's family, not bride or groom.	Wife's family must repay bride price to husband's family.	Bride price remains with wife's family.

Note: In either of the two separate property regimes, joint ownership can be available. Ownership shares are then part of the legal agreement and are usually 50–50. The table provides generic characteristics; actual conditions in particular countries may vary.

registered in her husband's name. Although a subset of countries with separate property regimes have provisions that allow such contributions from women to count toward the overall assets acquired during marriage—and these nonmonetary contributions can be used to entitle the wife to a portion of the assets—the share is rarely half and it does not always apply at divorce and inheritance.

Customary law.   Some countries' family codes and statutes include provisions regarding the marital regime; other countries have left the marital regime to be determined by customary law. Only three countries (Botswana, Burundi, and Swaziland) provide that customary regimes are the default regime for statutory marriages, though many more countries' statutes include provisions on customary marriages.

Several countries, including Comoros and Madagascar, preserve their unique customary law traditions through provisions in their family codes. In Comoros, on marriage, the wife's family is obliged to provide her with a house, which remains her personal property even on divorce or the husband's death. Other marital provisions are a hybrid of community and separate ownership regimes. For instance, any immovable property that is acquired during the marriage is jointly owned, though the wife's income and movable property are her personal property.

In Madagascar, the default legal regime is the customary tradition of *kitay telo an-dalana*, a variant of the community of property regime. On separation or death, two-thirds of the communally owned marital property goes to the husband and a third to the wife rather than the 50–50 split found in most other countries.[17]

Indicators.   Scoresheet 5 includes the following indicators:

- Whether community of property, separate property of property, or a customary regime is the default regime. (If only one regime is allowed, it is shown as the default. Given that the default regime in polygamous marriages is separate property, countries with community of property as the default that officially allow polygamy are shown as having both systems as the default.)
- Whether community of property is allowed as a marital regime

The default marital property regime is then used to group countries by the other indicators in this section:

- Despite the default property regime, whether some countries still give the husband additional powers over the administration of property
- Whether marriage statutes recognize customary marriages (interpreted in conjunction with statutory provisions of nondiscrimination, where they exist)
- Whether polygamy is formally allowed (the default regime for polygamous marriages is separate property)

Patterns across countries.

Community of property.   All civil law countries for which statutes were available allow community of property, although not always as the default regime
(see appendix A). Some countries offer universal community of property as an
option. Some common law countries, including Lesotho, Namibia, and South
Africa (whose colonial heritage actually makes them hybrid common/civil law
countries), also use community of property as the default regime.[18] South Africa's
default regime is universal community of property, which encompasses property
owned by either spouse before the marriage.[19] Half the common law countries do
not allow community of property as an option. Figure 2.15 shows the prevalence
of the different default marital property regimes.

Separate property.   A separate property default regime is prevalent in civil law
countries that have significant Muslim populations, allow polygamous marriage, or both. It is often the default regime where the marriage is polygamous,
as in Gabon and Senegal; parties to a polygamous marriage are not allowed the
option of a community of property regime. Taking together the community of

Figure 2.15 Distribution of Default Marital Property Regimes

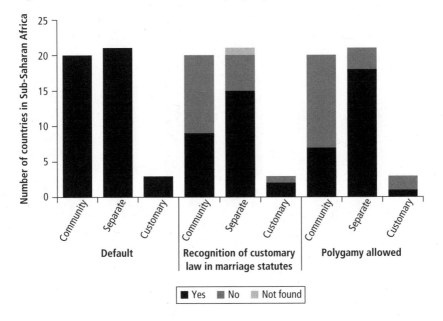

Source: Women–LEED–Africa.
Note: 44 countries are included here. Guinea does not provide a default regime and it was not found for the
Central African Republic and Equatorial Guinea.

property countries and countries that recognize polygamy, a substantial proportion of the population in several community of property countries lives under
a separate property regime.

Separate property regimes are widespread in common law countries, particularly countries that were British colonies and adopted the Married Woman's
Property Act. Many of these countries (including The Gambia, Ghana, Malawi,
Sierra Leone, Tanzania, Uganda, and Zambia) grant no option for community
of property by agreement. What is striking is that, even in separate property
regimes, the husband may still be given rights to administer marital property
and the private property of the wife.

Traditional regimes.   Traditional regimes overlap with statutory default
regimes (figure 2.16; box 2.7). Data were not found for all countries,[20] but these
regimes appear more prevalent in countries with separate property regimes.
Legislation in many countries recognizes the fact that dowry and bride price
are expected culturally but require that the sums paid are merely symbolic.

Figure 2.16 Statutory and Traditional Default Marital Property Regimes Overlap

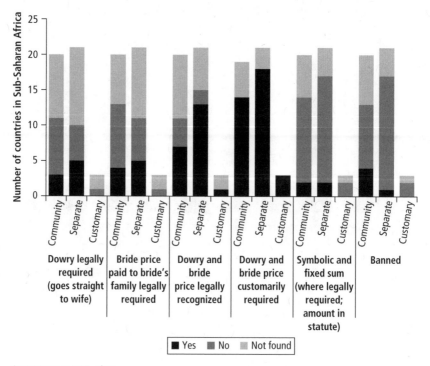

Source: Women–LEED–Africa.

BOX 2.7

Do Matrilocal and Matrilineal Communities Provide Stronger Rights for Women?

In some matrilocal societies (societies in which the married couple lives near the wife's family), ownership of land can pass to daughters rather than sons. Women in matrilocal societies tend to have higher status than women in patrilocal communities. And customary law in matrilocal communities could be more advantageous to women than formal statutory provisions.

In some matrilineal communities, although inheritance passes through the women's blood line, it is still generally given to males (the son of the husband's sister thus inherits). As such, this inheritance custom has little impact on promoting women's economic rights.

Source: USAID 2006.

Very few countries have banned the practices outright. Given that dowries offer women greater economic security than bride price (because women get to keep their dowries after the marriage ends), reducing the size of dowries rarely benefits them (box 2.8).

Women's Property Rights in Marriage

Issues captured.   Separate ownership of property regimes grants the husband no additional rights in administering a wife's property in marriage. In theory, community of property regimes recognize property to be owned by the spouses, usually equally, though many countries with such regimes give the husband additional powers in administering property. In these cases, even where community of property in marriage guarantees women a percentage of the property after dissolution of marriage because of divorce or husband's death, during marriage women have less legal control of marital property than under separate property regimes—or even none at all.

These head-of-household provisions can also apply to property owned jointly by the spouses under an agreement in which the spouses are under a separate property regime by choice or default. For instance, if a husband and wife who are under a separate marital property regime buy property in joint names and sign a written agreement reflecting the joint ownership, the head-of-household rules apply to that joint property.

Indicators.   Scoresheet 5 includes the following indicators:

- Whether the husband as head of household administers or manages community of property alone

BOX 2.8

Are Dowries and Bride Payments Bad for Women?

Dowry regimes are prevalent in countries with large Muslim populations; bride price regimes are required by customary law in several countries. Both regimes can be incorporated into a country's formal legal system though statutory provisions. Under a dowry regime, the husband's family usually pays a dowry to the bride. The assets are then hers and remain hers, even on divorce. Dowry regimes usually coexist with the property regimes outlined in this chapter; they are not default regimes. Examples are in the family and civil codes of Comoros, Guinea,[a] Mauritania,[b] and Senegal.

Senegal allows for three regimes: separate ownership of property, community of property, and dowry. Where the marriage is polygamous, only separate ownership and dowry are allowed. Under a dowry regime, all immovable and movable property given to the wife by people other than the husband has to be deposited in a dowry account in her name. The application of a dowry regime on a house has to be stated in the Land Registry. Administration of the dowry property is in the hands of the husband during the marriage. The wife can seek an order asking for a separate property regime if the husband mismanages the dowry property in a malicious or incompetent way, but doing so is time consuming and potentially expensive.

Under a bride price system, the groom or his family make a payment to the bride's family. The Democratic Republic of Congo has a statutory bride price dowry regime, although the amount of the dowry is legally limited in order to prevent bride price from being treated as a commercial operation by the bride's family and there are sanctions for breaching the limit. If the couple divorces, this sum has to be repaid—a disincentive for the woman to leave the marriage. Her family may also be reluctant to support her in this decision, undermining her bargaining power in the household.

Source: Women–LEED–Africa.

[a] The dowry is a precondition of marriage and must be paid to the wife's family.

[b] If the marriage has been consummated, the wife retains the whole amount. If not, she retains half the amount.

- Whether the husband as head of household requires the consent of the wife in managing marital property
- Whether the husband as head of household has powers to administer the personal property of the wife
- Whether the husband as head of household can pay community debts from the personal property of the wife
- Whether the personal debts of the husband can be paid from community property

Patterns across countries.   Seventeen countries have head-of-household provisions in family codes or statutes. The last four indicators are shown in table 2.2. In Cameroon, Guinea-Bissau, Madagascar, Niger, and Swaziland, the de jure legal status provides that the husband has the right as head of household to manage, control, and dispose of community property without the consent of the wife. In Cameroon and Swaziland, where the husband is allowed to manage even the personal property of the wife, women's ability to provide for collateral security is limited. By contrast, in Burundi, the Democratic Republic of Congo, the Republic of Congo, Gabon, Mali, Rwanda, and Senegal, the husband administers community property but has to obtain the wife's consent in any acts of disposition, putting women in a fairly advantageous position.

All common law countries except Swaziland that allow for community of property have outlawed the marital power of the husband over the person and property of the wife in civil marriages. Women in this system of marriage retain full legal rights during marriage; the husband has to seek the consent of the wife in dealing with marital property. On dissolution through death or divorce, women are automatically entitled to half the property.

Division of Marital Property on Divorce

Issues captured.   In the case of divorce, the division of property depends on the default marital property regime as well as statutory recognition of nonmonetary contributions.[21] Statutory protections can also vary by type of marriage (registered, customary, or consensual union).[22]

Community of property regimes.   Marriage under a community of property regime guarantees that a woman receives a share of the marital property on divorce. Because property is jointly owned (except for gifts and bequests

Table 2.2 Inequalities in Administration of Property During Marriage, by Type of Regime

Indicator	Community of property	Separate property	Customary
Husband does not require consent of wife in managing marital property.	Cameroon, Guinea-Bissau, Madagascar	Niger	Swaziland
Husband has powers to administer wife's personal property.	Cameroon	—	Swaziland
Husband can pay community debts from wife's personal property.	Cameroon	Mali, Togo	Swaziland
Husband's personal debts can be paid from community property.	Cameroon, Mauritius	Mali, Togo	Swaziland

Source: Based on data from Women–LEED–Africa.
Note: Insufficient information was available for the Central African Republic, Chad, Equatorial Guinea, and Somalia.
— = No examples found.

specifically designated to be the personal property of one spouse), both monetary and nonmonetary contributions are recognized; on divorce, women have property they can use as collateral to set up a business (box 2.9). Most countries provide for a 50–50 split of marital property on divorce.

In countries in which the husband has been given greater powers over the administration of marital property in the community of property regime, he can maliciously mismanage property because of marital conflict. Some of these countries have legal provisions that allow women to challenge mismanagement of community property,[23] but they require women to file a claim in court, which, as illustrated in box 2.6, is not easy.

Separate property regimes.   Under separate property regimes, parties are generally entitled to retain their share of assets but are not entitled to a share of the spouse's assets. Title and financial contributions determine how assets are divided.

Statutory recognition of nonmonetary contribution.   Many countries recognize that spouses may have indirectly contributed to buying assets. Their unpaid work in the household may have allowed the other spouse to earn income that then finances the purchase of the asset. These nonmonetary contributions can be considered in countries that provide for their inclusion in the division of assets. Most countries do not specify how nonmonetary

---

BOX 2.9

Protecting the Marital Home as a Woman's Place of Business

Laws that explicitly define property rights for women help safeguard their rights to property on divorce. In Burundi, for example, Article 172 of the Family Code 1993 provides the following:

> *During divorce proceedings and at the demand of one of the parties, the court will take into considerations the interest of the household and that of the children, on the separation of the residence of the spouses and the return of personal property. If the matrimonial home was used for the exercise of an art, liberal profession, artisanal works, trade or industry, the court will take all necessary measures to safeguard the interest of each of the spouses and the interest of the clients.*

Such laws help businesswomen protect their business on divorce. They are very important because in most civil law countries, especially in West Africa, most women have informal businesses, many of them in their marital homes. If they are forced to leave the marital home on divorce, they risk losing their businesses and clients.

contributions should be assessed, however, leaving this determination to the judge or jury (box 2.10).[24]

Indicators.   The database records laws on divorce and the default marital property regime (see figure 2.15). The indicators cover the following features:

- Provision of equal division of marital property on divorce
- Recognition of a wife's nonmonetary contribution in determining the share of property she receives in countries with a separate property regime
- Women's entitlement to some of the marital property on divorce in statutory marriages, customary marriages, and consensual unions

Patterns across countries.   Equal division of property on divorce is far more common under community of property regimes than other regimes (figure 2.17). By contrast, only a few countries with separate property regimes recognize the wife's nonmonetary contribution.

The benefits of legal protection to receive marital property on divorce generally accrue only to people in statutory marriages (figure 2.18). People in customary marriages or consensual unions rarely receive these protections.[25]

BOX 2.10

Divorce Laws Recognizing Women's Nonmonetary Contributions

South Africa's Divorce Amendment Act, No.7 of 1989, requires courts to consider what is just and equitable in dividing marital property. The court should consider the direct and indirect contribution to the maintenance or increase of the estate. Section 8(4) of South Africa's Recognition of Customary Marriages Act of 2000 confers equitable jurisdiction to deal with customary marriages with a separate property regime (such as polygamous customary marriages).

Tanzania's Law of Marriage Act of 1971 requires courts to consider the extent of contribution of each party in terms of money, property, and work toward asset acquisition. The act requires courts to consider equality as much as possible in dividing assets, particularly where there are minor children.

Zimbabwe's Matrimonial Causes Act of 1985 obliges courts to consider the direct and indirect contributions of each spouse to the family, including contributions such as looking after the home, in determining the division, apportionment, and distribution of the spouses' assets.

Source: Women–LEED–Africa.

Figure 2.17 Division of Marital Property on Divorce, by Default Marital Property Regime and Selected Indicators

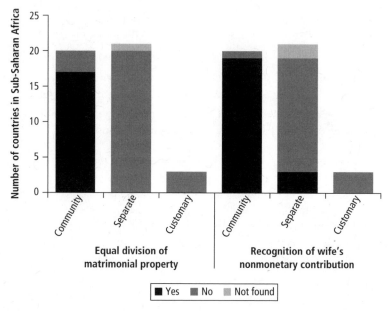

Source: Women–LEED–Africa.

Division of Marital Property on Inheritance

Issues captured. Inheritance is one of the main ways in which women access and control property. It is also one of the principal areas in which women encounter property disputes. The focus here regards cases in which the husband dies without a will. The legal framework for succession laws in Sub-Saharan Africa falls under constitutions, family laws, and customary laws. Religious laws also determine a woman's ability to access or control property on the husband's death. Judicial precedents also play a large role. All these factors determine the extent to which women can own and control property when the husband dies and thus their ability to use such assets in their business.

Community of property. Under a community or property regime, a widow generally automatically inherits 50 percent of the estate's community property. If she is one of the heirs to the estate, she can inherit an additional share. These shares can vary by country, based partly on the presence of children, parents, grandparents, siblings, and cousins.[26]

Figure 2.18 Woman's Entitlement to Marital Property on Divorce, by Default Marital Property Regimes and Type of Union

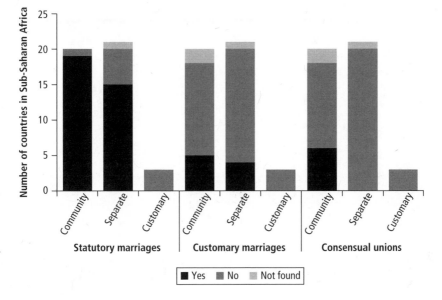

Source: Women–LEED–Africa.

Separate property.   Under a separate property regime, married women do not automatically inherit from their husband's estate. Some countries provide for some inheritance, but the share is usually far less than half. (As discussed in chapter 3, the courts can interpret unclear wording in these provisions to limit the assets widows receive.)

Statutory user rights to property.   A common practice in many countries is to provide the surviving wife with user rights rather than to transfer ownership. These rights allow the widow to occupy land, including the house, and cultivate it during her lifetime or until remarriage. This practice provides some protection of women's economic well-being, but it does not confer the same economic rights as inheritance, as the woman is not allowed to sell the land or bequeath it after her death.[27] Countries that allow women to inherit property (as opposed to granting user rights) thus provide more secure rights, as inheriting land allows a woman to use the land as collateral or to set up a business directly.

Division of property among wives in polygamous marriages.   Under separate property regimes, provisions can be made that entitle wives to a share of the husband's estate. The issue is more complicated when there are multiple wives, particularly if the statute's language uses words such as "spouse." The practice has been to have the wives as a group inherit the amount left to "the wife" or "the spouse," meaning that that share is divided among them. In Ghana, for example, "the wife" is entitled to use the marital home. Even if there were four wives, each in her own home, on the death of the husband, the wives would be entitled to only one home among the four of them.

Indicators.   Indicators focus on the laws of intestate succession—that is, how property is divided if the deceased dies without a will. They include the following:

- Whether the law recognizes the ability of a wife in a statutory marriage to inherit
- Whether the law recognizes the ability of a wife in a customary marriage to inherit
- Whether the law recognizes the ability of a wife in a consensual union to inherit
- Whether there is statutory recognition of a minimum share that a wife inherits on the death of her husband
- Whether the law recognizes a wife's portion in joint property in distribution on her husband's intestate death
- Whether the law recognizes user rights

Patterns across countries.   Consistent with the recognition of customary law in the constitutions, succession or inheritance acts in common law countries are more likely than succession or inheritance acts in civil law countries to discuss customary law practices and include provisions that make women in customary marriages eligible to inherit at least some assets (figure 2.19). Many of the legal protections of women's inheritance depend on the marital regime, with statutory marriages usually offering far more protections than customary marriages or consensual unions. Like property rights on divorce, women's inheritance rights are generally weaker under separate property regimes and stronger where specific legal provisions in inheritance laws provide them with a share of the estate (figure 2.20).

The rights of widows to inherit property vary by marital property regime. Widows often have the right to use the marital home and the land of the deceased; less often, they have rights to maintenance from the estate of the deceased (figure 2.21). In many countries, these benefits end when the widow remarries.

Figure 2.19 Widows' Entitlement to Inherit Marital Property When Husband Dies Intestate, by Default Marital Property Regime and Type of Union

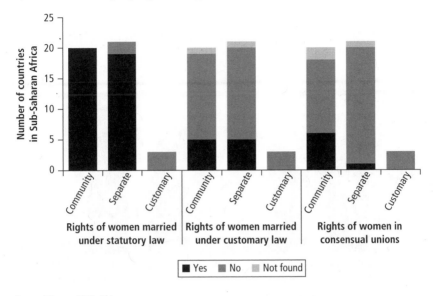

Source: Women–LEED–Africa.

Figure 2.20 Different Types of Default Marital Property Regimes Grant Women Very Different Rights to Inherit Marital Property

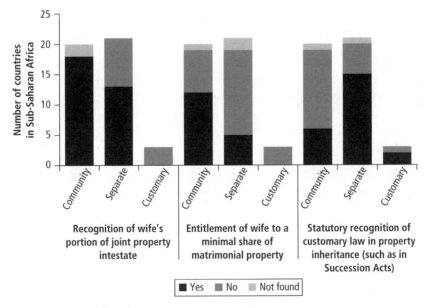

Source: Women–LEED–Africa.

Figure 2.21 Widow's Entitlement to Use Marital Property, by Default Marital Property Regime

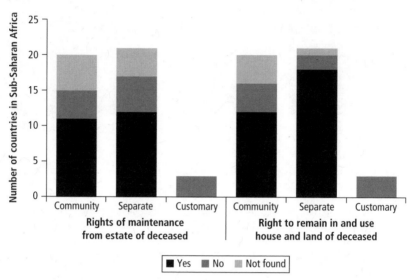

Source: Women–LEED–Africa.

Scoresheet 6: Land Law and Land Rights

Issues Captured

This section focuses on title, the assertion of customary rights, the ability to inherit, and the ability to access property that can be used in a business or as collateral for loans.[28] Especially in Sub-Saharan Africa's collateral-based banking systems, these issues are key to enterprise development.

The introduction of formal land titling systems was particularly disadvantageous to women in many countries, because it increased men's control over land through registration, which was (and is) often allowed in only a single name—the head of household. Even where joint names were (and are) allowed, social norms meant that women did not add their names to the title. Women's customary user rights to land were also sidelined by titling systems, which often failed to acknowledge women's user rights (box 2.11).

Gender differences in accessing and controlling land remain a major problem in Sub-Saharan Africa (Joireman 2009, Peters 2009). Whereas most men reported unfettered rights to give land to family members, less than 5 percent of women did do so in Burundi, Uganda, and Zambia (Place 1995). Women are rarely allowed to inherit land, even in matrilineal systems; they seem to fare better in acquiring short-term rights to land through renting or sharecropping markets. A few exceptions stand out. In cocoa-growing areas of Ghana, for example, women are granted rights to land and trees through gifts (see Lastarria-Corhiel 1997; Quisumbing and

BOX 2.11

Stripping Women of Customary Rights to Land through Titling in Kenya

After independence, the government of Kenya maintained the formal and individualized titling of the colonial era: the 1963 Registered Land Act eliminated and replaced the customary systems of communal ownership with the formal British style of individual ownership. The rights of title holders are set out in gender neutral language. But title deeds are registered in the names of men even though titles can be held in the name of more than one person. The vesting of absolute ownership to land in the title holder excludes all claims by women, including customary rights of access and usage.

Source: Kamangu 2009.

others 1999). The avenues available to women in accessing land include purchase, allocation (with customary land tenure), distribution (on divorce), and inheritance. Intestate succession laws in several countries, such as Ghana and Zambia, exclude customary or lineage land from property widows can inherit. Instead, the land follows customary rules of inheritance, usually going to a male heir. As a significant percentage of land is customary land in many countries (60 percent in Swaziland, 72 percent in Malawi, 80 percent in Mozambique, and 81 percent in Zambia [UNECA 2003]),[29] this exclusion represents a significant impediment.

Indicators
Scoresheet 6 reports on land laws (protections in the constitutions are in scoresheet 2). Some land laws are gender neutral, others recognize the rights of women to own land. Indicators include the following:

- Availability of any form of statutory protection for women's land rights under land laws
- Statutory recognition of customary law applying to ownership of land, distribution of land, or both
- Exemption of customary land from succession statutes
- Availability of co-ownership (based on marriage) to women

Patterns across Countries
Customary ownership of land is widely recognized in statutes (figure 2.22). In common law countries, only Seychelles does not recognize customary ownership; in civil law countries, almost two-thirds do so. In many cases, customary ownership of land is patriarchal and keeps women from owning and inheriting land. But customary ownership can also provide important user rights, particularly after divorce or on inheritance.

Figure 2.22 Only a Minority of Countries Provide Statutory Protections to Women's Land Rights

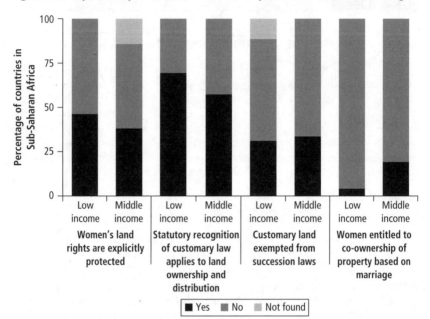

Source: Women–LEED–Africa.

Fewer than half the countries explicitly grant women the right to own land. Providing for co-ownership of land on the basis of marriage is even less common, albeit more prevalent in middle-income than in low-income countries. Among countries that recognize customary land ownership, half have statutory provisions for women's land rights.

Scoresheet 7: Labor Laws

Scoresheets 1 and 2 examine protection of women's rights to equal work and equal pay provided in constitutions and ILO conventions. This section complements the discussions there by examining statutory protections.

Issues Captured

Labor laws directly affect employees. They can also affect rates of entrepreneurship by increasing or decreasing the availability and attractiveness of wage employment (Altonji and Bank 1999; World Bank 2011).

In many countries, laws and regulations restrict the kind of work women may perform or limit the hours they are permitted to work. Some restrictions apply to all women, others only to pregnant women. These restrictions—adopted in order to protect women—can actually hurt them.

Indicators
Scoresheet 7 includes the following indicators:

- Whether there is statutory protection of equal pay for equal work
- Whether there are restrictions on the industries in which women may work, on the hours women may work, or both
- Whether there are statutory requirements to provide maternity leave and provisions relating to the duration of such leave and how such leave is funded
- Whether there are restrictions on the industries in which pregnant women can work, the hours pregnant women may work, or both
- Whether there are provisions for maternity leave

Patterns across Countries
Most countries' statutes provide for the equal right to work (39 countries) and stipulate equal pay for equal work (37 countries). Labor laws in Botswana, Mauritius, and Zambia do not provide for the equal right to work or for equal pay. By contrast, Liberia, Seychelles, and Sudan refer to labor rights such as equal pay for equal work in their constitutions (figure 2.23).

Figure 2.23 Constitutional Recognition of Nondiscrimination in the Workplace

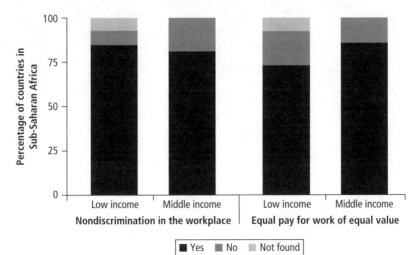

Source: Women–LEED–Africa.

All but four countries that provide constitutional protections for the equal right to work and the right to equal pay have corresponding statutes. Some countries have statutory but not constitutional protections. Taken together, middle-income countries and countries with a stronger rule of law are more likely to lack equal pay protections (figure 2.24). This pattern reflects the fact that fewer common law countries include these protections in their statutes.

Twenty-six countries restrict the industries in which women may work; another 10 restrict the rights of pregnant women (figure 2.25). Seventeen countries restrict the hours women may work; another 18 apply this restriction to pregnant women only. These restrictions, combined with other limits resulting from head-of-household provisions, constitute a significant obstacle to women participating in the labor force as wage workers. They may be one of the factors contributing to the fact that most women not employed in agriculture are self-employed in informal and small-scale enterprises.

Figure 2.24 Statutory and Constitutional Protection of the Right to Equal Pay for Work of Equal Value

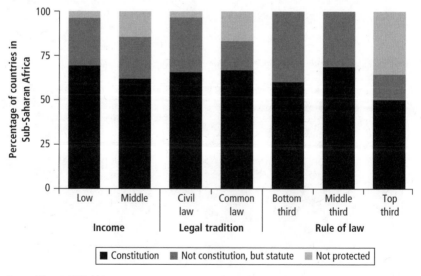

Source: Women–LEED–Africa.

Figure 2.25 Many Countries Restrict the Type of Work Women Can Perform and Women's Hours

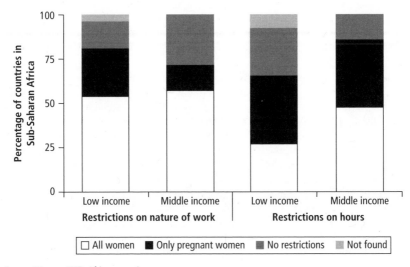

Source: Women–LEED–Africa.

Conclusion

Every country in Sub-Saharan Africa recognizes nondiscrimination as a constitutional guiding principle—but numerous exceptions are formally allowed. Many countries have head-of-household statutes or recognize customary law in matters of property and inheritance and exempt it from nondiscrimination protections. The choice of marital regime (statutory, customary, or consensual union) can thus have important implications for women's rights.

Gender gaps in legal rights do not necessarily close when the rule of law is stronger. Gaps in legal capacity are more common and protection of labor rights weaker in countries in which the rule of law is weak. But the exemption of customary law from nondiscrimination provisions is often more common where the enforcement of the rule of law is strong.

Gaps in legal rights are also not closely associated with income: similar proportions of middle-income countries have gender gaps as low-income countries. Economic growth alone will thus not improve conditions for women. More interventionist measures, described in chapter 5, are needed.

Notes

1. This database examines the de jure situation based on the letter of the law. Case law, which also determines de jure rights, is examined in later chapters. It is not part of the database, however, because it is not possible to implement an exhaustive review of court decisions. The database does not measure the extent to which provisions of the law are carried out-and, as chapter 4 documents, there can be substantial gaps between the de jure and de facto situation. Even for gender-blind laws, such as laws covering banking and business laws, this study does not address whether their practical effect is gender neutral (that is, whether banks assess certain requirements, such as documents of title for collateral, differently for men and women). The companion volume, *Enterprising Women: Expanding Opportunities in Africa* (2013), addresses these areas through surveys of entrepreneurs.
2. Customs or traditions, as opposed to formal customary law, affect de facto outcomes. They are discussed in chapter 4.
3. The entire database is available online, at http://documents.worldbank.org/query? title=Women+LEED+Africa+Database.
4. Customary and religious laws do not necessarily weaken nondiscrimination provisions, but simply having multiple systems creates room for potentially divergent views that render uncertain the strength of any provision. At a certain level, all countries have multiple systems, but the issue is particularly relevant in Africa, where customary law is recognized as a formal source of law in many countries and prevails in large areas of the law.
5. Some countries are hybrid systems, with features of both common and civil law. Cameroon formally recognizes both systems. Ethiopia, Mauritius, and countries in southern Africa are hybrids. Rwanda is switching from a civil system to a hybrid system as it seeks to join the East African Community. In these cases, the predominant system is chosen (see scoresheets in appendix A).
6. However, the average GDP per capita ignores underlying variations in the structure of the economy and other factors that may affect growth but do little to change women's ability to share in this growth.
7. In monist states, ratifying an international treaty binds a state by its provisions. Legislative approval is gained before signing the treaty; once it is signed it has the force of law domestically (as well as in international forums). Dualist states require a formal domestication procedure: domestic laws need to be changed to bring them into line with the treaty. The purpose of the Vienna Convention on the law of treaties is to ensure that states that ratify international instruments take measures to domesticate and allow the implementation of ratified treaties in their territories.
8. In addition, Mauritania and Niger have substantive reservations, and Ethiopia and Mauritius have reservations about the arbitration procedure.
9. CEDAW requires countries to file reports on the progress they have made in achieving the requirements of the treaties. The reports include a discussion of where countries still need to make progress.
10. These earlier conventions are from 1919, 1934, and 1948, and so are long-standing conventions. Newer conventions—such as Convention 171 (1990) and the 1990 Pro-

tocol to Convention 89—lift restrictions on nonpregnant women. However, Madagascar is the only one to have signed them.

11. Indicators on the standards needed to show standing, which are found in administrative laws, are not included. They can vary across subject areas and be interpreted in conjunction with other statutes and regulations, making it difficult to establish standardized measures.

12. Botswana has no written provisions for heads of household, but customary law applies as the default marital regime—and the Repeal of the Marital Power Act does not apply to customary marriages. Botswana also recognizes customary law in the constitution and exempts it from nondiscrimination provisions.

13. Other countries had similar provisions but reformed their marital powers acts.

14. Within the region, Sharia is the most common source of religious law recognized. Because it applies to larger shares of the population in more countries than other sources of religious law, most of the discussion here is devoted to it.

15. The repugnancy test is a legal doctrine dating from the British colonial era. Its original purpose was to give the colonial administrators a level of oversight over the customary and religious legal system. Customary laws could be challenged, and the courts could decide not to enforce them, if they were found to be repugnant to natural justice, equity, or good conscience.

16. The rule of law measure comes from the Global Governance Indicators. This measure is based largely on enforcement and the role that rules and law play in settling disputes; it is not based on the quality or content of the laws themselves. Thus there is no circularity between this measure and indicators of gender gaps in legal rights.

17. Titre Préliminaire, Article A, Law No. 67-030 (December 1967) relates to marital regimes and succession.

18. Many Namibians fall under the apartheid-era Native Administration Proclamation Act 15 of 1928, which applies to black Namibians north of the old "police line" (the historically black territories under apartheid). The majority of poor black women live in this region. Civil marriages in this region are by default under a separate ownership regime. The High Court of Namibia has declared provisions of this act to be unconstitutional and has ordered the government to reform this law. The government has yet to finalize its efforts.

19. Section 7(2) of the Recognition Act (2000) of South Africa extends the default regime of community property to monogamous customary marriages. The parties to a civil or monogamous customary marriage can opt out of the default universal community of property regime by a prenuptial agreement and select either a separate property regime or a separate property regime with accrual of profits (similar to a simple community of property regime).

20. It should also be kept in mind that the characterization of countries most often represents some tribes or ethnic groups, but may not be applicable to the whole country.

21. Other issues—such as whether divorce is "allowed" and whether the issue of "fault" affects what happens to assets (and children)—may also matter. These issues were beyond the scope of this study.

22. Customary marriages are marriages recognized by the performance of customary rites; they may or may not be formally registered with the state. Consensual unions

are couples who live together but are not married according to religious or customary practices or registered with the state. Most relationships in many countries are customary marriages or consensual unions.

23. For example, Article 87 of Côte d'Ivoire's 1983 Marriage Code allows the wife to bring a claim before the court to revert to a separate property regime if the husband mismanages community property.

24. This issue is likely to make it to court only for wealthier couples. However, it is an important signal for the wider population about how nonmonetary contributions are treated.

25. An exception is couples in matrilocal communities (communities in which the husband moves to his wife's village).

26. The United Nations Convention on the Rights of the Child stipulates that children born out of wedlock fall under succession. The laudable intention was to provide for all the deceased's children; the effect, however, was to further diminish the property rights of the widow.

27. Depending on the nature of the ownership arrangements of the land, similar restrictions may also pertain to men. But the more common pattern is that women have user rights in land that belongs to the husband's family—rights that do not confer to their children and often "expire" when they remarry.

28. The two major land tenure systems in Sub-Saharan Africa are customary and statutory tenure. Current land tenure regimes, which generally include a mix of customary, statutory, and legal arrangements, have their origins in the early colonial period of land consolidation, when colonialists left family and community concerns such as land under the jurisdiction of customary law and customary courts. After the 1930s, customary tenure arrangements became an obstacle to changing colonial objectives, which incorporated the promotion of economic growth through agricultural production. The new goals were predicated upon the state's fostering the emergence of a freehold system and individual property of land ownership. With the introduction of private property systems, women lost out, because their rights to land through husbands, fathers, or sons diminished in importance.

29. In 2006, Zambia's Land Ministry estimated the share of customary land at 93 percent 2006 (Ministry of Lands of the Republic of Zambia 2006). Whatever the exact figure, the vast majority of land in Zambia is customary land.

References

Altonji, Joseph, and Rebecca Bank, 1999. "Race and Gender in the Labor Market." In *Handbook of Labor Economics*, vol. 3, Part C, ed. Orley Ashenfelter and David Card, 3143–259. Amsterdam: Elsevier.

Diarra, Marthe, and Marie Monimart. 2006. "Landless Women, Hopeless Women: Gender, Land and Decentralisation in Niger." IIED Issues Paper 143, International Institute for Environment and Development, London.

Henrysson, Elin, and Sandra F. Joireman. 2009. "On the Edge of the Law: Women Property Rights and Dispute Resolution in Kisii Kenya." *Law & Society Review* 43 (1): 39–60.

Joireman, Sandra F. 2008. "The Mystery of Capital Formation in Sub-Saharan Africa: Women, Property Rights and Customary Law." *World Development* 36 (7): 1233–46.

———. 2009. Comment made at workshop on "Law, Custom and the Investment Climate for Women Entrepreneurs in Africa," World Bank, Washington, DC, July.

Kamangu, Jane. 2009. "The Principles of Non-Discrimination and Equal Protection of the Law: A Case Study of Unwed Mothers and Children Born out of Wedlock in Kenya." Paper presented at the meetings of the 2008/09 Leadership and Advocacy for Women in Africa Fellows, Georgetown University, Washington, DC.

Kane, Minneh, J. Oloka-Onyango, and Abdul Tejan-Cole. 2005. "Reassessing Customary Law Systems as a Vehicle for Providing Equitable Access to Justice for the Poor." Paper presented at the conference "New Frontiers of Social Policy," Arusha, Tanzania, December 12–15.

Kuruk, Paul. 2002. "African Customary Law and the Protection of Folklore." *UNESCO Bulletin* 36 (2): 4–32.

Lastarria-Cornhiel, Susana. 1997. "Impact of Privatization on Gender and Property Rights in Africa." *World Development* 25 (8): 1317–33.

Ministry of Lands of the Republic of Zambia. 2006. *Zambia Draft Land Policy*. Lusaka: Ministry of Lands.

Nhlapo, Thandabantu. 1995. "Indigenous Law and Gender in South Africa: Taking Human Rights and Cultural Diversity Seriously." *Third World Legal Studies* (1994–95): 49–71.

Peters, Pauline E. 2009. "Challenges in Land Tenure and Land Reform in Africa: Anthropological Contributions." *World Development* 37 (8): 1317–25.

Place, Frank. 1995. "The Role of Land and Tree Tenure on the Adoption of Agroforestry Technologies in Zambia, Burundi, Uganda, and Malawi: A Summary and Synthesis." Land Tenure Center, University of Wisconsin–Madison.

Platteau, Jean-Philippe, Anita Abraham, A. Brasselle, F. Gaspart, A. Niang, J. Sawadogo, and L. Stevens. 2000. "Marriage System, Access to Land and Social Protection for Women." Centre de Recherche en Economie du Développment, Namur, Belgium.

Quisumbing, Agnes, Ellen Payongayong, J. B. Aidoo, and Keijiro Otsuka. 1999. "Women's Land Rights in the Transition to Individualized Ownership: Implications for the Management of Tree Resources in Western Ghana." FCND Discussion Paper 58, International Food Policy Research Institute, Food Consumption and Nutrition Division, Washington, DC.

Republic of Botswana. 2008. "Botswana Report on the Implementation of the Convention of the Elimination of All Forms of Discrimination against Women." CEDAW/C/BOT/3, Gabarone.

Simavi, Sevi, Clare Manuel, and Mark Blackden. 2010. *Gender Dimensions of Investment Climate Reform: A Guide for Policy Makers and Practitioners.* Washington, DC: World Bank.

Sowsidibe, Amsatou. 1994. "Senegal's Evolving Family Law." *University of Louisville Journal of Family Law* 32 (2): 421–30

UNECA (United Nations Economic Commission for Africa). 2003. "Land Tenure Systems and Sustainable Development in Southern Africa." UNECA, South Africa Office, Lusaka, Zambia.

USAID (U.S. Agency for International Development). 2006. "Study on Women and Property Rights: Project Best Practices." USAID, Washington, DC.

Wing, Susanna D. 2009. "Exploring Democracy, Women's Rights, and Legal Reform in Francophone Africa." Paper presented at the conference on "Rethinking Development: Societal Transformations and the Challenges of Governance in Africa and the Middle East," Yale University, New Haven, CT.

Women–LEED–Africa (Women's Legal and Economic Empowerment Database), http://documents.worldbank.org/query?title=Women+LEED+Africa+Database developed by Mary Hallward-Driemeier, Tazeen Hasan, Jane Kamangu, Emila Lobti, and Mark Blackden. Development Economics, World Bank.

World Bank. 2011. *World Development Report 2012: Gender Equality and Development.* Washington, DC: World Bank.

Chapter 3

Legal Pluralism: Multiple Systems, Multiple Challenges

Sub-Saharan countries draw their rules and institutions of laws from more than one normative tradition. In both common and civil law countries, international, constitutional, and statutory systems of laws coexist to different degrees with religious and indigenous customary laws and institutions. These religious and customary laws are often part of the formal system—sources of law that are legally recognized and that have formalized procedural rules and enforcement provisions. Irrespective of the content of the laws, the very existence of overlapping sources of law introduces uncertainty regarding how strongly particular rights are protected.

Formal customary law may play a larger role in Africa than elsewhere, but the issue is not unique to Africa: inconsistent and conflicting sources of law permeate every legal system in the world. To reduce uncertainty, a legal system has to have a clear hierarchy regarding which law prevails when a conflict arises. To reduce discrimination within a legal system, it is essential that the principle of nondiscrimination be regarded as paramount and that it supersede conflicting provisions.

This chapter looks at the extent to which countries in the region define this hierarchy. It uses case law to illustrate how courts have interpreted cases at the intersections of different sources of law and conflicting provisions on the books. Case law is itself a formal source of law in common law systems and an integral part of the legal landscape, as judicial decision making and precedent can shape rights to property as much as any other source of law. Judicial precedent exists to a lesser degree in civil law systems. For this reason, this chapter gives more coverage to case law in a common law framework.

The Role and Interplay of Various Sources of Law

To understand the challenges inherent in a pluralistic legal system, it is helpful to look at the individual sources of law and how they enhance or restrict the principles of nondiscrimination and gender equality in both civil and common law systems.[1] Cases in which property is divided on inheritance and divorce offer insights into how women's claims to property have evolved or been restricted by courts as they grapple with legal pluralism. Judges have been called on to interpret various sources of law. Their rulings can either reinforce existing discriminatory laws, including customary law, or set them aside in favor of more equitable provisions. As will be seen from the cases cited throughout this chapter, the approach has often been inconsistent, rendering evolution of the law dependent on the mindset of a particular bench of judges.

The cases cited are in areas with important implications for women's entrepreneurship. They affect women's access to and control over assets that they can use directly in their business or as collateral for loans. These laws are critical because, as chapter 2 shows, when their rights are restricted, women are less likely to operate as employers.

Appealing to International Law in Domestic Courts

International treaties that have been ratified and are part of the national law through direct implementation or domesticating legislation can exert a positive influence in overturning historically entrenched legal norms. Domestic courts in several countries have referred to international conventions such as the Convention on the Elimination of All Forms of Discrimination against Women (CEDAW) and the Protocol to the African Charter on Human and Peoples' Rights on the Rights of Women in Africa as direct authority for setting aside discriminatory statutory and customary laws.

Lack of direct national implementation is not always a barrier to domestic courts' use of treaties. Some judges in Kenya have categorized the CEDAW principles as norms of customary international law, which can have direct force in the national legal system without requiring further legislation:

- In *Wachokire* (2002), the Chief Magistrates' Court at Thika held that a provision under Kikuyu customary law that deprived unmarried women of equal inheritance rights violated Section 82(1) of the Constitution, which prohibits discrimination on the basis of gender. The court also held that the provision violated Article 18(3) of the Banjul charter and Article 15(3) of CEDAW, which provides for gender equality.

- In *Andrew Manunzya Musyoka* (2005), the High Court applied the principles of equality and nondiscrimination in CEDAW to set aside a discriminatory Kamba custom that held that a daughter is not allowed to inherit from her father's estate.

- In *Mary Rono v. Jane Rono* (2005), the Court of Appeal held that there was no reasonable basis for drawing a distinction between sons and daughters in determining inheritance. The principles of equality and nondiscrimination prevailed over customary law that disinherited daughters. The court applied international law directly to Kenya, a dualist state, and justified it based on the common law theory, allowing for application of customary international law and treaty law where there is no conflict, even if such laws have not been domesticated.

Using the Constitution to Set Aside Discriminatory Law

The constitutional principles of nondiscrimination and gender equality are integral tools in enabling citizens to challenge discriminatory statutory and customary or personal law provisions. The principle of nondiscrimination, cited in every constitution in Africa, is a starting point that can be used creatively to set aside discriminatory laws. In addition, specific constitutional provisions on gender equality, found in several constitutions in Sub-Saharan Africa, may facilitate the promotion of proactive policies to achieve equality and enhance the ability of women's groups to bring suit against discriminatory laws (Lambert and Scribner 2008).

Constitutional provisions relating to the right to property and the recognition of human rights also reinforce women's legal rights in inheritance and in registering property in their own names:

- In the *Benin Constitutional Court Decision No. DCC 02-144* (2004), Rosine Vieyra, a member of parliament, successfully challenged the constitutionality of provisions that allowed polygamy in the new Family Code approved by the National Assembly in June 2002. She argued that the provisions were discriminatory, violated the constitutional principle of equality between a man and a woman, and were contrary to the African Charter on Human and Peoples' Rights (the Banjul Charter) and the Maputo Protocol on the Rights of Women in Africa. The Family Code was subsequently reviewed and polygamy outlawed, with beneficial implications for wives' inheritance and the division of marital property.

- In *Uganda Association of Women Lawyers and others v. Attorney General* (2002), the Constitutional Court declared provisions of the 1904 Divorce Act discriminatory and thus unconstitutional where they provided for differing grounds for divorce, recovery of legal costs, financial relief, and alimony for women and men.[2] The Act had made divorce more difficult for women to obtain and limited their right to financial relief.

- In *Bernado Ephraim v. Holaria Pastory and Another* (2001), the High Court in Tanzania held that women can inherit land, including clan land, even when Haya customary law bans such inheritance and that they are thus able to dispose of such land without any discrimination based on gender. The court upheld the constitutional principle of nondiscrimination to the exclusion of Haya customary law.

- In *Ndossi v. Ndossi* (2001), the High Court in Tanzania held that a widow was entitled to administer her estate on behalf of her children under the Constitution, which provides that that "every person is entitled to own property and has a right to the protection of that property held in accordance of the law." The judge further held that Article 9(a) and (f) of the Constitution recognizes human rights by requiring "that human dignity is preserved and upheld in accordance with the spirit of the Universal Declaration of Human Rights," explaining that this clause generally domesticated human rights instruments ratified by Tanzania, including the antidiscrimination principles of CEDAW, Articles 2(b) and (f), and the best interest of the child principle found in Article 3 of the Convention on the Rights of the Child.

- A coalition of woman's groups from across the political spectrum in Sudan opposed an Act passed by the governor of Khartoum as unconstitutional. The Act prohibited women from working after 5 p.m. and from participating in work that "damaged their reputation," including work in hotels, service stations, and cafes. The case was contested in the Constitutional Court: the Act was withdrawn and the governor replaced (Badri 2005).

Expanding the Constitutional Power Vested in Certain Courts

Courts in many countries can use the constitution to set aside discriminatory legislation, but they do not have the authority to change it or refer to alternative provisions. South Africa and Swaziland are two examples where additional powers are given to Supreme Courts.

The Constitution of South Africa, widely acclaimed as among the most progressive in the region, subjects all statutory and traditional laws to overarching constitutional principles of equality and nondiscrimination.[3] Moreover, under the Constitution, the Supreme Court of Appeal and High Courts (or equivalent) have the power to declare a law or conduct constitutionally invalid and to set aside discriminatory customary provisions, whether codified or not.[4] The courts even have the discretion to refer to nondiscriminatory legislation instead of the discriminatory provisions that would normally have been applicable.[5]

Two rulings illustrate the scope of the courts:

- In 2004, the Constitutional Court in *Bhe v. Khayelitsha Magistrate and the President of the Republic of South Africa* set aside Section 23 of the Black Administration Act (1927), which stated that customary law should apply to the estates of Africans who died intestate—and excluded the application of the Intestate Succession Act (1987). The customary law of succession was the rule of primogeniture or inheritance by other male relatives. The court concluded that the official system of customary law of succession was incompatible with the Bill of Rights and applied Section 1 of the Intestate Succession Act instead.

- In *Elizabeth Gumede v. President of South Africa and others* (2008), the Constitutional Court held that a rule of customary law under which the husband was the family head and the owner of all family property violated the wife's right to dignity and equality, which is protected by the Constitution. In this case, customary law was codified in the KwaZulu Act and the Natal Code, which provided that in a customary law marriage, the husband was the family head and owner of all family law property, which he could use at his exclusive discretion. The Gumedes had married under customary law in 1968. They were therefore excluded from the provisions of the Recognition Act 2005, which extended the default marital regime of community of property to all customary marriages entered into on or after November 15, 2005. The Court was able to set aside the offending provisions of customary law and the provisions of the Recognition Act, which prevented it from applying to earlier customary marriages.

The courts in Swaziland have even stronger powers: they can change the wording of offending legislation. Swaziland took a major step toward gender equality in 2005, when it amended its constitution to include a nondiscrimination clause.[6] In 2010, the High Court allowed women married in community of property to register property in their own names for the first time.

The High Court case of *Mary-Joyce Doo Aphane v. Registrar of Deeds, Minister of Justice and Constitutional Affairs and the Attorney General* (2010) concerned a couple married under a community of property regime. The wife's request to register property jointly in their names was not allowed under a provision of the Deeds Registry Act. The High Court upheld Aphane's request and declared the provision unconstitutional. Significantly, the judge used her powers under Section 151(2) of the Constitution that gives the High Court jurisdiction to enforce fundamental human rights and freedoms guaranteed by the Constitution to change the wording of the offending provision to allow registration of community property by women. The Supreme Court in May 2010 upheld the unconstitutionality of the discriminatory provision, but overturned the High Court Judge's decision to "severe" and "read in" the Act on this occasion. It suspended the declaration of illegality for a year, allowing married women to register property in the interim, and allowing for Parliament to amend the legislation in the meantime. However, two years later, parliament has not amended the legislation and there has been no follow-up action in the courts.

As important as this victory was for gender equality in Swaziland, barriers to land ownership remain. Most women are married under customary law and are still not legally entitled to register property under their name. The court had the jurisdiction only to set aside the discriminatory provisions that the litigants asked it to adjudicate on; it could not carry out wholesale reform of the Deeds Registry Act.

Catalyzing the Effect of Impact Litigation

Discriminatory provisions remain in force in many countries; courts can strike down only a few provisions at a time. The aim of "impact litigation" is to strategically choose cases to bring to the highest courts in order to maximize the chances of changing the legal precedent in an area of law important to the affected group and its supporters.[7] It has a catalytic effect on mobilizing reform movements to pressure governments into comprehensive legislative reform.

Impact litigation that successfully challenges discriminatory laws based on unconstitutionality in one country can influence the interpretation and application of constitutional provisions by courts in other countries. For this potential to be realized, it is important that the case address the key legal issue in question. A ruling is likely to have a greater effect if it affects a large class of women, can be linked to interests of other groups, and captures the attention of the media.

The judgment in *Uganda Association of Women Lawyers and others v. Attorney General* (2002) cited the Tanzanian case of *Ephraim v. Pastory* (1989) and the Botswana case of *Attorney General of the Republic of Botswana v. Unity Dow* (1994) (described in box 3.2) as support for setting aside discriminatory divorce laws in the Ugandan case. Drawing on similar challenges in neighboring countries, in 2009 the Women's Law Association for Southern Africa filed a case before the Constitutional Court of Malawi (*Registered Trustees of the Women and Law in Southern Africa Malawi v. the Attorney General* [2009]) arguing that the failure to recognize nonmonetary contributions under the Married Women's Property Act 1882 is discriminatory and thus unconstitutional.

Statutory Law

Different statutes or codes in a country can have conflicting provisions. For example, in Chad, the French Civil Code of 1958 sets the default marital regime as community of property, whereas Order O3/INT/ 61 of June 21, 1961, states that the default regime is a separate property regime. The French Civil Code allows only monogamous marriages, but the 1961 Order permits polygamy (Center for Reproductive Rights 2003). It is unclear how these conflicting laws interact in practice.

Reform can lead to more equitable provisions. But discriminatory legislation persists, in the ways described below.

Preindependence statutory laws are generally more likely to discriminate than recently drafted laws.   Many countries still have statutes that originated more than a century ago that were long since replaced or amended in the country of origin. These earlier statutory laws are more prone to be discriminatory, as they reflect the gender attitudes of the era. The English Married Women's Property Act of 1882 and the Matrimonial Causes Act of 1941 are currently applicable legislation in Kenya. In Nigeria, the Federal Interpretation Act states that any statute of general application in force in England before January 1, 1900, and not subsequently replaced by domestic Nigerian law is binding in Nigeria, even if Britain repealed or amended the law (Emery 2005). With little reform, only a few anglophone countries statutorily recognize relatively recent concepts, such as the inclusion of the wife's nonmonetary contribution to a household's assets in determining a settlement following divorce.

Many francophone countries took the French Civil Code of 1958, including its head-of-household provisions, as their starting point. Many of these countries retain these provisions on the books, though countries such as Benin have tackled most of them with family law reforms.

Racially and ethnically based legislation continues to affect segments of the population. Antiquated apartheid-era legislation continues to divide populations according to classifications based on ethnic differences in Botswana and Namibia. Different and discriminatory marriage regimes and inheritance provisions still apply to the population north of the apartheid-era Police Line in Namibia, even though they have been successfully challenged as unconstitutional (box 3.1). Default marital regimes are also based on ethnic lines in Botswana, where customary law is the default for indigenous Botswana citizens and a separate property regime is the default for Botswana citizens of European descent.

Many statutory provisions are inadequate and discriminatory, although statutory legislation offers some protection. The inheritance provisions stipulated in many countries' statutory intestacy laws do not enable widows to be self-sufficient and maintain their children. The underlying assumption, which mirrors customary law, is that members of their own family will look after them. In Gabon, a widow receives no share of her husband's estate if she has children. She receives a share if she has no children but if she remarries into a family other than her husband's, she is deprived of her right to inheritance (Article 692 of the Penal Code CEDAW Committee Observations regarding UN [2005a]).

A common feature in conflict and postconflict countries is the lack of statutory legislation in certain sectors, which may stem from several factors. Colonial-era laws or later legislation enacted by a previous regime may have been repealed by the incoming government but not replaced. Legislation relating to land, for example, may not have been enacted at the time of independence, as it was not required then. Burundi, for example, has no statutory law governing women's inheritance rights, and, under customary law, women cannot inherit land (Kamungi, Oketch, and Huggins 2004). Niger has been preparing a family code since 1976 but has yet to adopt it; the status of the French Civil Code of 1804, which applied after independence, is unclear (an order from 1962 states that customary law applies to marriage and inheritance). Customary law is the only practical alternative, but in these countries it rarely gives women an equitable share of household assets (Kamungi, Oketch, and Huggins 2004; Diarra and Monimart 2006).

BOX 3.1

Apartheid-Era Legislation in Namibia Continues to Differentiate among Ethnic Groups

Namibians of European descent are covered by statutory succession and marital property laws—statutes that do not apply to the indigenous population. In the case of *Berendt and Another v. Stuurman and Others* (2003), the High Court declared that several sections of the Native Proclamation 15 of 1928 were unconstitutional. The proclamation treated the estates of deceased indigenous Namibians as if they were European in some circumstances but decreed that their estates should be distributed according to native law and custom in others. The court gave the government a deadline of June 30, 2005, to replace the legislation. The government passed the Estates and Succession Amendment Act (2005), but the new law did not change the "native law and custom" provisions, which generally exclude women and girls from inheritance.

Marital regimes also vary across ethnic groups. For indigenous Namibians married north of the apartheid-era Police Line, the marital regime continues to be separate property; in the rest of the country, the regime is community of property. Most black women live in the poorer rural areas of the north, where Section 17(6) of the Native Proclamation allows husbands to exert unilateral control over marital property and husbands are not required to obtain the consent of their wives even for transactions concerning the marital home.

These laws have not been repealed, even though the government acknowledges the pressing need for reform. In essence, statutory laws relating to marriage and inheritance that continue to apply to the Namibian population are based on skin color and where a person lives.

Source: Legal Assistance Centre and International Women's Human Rights Clinic 2008.

Women may receive greater protection in marital and inheritance disputes when they fall under the umbrella of statutory legislation than under customary law. They may be entitled to ownership of marital property on divorce and in inheritance, rights usually denied to them in customary law.

In the Nigerian case of *Obusez v. Obusez* (2001), the brothers of the deceased argued that under Agbor customary law, the widow was regarded as a chattel to be inherited and thus could not be an administrator of her deceased husband's estate. The Court of Appeal confirmed the lower court's decision that, as the widow had been married under the Marriage Act, she was not a chattel and could therefore administer the estate. It suggested that had she been married under customary law, Agbor customary law would have applied and she would indeed have been chattel and barred from taking up letters of administration (Nwabueze 2010).

Statutory protections can also be important in protecting women's rights in labor and land. Labor laws that prohibit discriminatory practices in the workplace are integral to women's entry into and progress in the formal labor market. These rights are hard to safeguard without statutory protections. If enforced, land laws that oblige—or at a minimum allow—spouses to title property in their joint names can change patterns of land ownership (as the case in Ethiopia described in box 5.2 in chapter 5 illustrates).

Rewriting statutes is not enough to catalyze social change without the parallel strengthening of enforcing institutions. Still, statutory reform that repeals offending legislation or promotes equality and the protection of women sets a benchmark for treating women in society, even if it is not adequately enforced. Examples include laws in Ghana and Malawi protecting widows from being evicted from the marital home and penalizing property grabbing by relatives. Liberia reformed intestacy laws in 2003 (UNHCR 2003). Since reform, widows married under customary or civil law, who previously did not inherit, have been entitled to 30 percent of the husband's estate.

Laws on gender discrimination and equality can be important in enforcing gender rights in the workplace and beyond. In South Africa, the Promotion of Equality and Prevention of Unfair Discrimination Act (2000) places a positive duty on both state and nonstate actors to redress discrimination. The Sex Discrimination Act (2002) in Mauritius also provides protection against discrimination. The Sex Discrimination Division the government established in accord with the Act has jurisdiction to make enquiries and determinations regarding complaints it receives on alleged infringements of the Act. The Act provides various penalties for people judged to have violated its provisions, but according to the 2006 report of the Convention on the Elimination of All Forms of Discrimination against Women Committee, enforcement is weak. The division apparently prefers mediation to referring cases for prosecution. The Committee recommended that serious breaches should be forwarded for prosecution.

Judicial Precedent

The principle of judicial precedent obliges a court to follow a ruling made by an earlier court of equal or superior standing unless the facts of the case before it can be distinguished. This binding nature of case precedent makes it a formal source of law. Its role is clearest in common law systems; judicial precedent also exists under various guises in civil law systems, where it arguably plays a less prominent role.

Judges and magistrates can have wide discretion in interpreting the law, using tools such as the analysis of legislative intention (that is, the spirit of the law). Their interpretations can have a profound and long-lasting effect on a country's legal framework (box 3.2).

BOX 3.2

Using the Constitution to Challenge Gender Discrimination: The Case of Unity Dow

In the milestone case of *Attorney General of the Republic of Botswana v. Unity Dow* (1994), the High Court and the Court of Appeal extended the ambit of the nondiscrimination clause in Botswana's constitution. The clause outlawed discrimination on several grounds but did not specifically mention gender. Unity Dow, a citizen of Botswana, challenged the 1982 Citizenship Law as discriminatory on the grounds that it denied citizenship to the children of Botswana women married to foreigners.

The High Court held that the Constitution prohibited discrimination on the grounds of gender and that "the time that women were treated as chattels or were there to obey the whims and wishes of males is long past, and it would be offensive to modern thinking and the spirit of the Constitution to find that the Constitution was framed deliberately to permit discrimination on the grounds of sex."

Ironically, almost 20 years after the decision, the Constitution still exempts personal law—including marriage, divorce, and inheritance—from its nondiscrimination provision. Even so, the *Unity Dow* ruling may offer scope for a constitutional challenge to discriminatory provisions of personal law.

One area illustrating the power of judicial interpretation is recognition of a spouse's nonmonetary contribution to marital assets. In some countries where the default regime is separate marital property, statutory law is silent on this issue. As chapter 2 showed, such silence excludes not only the contribution of household work but also unpaid work in the family enterprise in the division of marital property. Failure to recognize nonmonetary contributions reduces the assets a woman has to start or run a business after a marriage ends. It denies women access to assets or businesses to which they contributed during their marriage but did not have registered in their name.

The Married Women's Property Act of 1882, which applies in several common law countries, has no specific provisions for recognition of nonmonetary contribution. Its applicability to property ownership has been questioned in the face of domestic laws that govern ownership of property in matters such as contracts.[8] The courts in Malawi have interpreted the provisions of the Act restrictively, not recognizing the nonmonetary contribution of the wife on divorce. Property is held jointly only if both spouses made a direct financial contribution to its acquisition.[9] The approach of the courts, stated in *Nyangulu v. Nyangulu*, is that "an inference of joint ownership of property is not to be made from a mere fact of marriage."

The lack of a clear regulation in law on the mode of distribution of marital property on divorce may allow a superior court (or even a lateral court) to overturn earlier decisions that recognized nonmonetary contributions and set a new precedent. There may also be conflicting precedents that can allow judges to select the line of argument they prefer, as they did in Kenya (box 3.3).

In Nigeria, which adopted a 1970 version of the Matrimonial Causes Act from the United Kingdom, the momentum has moved in the opposite direction. Although the wording of the Act is more flexible than the 1941 version adopted by Kenya and allows the court to make "just and equitable" provision for the wife, the courts originally took the line that the wife had to show financial contribution to marital property and provide receipts as evidence.[10] But in the 1986 case of *Kaffi v. Kaffi*, the Court of Appeal held that the wife's contribution to marital property could consider the fact that she had taken care of her husband and family and that the husband consequently enjoyed the peace of mind to acquire the property.

The doctrine of precedent offers flexibility, but it also generates uncertainty. Laws reinforcing judicial precedent are therefore needed to safeguard against discrimination. The existence of an unequivocal law also ensures uniformity in decisions, thereby contributing to greater certainty in expectations. Clear language has many benefits. In Tanzania, the Law of Marriage Act (1971) offers flexibility and a presumption in favor of equal division of property (box 3.4).[11] Zambia enacted a new version of the Matrimonial Causes Act in 2007, which explicitly recognizes nonmonetary contribution.[12]

Where statutes are silent, judges can use principles of common law to fill the gaps. Common law was the ancient law of England, based on societal customs and reinforced by judgments and decrees of the court. It establishes the importance of judicial precedent and is an important modern-day feature of common law legal systems.

Common law doctrines give courts some flexibility in offering "just" solutions to situations not covered by statutory law. One example is the treatment of committed couples who lived together as if married but did not have a formal ceremony and did not register their relationship. In South Africa, courts have applied the common law doctrine of universal partnership to cohabiting couples and extended it to customary marriages, particularly in cases where legal requirements such as registration for customary marriages have not been met. The courts have gotten around the fact that cohabitation is not legally recognized in South Africa by declaring that an express or implied partnership exists between the parties. Significantly, this doctrine recognizes nonmonetary contributions

BOX 3.3

Changing Precedents Regarding the Status of Marital Property in Kenya

Before 2005, the courts in Kenya have sometimes interpreted the Married Women's Property Act and the Matrimonial Causes Act (1941) as securing women's property rights on divorce and recognizing nonmonetary contributions in civil, religious, and customary marriages:

- In *Karanja v. Karanja* (1976), the High Court rejected the argument that under Kikuyu customary law, married women do not own property because they have no independent legal identity. The court applied the Married Women's Property Act to award the wife a third of the couple's property.

- In *Kivuitu v. Kivuitu* (1991), the Court of Appeal applied the principle of nondiscrimination and equal protection of the law in recognizing the wife's nonmonetary contribution in the form of domestic chores and subsistence farming.

- In *Essa v. Essa* (1996), the High Court relied on the Married Women's Property Act to award property after divorce to a wife married under Islamic law. The court reiterated in its earlier judgment in *I v. I* (1970) that the Married Women's Property Act applies equally to Muslims and non-Muslims in Kenya.

- In *Omar Said Jaiz v. Naame Ali*, the High Court took *Kivuitu v. Kivuitu* one step farther to rule that property acquired through a joint venture would be considered joint property even without clear evidence of the extent of actual contribution made by each spouse (Baraza 2009).

Echaria v. Echaria (2007) was decided by a five-judge bench on the Court of Appeal, which overturned earlier decisions of the High Court and Court of Appeal on recognition

---

by women. Four requirements must be met for the universal partnership to exist:

- The partnership must aim to make a profit.[13]
- Both parties must contribute to the partnership, either monetarily or in other ways (by contributing labor or skills, for example).
- The partnership must operate for the benefit of both parties.
- There must be an agreement, either expressly in writing or implied from the conduct of the parties.

If a universal partnership is established, the property regime is similar to that of community of property, though the exact distribution of the partnership's assets is surmised from the terms of the agreement. It is important for cohabiting couples to draw up a written agreement—either before or during the period of cohabitation—that sets out the property distribution on separation or death.

of nonmonetary contributions. The court held that division of property in marriage would be determined under the general laws of contract in Kenya and that a woman must demonstrate her monetary contribution. (The requirement of proof of monetary contribution to matrimonial property had been upheld in the cases of *Beatrice Wanjiru Kimani v. Evanson Kimani Njoroge* [1995] and *Tabitha Wangechi Nderitu v. Simon Nderitu Kariuki* [1997], among others.)

In *Echaria v. Echaria*, the spouses had been married for 23 years. The wife was university educated and had worked outside the home for some time but had spent much of her married life looking after the couple's four children and supporting her husband, who had risen in the diplomatic service to become an ambassador. On the family's return from abroad, the wife worked as a senior education officer. In divorce proceedings, she claimed a 50 percent share of the marital property. The Court of Appeal awarded her only a 25 percent share, ruling that the "only contribution toward the acquisition of the property that Mrs. Echaria could have made was by payment of monthly installments of the loan." The court went on to state that "merely the status of marriage does not entitle a spouse to a beneficial interest of the property registered in the name of the other nor ... [does] the performance of domestic duties."

Kenya is a common law country; a judgment by a five-judge bench in the Court of Appeal is therefore binding on a smaller bench in the Court of Appeal, the High Court, and all subordinate courts. Exclusion of the wife's nonmonetary contribution in *Echaria v. Echaria*—the current legal position in Kenya—will adversely affect thousands of women until parliament enacts a new law.

Note: In light of the new Constitution of 2010 and subsequent legislative reform efforts (such as the Land Act No. 6 of 2012 and the current Matrimonial Property Bill) the right to nonmonetary contributions is open to reassessment.

The following cases in Botswana and Zimbabwe illustrate the concept of universal partnership where the agreement is implied from the conduct of the parties:

- In *Mogorosi v. Mogorosi* (2008), which originated in the customary courts, the Court of Appeal in Botswana applied the common law principle of universal partnership in recognizing the woman's nonmonetary contribution to the business incorporated and run by the man with whom she cohabited for about 15 years. The man had paid a customary dowry to the woman's family. The woman had worked for the business and carried out household duties, including caring for the couple's children. The court ruled that she was thus entitled to a 20 percent share of the man's estate valued at the date at which the cohabitation ended.

- In *Ivy Mbenge v. Jele Mbenge* (1996), the Court of Appeal in Botswana awarded the woman 50 percent of her ex-partner's assets acquired through their joint effort during the 28 years during which they cohabited. The case report

BOX 3.4

Recognition of Nonmonetary Contributions in Marriage in Tanzania

The courts in Tanzania have generally considered nonmonetary contributions in marriage, not only in statutory but also in customary and religious marriages:

- In *Keticia Bgumba v. Thadeo Maguma and Another* (1989), the High Court recognized the nonmonetary contribution of a woman during the two years she had cohabited with her husband, even though the couple had celebrated no formal or customary marriage. The court held that the woman had established the existence of a marriage by cohabitation and repute and that she could still claim a share or interest in a house in dispute by virtue of Section 160(2) of the Law of Marriage Act.
- In *Mohamed Abdallah v. Halima Lisangwe* (1988), the marriage was contracted under Islamic law. The High Court recognized the wife's clearing of the site where a house was built as a nonmonetary contribution. The court also observed that during the time the house was built, the wife bore children, reared them, and took care of the marital home. These activities freed her husband for his economic activities and entitled her to the fruits of his labor.
- In *Bi Hawa Mohamed v. Ally Sefu* (1983), the Court of Appeal recognized the domestic role of a housewife as a legitimate contribution to marital welfare, thus entitling the wife to part of that property.
- In *Richard Wilham Sawe v. Woitara Richard Sawe* (1992), the Court of Appeal held that, at divorce, marital property should be divided 50–50.

---

presents no evidence of customary marriage. The woman had run various commercial enterprises, including a cattle post and a general dealer shop, thereby satisfying the condition of having established a universal partnership.

- In *Chapeyama v. Matende* (2000), the High Court in Zimbabwe held that a wife married under customary law for 10 years was entitled to a fair distribution of all assets in the marital house on the breakdown of the marriage. The husband had tried unsuccessfully to overturn the joint registration of the couple's house. The court held that the application of the concept of a tacit partnership was fully justified. The husband appealed to the Supreme Court, which dismissed his appeal and recommended a review of marriage laws specifically to recognize unregistered customary marriages (Government of Zimbabwe 2009).

As these cases show, judicial decision making can be a progressive instrument for change, interpreting statutes equitably or creatively filling in legal ambiguities to advance women's rights. But judges can reinforce the status quo or, as in *Echaria*, reverse earlier gains.

To reduce the potential for discrimination, legislators need to craft legislation in harmony with constitutional principles of gender equality or non-discrimination. In the areas of family law and inheritance, women's rights to marital and inheritance property under statute should be unequivocally equal to those of men.

Customary Law

Customary law forms part of the legal framework in almost every Sub-Saharan country, as noted in chapter 2. A study of Sierra Leone suggests that up to 85 percent of the population used customary law as part of the formal and informal legal system (Kane and others 2004).

Customary law is generally not codified (some have argued that this is one of the features that has allowed it to evolve). But there are exceptions: the 1931 Customary Code of Dahomey in Benin, compiled by French authorities in colonial times, was in force until the new Family Code of 2004 effectively repealed many of its discriminatory provisions (UN 2005b). Some states in South Africa—such as KwaZulu Natal as the *Gumede* case illustrates—and Tanzania have also codified provisions of customary law.

Customary tribunals are normally based in or near villages. They are therefore more accessible than the formal statutory courts, which are usually in urban centers. In some countries, such as Cameroon, they are legally recognized by the state and part of the formal hierarchy of courts. Cameroon has a mixed legal system, comprising a civil law system in the francophone part of the country and a common law system in the anglophone part. Customary courts operate in both regions. The Customary Courts Ordinance establishes customary courts in the anglophone region. In the francophone region, Article 7(1) and 8(1) of the Decree of 1969 and Article 3 of the Law of 1979 sets out the composition of traditional courts to comprise a presiding officer; a civil servant or local dignitary, such as a traditional chief with reasonable knowledge of customary law; and assessors.[14] Assessors are elders who have lived for a long time in the area covered by the jurisdiction of the court and who have been chosen by the Ministry of Justice as people believed to have both moral integrity and in-depth knowledge of the customary law they are called on to represent. All parties must accept the competence of the traditional court for it to have jurisdiction.

In Côte d'Ivoire, village tribunals play a quasi-formal role. The constitution provides for the office of a grand mediator, who decides disputes that cannot be resolved by traditional means (UN 2007).

In Madagascar, the state recognizes customary tribunals, whose decisions can be appealed in the formal court system. These tribunals can adjudicate local village disputes relating to land use, for example. They have been co-opted by the state as an effective instrument in coastal marine resources management (Rakotoson and Tanner 2006).

Customary courts can also serve as nonstate justice systems. Proceedings are usually conducted informally, without lawyers and in the local vernacular language (formal legal proceedings are conducted in English, French, Portuguese, or Spanish). The costs are low, and decisions are rendered more quickly than in the formal system. The customary system may also be viewed by the local population as having greater legitimacy.

In Liberia, where long-running civil conflicts incapacitated the already weak formal justice system, the majority of the population resorted to traditional dispute settlement mechanisms. The types of cases that were most likely to be tried formally were bribery, property, and land disputes, although even in these instances the number of cases was very small and the majority of cases that were tried were tried in informal forums (table 3.1).

The adjudication of disputes usually takes a restorative approach—one that addresses grievances in terms of harm done to the community—rather than a retributive one. In nomadic pastoralist communities in northern Kenya, for example, the theft of livestock is seen as a crime against the community. A restorative approach is taken in which the kin group of the perpetrator compensates the victim and the victim's kin group. The communities prefer to follow this approach, which helps ease conflict, restore good relations, and strengthen

Table 3.1 Forums for Resolving Civil Disputes in Liberia, 2008–09

Dispute	Number of cases	Proportion of all cases taken to		
		No forum (percent)	Informal forum (percent)	Formal forum (percent)
Bribery and corruption	14	57	29	14
Debt dispute	1,497	67	31	2
Family and marital dispute	788	58	41	1
Child custody	21	62	38	0
Child and wife neglect	181	59	41	0
Divorce and separation	131	34	61	5
Other	455	64	35	1
Labor dispute	157	65	34	1
Land dispute	430	32	60	8
Property dispute	68	53	37	10
Witchcraft	227	56	41	4
Total	3,181	59	38	3

Source: Isser, Lubkemann, and N'Tow 2009.

kin relations, than to pursue the matter in the formal court system (Chopra 2008). The element of compromise inherent in the customary law system can reinforce social norms that discriminate on the basis of gender, age, or marital status (Penal Reform International 2000).

Informal customary courts, though not officially recognized, continue to operate in many civil law countries, including Benin, Burkina Faso, Gabon, and Guinea Bissau. Difficulties of access to formal systems allow these systems to continue to play an important role in civil law countries (Frémont 2009).

In common law countries, both formal and informal systems may refer to customary law. In some countries, such as Botswana, Nigeria, South Africa, and Zambia, specialized customary courts have been established under formal law. In others, such as Kenya, magistrates' courts have the jurisdiction to rule on customary law matters. In almost all common law countries, informal customary courts that are not officially recognized by the state continue to operate.

Advantages of customary law for women.   The range of customary law is vast, and provisions of customary law can sometimes help women access property. Under the same Yoruba customary law in Nigeria highlighted as discriminatory in *Akinnubi v. Akinnubi* (1997) below, women can be selected as heads of households and, as head, can control the arrangements for their husband's burial.[15] Under Yoruba customary law, both sons and daughters can inherit land (see *Amusan v. Amusan* 2002).

Customary law can also allow the marginalized and poor to voice their grievances where the formal system is out of reach because of cost, inaccessibility, or lack of local legitimacy because it is seen as corrupt, inefficient, or captured by the elite.[16] Kenya and Sierra Leone provide two examples. User rights granted to women by customary law in Kenya can give protection to marginalized women who are, for all practical purposes, disenfranchised from the statutory land-titling system. In Sierra Leone, where formal statutory laws on maintenance are inadequate, customary law may reinforce the obligation of the husband's family to provide for his children on divorce, especially when the ex-husband cannot be located (Kent 2007).

Customary law is not static; it can evolve to reflect changing societal norms. Formal courts in some countries have recognized these changes.

Under customary law in Botswana, after divorce, marital property is allocated based on the way it was acquired. In *Moisakomo v. Moisakamo* (1980), the High Court held that the wealth was produced principally by the effort of the wife and her use of property she had brought to the marriage. The chief justice made some observations about customary law:

> Custom of course plays an important role in how people choose to live but changing social and economic conditions affect and mould customs. One

of the changes is increasing urbanization. In the rapidly changing conditions of social life that is occurring in Africa, the need to examine the social utility of each rule of Customary Law is imperative. A rule that may have been just and suitable in a subsistence farming community may work grave hardship in a commercial farming economy (Griffiths 1983, 157).

In Malawi, customary law in some societies require the husband to move to their wife's village on marriage (a custom known as *matrilocality*). No bride price (sometimes known as *lobola*) is paid to the bride's family. Under customary law, the household property is jointly owned and subject to joint control. The marital home belongs to the wife.

Customary law in some matrilocal societies can be particularly favorable to women. In some countries, land can devolve to women or girls in a community under matrilocal inheritance rights (in others, such as Ghana, inheritance follows female bloodlines but the male relative inherits). Matrilocal societies exist in the Comoros Islands, Malawi, Zambia, and elsewhere in Africa. [17]

In Malawi, divorce is easier to obtain by both spouses in these matrilocal societies. Custody of the children goes to the wife, and the house remains under her ownership. Each spouse retains all its personal belongings, including livestock and traditional gifts given by the other spouse. Household property is equally divided, and the husband is entitled to remove doors, windows, and valuable fixtures that do not affect the main structure if he provided for them. Land cultivated by the husband is returned to the wife and, in essence, to her family. Inheritance also passes through female offspring (Mwambene 2005). By contrast, in Malawi's patrilineal societies, under customary law the wife requires her guardian's assistance to pursue divorce proceedings.[18]

The courts in Malawi have recognized customary property rights. In *Poya v. Poya* (1979), the High Court in Malawi held that the marital home built by the husband in the wife's village belonged to the wife under customary law. In recent years, some courts have taken a modified approach to customary law in matrilocal societies. Matrimonial property has been divided equally between the spouses under customary law on divorce.[19]

In *Shilubana and Others v. Nwamitwa* (2008), the Constitutional Court of South Africa stressed the importance of allowing traditional authorities the power to develop customary law to bring it in line with the contemporary needs of their communities:

> As has been repeatedly emphasised by this and other courts, customary law is by its nature a constantly evolving system. Under pre-democratic colonial and apartheid regimes, this development was frustrated and customary law stagnated. This stagnation should not continue, and the free development by communities of their own laws to meet the needs of a

rapidly changing society must be respected and facilitated. . . . "Living" customary law is not always easy to establish and it may sometimes not be possible to determine a new position with clarity. However, where there is a dispute over the law of a community, parties should strive to place evidence of the present practice of that community before the courts, and courts have a duty to examine the law in the context of a community and to acknowledge developments if they have occurred (page 22).

In Zambia, local courts have the jurisdiction to decide on matters of customary law in relation to family disputes. According to customary traditions in the region, families agree on a bride price and a verbal agreement is made, witnessed by the families. There is no written record. In divorce, women do not have the right to demand anything, and, in some customs, the children are taken away from the mother. According to a local lawyer, Manfred Chibanda, "It is precisely for these reasons that men prefer customary unions . . . because the mind-set is I do not want my wife to get anything of mine, if she leaves my house, she goes the way she came" (IRIN 2005).

In a landmark case in December 2005, a local court ruled that women married under customary law have the right to a share of marital property on divorce or husband's death. In *Martha Mwanamwalye v. Collins Mwanamwalye* (2005), Magistrate Mwaba Chanda stated that "notwithstanding that the parties married under customary law, justice demands that when a marriage has broken down, the parties should be put in equal position to avoid any of them falling into destitution." Another woman who had been married under customary law for 30 years but was awarded nothing in her settlement is using the case to make a fresh claim (IRIN 2005).

Disadvantages of customary law for women.   Customary law can also discriminate against women and be unsupportive of gender equality (Ayuko and Chopra 2008a, 2008b). Under Article 127 of the Code of Dahomey 1931 in Benin (repealed only in 2004), "a woman has no legal rights. Only in practice is she given some importance. She is often in charge of the administration of the household and can create some savings through the sale of her items. She is part of a man's property and heritage." Under this Code, women were considered legal minors and did not have the right to inherit from their parents or spouses. The *Benin United Nations Human Development Report 2003* reports that 231 of 419 women included in their study had been denied loans specifically for these reasons and were forced to resort to informal financing.

The Modogashe Declaration, drawn up to help bring peace to tribes in northern Kenya, sets out the traditional laws of these communities. According to the declaration, killing a man engenders compensation of 100 camels or cows, and killing a woman involves half that amount. When some women protested, they were told that this was the traditional way and were overruled by the men in the community (Chopra 2008).

Customary rights to succession are patrilineal in many communities (see, for example, *Bhe v. Khayelitsha Magistrate and the President of the Republic of South Africa* 2004). A widow may even be "inherited" by her brother-in-law. If she opposes the marriage, her only option is to leave her home, with her children and livestock retained by the husband's family. Sons also inherit in preference to daughters (Ayuko and Chopra 2008a).

Courts adjudicating family and inheritance disputes have sometimes upheld discriminatory provisions:

- In the case of *Ashu v. Ashu* (1986), Cameroon's High Court held that the wife was not entitled to her share of property because she herself was property according to customary law.

- In *Akinnubi v. Akinnubi* (1997), Nigeria's Supreme Court upheld the Court of Appeal's judgment that a widow married under Yoruba customary law could not administer her deceased husband's estate. It observed that "under Yoruba customary law, a widow under an intestacy is regarded as part of the estate of her deceased husband to be administered or inherited by the deceased's family; she could neither be entitled to apply for a grant of letters of administration nor to be appointed as co-administratrix."

- In *Scholastica Benedict v. Martin Benedict* (1993), Tanzania's Court of Appeal decided, after 17 years of litigation, to uphold the supremacy of the rights of the male heir under customary law to a property occupied by the second wife and her unmarried daughter. The second wife and her daughter had been living on the property in question for more than 15 years. Their right to continue living there was successfully challenged by the eldest son of the first wife, even though he lived in a separate house with his mother and family. The second wife and daughter were evicted from the property, and ownership was transferred to the son.

Religious Law
A country's colonial history influenced personal laws and their codification. Various anglophone countries in Africa adopted marriage acts pertaining to Muslim and Hindu marriages that the British codified in India. (Chapter 2 discusses specific aspects of Sharia law.)

Several countries exempt religious laws from constitutional provisions of nondiscrimination, making it impossible for women to appeal decisions of a religious court on the basis of discrimination. Kenya's new Constitution, for example, removed the exemption from nondiscrimination for customary law but retains the exemption for religious laws.

Countries have adopted different approaches to the application of religious laws and to the individual's ability to choose between legal systems:

- In the Gambian case of *Saika Saidy Theresa Saide, Albert Shrunsole and Jukba Saidy* (1974), the testator was a Muslim who willed all his property to his wife. His brother challenged the will. The Supreme Court ruled that the deceased could not dispose of his property under the Wills Act (1837) and that it had to be bequeathed according to Sharia law.

- In the Cameroonian case of *Baba Iyayi v. Hadija Aninatoou* (2000), the court ruled that French laws of inheritance supplanted Sharia law, because the deceased had been married under civil law.

- In the Cameroonian case of *Gbaron v. Yaccoumba v. Anemena Suzanne v. Mbombo Asang v. Nadam Emile* (1997), the Court of Appeal rejected the widow's claim for an entitlement from her deceased husband's estate under Sharia law and instead applied customary law, which did not give inheritance rights to wives.

The statutory requirement of women's consent to the jurisdiction of the Sharia court may act as a safeguard for women who prefer to opt out of a religious law regime (see the *Mrs. Kedija Beshir v. 3rd Naiba Court* [2004] case in Ethiopia, described later). In practice, however, many women may be unable to resist social pressure not to sidestep religious courts.

Challenges of Multiple Legal Systems and Inconsistent Laws

The presence of customary, statutory, and religious laws in all Sub-Saharan countries, whether formal or informal, creates a number of challenges. First, the very existence of multiple systems of law and sources of jurisprudence provides space and opportunity for discrimination and bias by raising questions as to which systems prevail in which circumstances. Second, even if plurality gives discretion to participants to select the system that offers the greatest advantages—through forum shopping (discussed at the end of this section)—this choice is not equally available to everyone in practice. A plural legal system that does not make nondiscrimination its cornerstone will always be disadvantageous to women.

Which Court and Which Law?

Jurisdictional issues can arise as to the appropriate forum for hearings, which can itself be the basis for litigation. Plural legal systems can fail to define jurisdictions, and some judicial officers may be unaware of their jurisdiction's limits

(Isser, Lubkemann, and N'Tow 2009). Local council courts (formal, state-recognized customary courts) in Uganda are on record as routinely deciding cases outside their jurisdiction because they lacked knowledge of formal law and could not identify which types of cases were covered solely by customary law and were within their ambit (Penal Reform International 2000).

Even where traditional leaders are aware of the limits of their jurisdiction, they may feel pressured by the local community to decide on the dispute or believe that they are better equipped to deal with the case. In some instances, the motivation behind claiming jurisdiction is simply income generated by fees for adjudicating disputes (Penal Reform International 2000).

In 2004, the House of Federation of Ethiopia (the upper house of the Ethiopian parliament) approved the Council of Constitutional Inquiry's decision that a woman had the right to choose between a civil court and a Sharia court (Ashenafi and Tadesse 2005). The case, concerning an inheritance dispute, had begun in the Sharia Court of first instance, which had decided the case and overridden the woman's objections to the court's jurisdiction. With the support of the Ethiopian Women Lawyers Association, the applicant, Kedija Bashir, appealed all the way up to the Supreme Sharia Court and finally to the Federal Supreme Court (Ashenafi and Tadesse 2005).

Even when the jurisdiction of the court is uncontested, the applicable law may generate further disputes. The formal legal system uses various tools, such as the repugnancy test and the mode of life test (described below), to determine whether statutory civil law, customary law, or religious law applies. Because it often does so case by case, the same or similar sets of facts can lead to conflicting decisions, making outcomes complex and unpredictable. One way to avoid such outcomes is to encourage women to register their customary marriages where statutory law allows for registration and specifically grants greater inheritance rights or a more equitable share of marital assets to a spouse than under customary law.

Repugnancy Test

The repugnancy test is a legal doctrine that dates from the British colonial era. It appears in the statutes of several anglophone countries in Africa. Its original purpose was to provide colonial administrators and courts with the ability to challenge and refuse to enforce customary laws on the grounds that they were repugnant to natural justice, equity, or good conscience. Repugnancy test provisions carried over after independence in Kenya, Malawi, Nigeria, Tanzania, and Uganda.

Even where customary law is exempt from the constitutional principle of nondiscrimination, courts have used the repugnancy test to set aside discriminatory customary provisions. As a tool for countering discrimination, the test can be inconsistent, however, because the interpretation of what is contrary to natural justice, equity, or good conscience can be subjective and

BOX 3.5

Same Facts, Different Conclusions: The Case of *Mojekwu v. Mojekwu*

In 1997, Nigeria's Court of Appeal rejected as repugnant the Oliekpe custom that disentitles a daughter from inheriting the property of the father where no son survives him. In 2004, the Supreme Court overturned this decision on the grounds that the parties had not challenged the custom's validity. The judge criticized the lower court's finding of repugnancy, stating that the "language used made the pronouncement so general and so far-reaching that it seems to avail at and is capable of causing strong feelings against all customs which fail to recognize a role for women which with due respect is not justifiable."

Source: FIDH 2008.

---

vary from one court to another, as the case of *Mojekwu v. Mojekwu* (1997) illustrates (box 3.5).

Courts in some countries have hesitated to use the repugnancy test to reject provisions of religious law. In the case of *Saika Saidy Theresa Saide, Albert Shrunsole and Jukba Saidy* (1974), the Gambian court held that the repugnancy test applied only to customary law and not to Sharia law.

Use of the repugnancy test is also sensitive because of its associations with the colonial past and the sense that indigenous culture was subject to foreign oversight (Banda 2003). For these reasons, Ghana and Tanzania repealed the statute after independence and use alternative tools and terminology to counter inequity.

In South Africa, the approach taken by the courts has been to discard the repugnancy test and make constitutionality the ultimate arbitrator. In *Mabuza v. Mbatha* (2003), Judge President John Hlophe commented, "The starting point is to accept the supremacy of the Constitution and that law and/or conduct inconsistent with therewith is invalid. Should the Court in any given case come to the conclusion that the customary practice or conduct in question cannot withstand constitutional scrutiny, an appropriate order in that regard should be made. The former approach, which recognizes African law only to the extent that it is not repugnant to the principles of public policy or natural justice, is flawed. It is unconstitutional."

Mode of Life Test

The mode of life test is a statutory tool courts may use to determine whether a person, because of changes in his or her lifestyle, is still subject to customary law. In divorce cases, for example, the courts have held that customary law does not apply where the parties were educated and lived in urban settings.

In *Molomo v. Molomo* (1979), Botswana's High Court applied the mode of life exemption under Section 2 of the Dissolution of African Marriage Act (Griffiths 1983).[20] In applying the exemption, the judge emphasized that the parties were educated, had traveled abroad, lived in a modern dwelling in the capital city, and had business interests. Conflicting decisions have arisen on whether the mode of life exemption applies, however, and factually similar cases have had different outcomes.

Forum Shopping

Forum shopping by people with power usually disadvantages women, most of whom lack access to the necessary resources (Odinkalu 2005).[21] However, this is not always the case. In Niger, Muslim women have claimed land rights under Sharia law that have been denied under customary law. They have been able to claim these rights without incurring social stigma, as the wider community endorses religious values (Diarra and Monimart 2006). Most women in Sub-Saharan Africa, however, lack the ability to pick and choose between systems.

Conclusion

Legal pluralism brings additional challenges to ensuring equal rights for women and reinforces the need for certain principles in the constitution, such as nondiscrimination, to prevail and guide all sources of law. As many areas of intersection between statutory and customary law pertain to how the rights of women and men may differ, they are of prime concern for ensuring that women's property rights are protected and they can pursue the same economic opportunities open to men.

De jure legal economic rights are not static. It is not just that statutes on the books are reformed over time—legal decisions are also instrumental in defining legal economic rights. As the many examples in this chapter illustrate, judicial interpretations vary across countries and even over time in the same country. Case law can help push for more progressive decisions, but the best way to reduce uncertainty in economic rights is to pass clear legislation and effectively enforce the law.

Customary law also evolves. It cannot be ignored, because it touches the lives of most of the population in many parts of Africa. By promoting positive core values in local traditions, such as protection of women, and recognizing and encouraging the evolution of customs, customary law can play an important role in empowering women and giving them equitable rights to property.

Cases Cited

Adeyemi v. Adeyemi (1985), Suit No. CB/354D/85

Akinnubi v. Akinnubi (1997), 2 NLWR

Amusan v. Amusan (2002), FWLR 1385

Andrew Manunzya Musyoka (2005), eKLR,7 (HC at Machakos)

Ashu v. Ashu (1986), BCA/62/86

Attorney General v. Aphane [2010], SZSC 32

Attorney General of the Republic of Botswana v. Unity Dow (1994), Case Report Court of Appeal (6) BCLR 1

Baba Iyayi v. Hadija Aninatoou (2000), Arrêt No. 083 of 32 March 2000

Beatrice Wanjiru Kimani v. Evanson Kimani Njoroge (1995) [1998], eKLR

Benin Constitutional Court Decision No. DCC 02-144 (2004), AHRLR (beCC 20202)

Berendt and Another v. Stuurman and Others (2003), NR 81 (HC)

Bernado Ephraim v. Holaria Pastory and Another (2001), AHRLR 236

Bhe v. Khayelitsha Magistrate and the President of the Republic of South Africa (2004), Case CCT 50/03

Bi Hawa Mohamed v. Ally Sefu (1983), TLR 32

Chapeyama v. Matende (2000), (2) 356 (s)

Echaria v. Echaria (2007), Eklr KECA 1

Elizabeth Gumede v. *President of South Africa and others* (2008), Case CCT 50/08 ZACC 23

Ephraim v. Pastory (2001), AHRLR 236

Essa v. Essa (1996), EA 53

Gbaron v. Yaccoumba v. Anemena Suzanne v. Mbombo Asang v. Nadam Emile (1997), Arrêt No. 002/c23, October

Georgina Mazunyane v. Rodney Chalera (2004), 76 Civil Cause No. 75 of 2004, Mulunguzi Magistrate Court (unreported)

I v. I (1970)

Ivy Mbenge v. Jele Mbenge (1996), BWCA 26; [1996] BLR 142 (CA), February 5

Kaffi v. Kaffi (1986), cited in 3 *Nigeria Weekly Law Report*, part 2, p. 175

Karanja v. Karanja (1976) [2008], 1 KLR (G&F) 171; (1976–80) 1 KLR 389

Mrs. Kedija Beshir v. 3rd Naiba Court (2004), House of the Federation, Appeal of Mrs. Kedija Beshir against being judged by Sharia Court and decision of House of Federation by which decision of 3rd Naiba Court Repealed (2004), 9 Federal Supreme Court Cassation Division File No. 12400/1999, May 15

Keticia Bgumba v. Thadeo Maguma and Another (1989), High Court, Mwanza, Mwalusanya J., Civil App. No. 8/89, July 18

Kivuitu v. Kivuitu (1991), 2 KAR 241

Mabuza v. Mbatha (2003), (4) SA 218 (C)

Malinki v. Malinki (1994) MC 9MLR 441

Mary-Joyce Doo Aphane v. Registrar of Deeds, Minister of Justice and Constitutional Affairs and the Attorney General (2010), Civil Case No. 383/2009

Mary Rono v. Jane Rono (2005) 1KLR (G&F)

Martha Mwanamwalye v. Collins Mwanamwalye (2005), cited in INSTRAW review news ticker "Zambia—ruling for women married under customary law—Property Rights," http://www.un-instraw.org/revista/hypermail/alltickers/en/0138

Mogorosi v. Mogorosi (2008), BWCA 18

Mohamed Abdallah v. Halima Lisangwe (1988), TLR 197 Tanzania

Moisakomo v. Moisakamo (1980), MC 106, cited in "Legal Duality: Conflict or Concord in Botswana?" *Journal of African Law* 150 (1983)

Mojekwu v. Mojekwu (1997), 7 NWLR: Pt 512: 283

Molomo v. Molomo (1979), 80 BLR 250

Mtegha v. Mtegha (1994), MC No. 9 of 1994

Ndossi v. Ndossi (2001), High Court Civil Appeal No. 13 of 2001, High Court of Tanzania at Dar Es Salaam, February 13

Nyangulu v. Nyangulu, 10 Malawi Law Reports 435

Obusez v. Obusez (2001), 15 N.W.L.R. 377

Omar Said Jaiz v Naame Ali, cited in "Family Law Reforms in Kenya: An Overview," paper presented by Nancy Baraza at the Heinrich Böll Foundation's Gender Forum, Nairobi, April 30, 2009

Poya v. Poya (1979), Civil Appeal No. 38 of 1979 N.T.A.C.

Registered Trustees of the Women and Law in Southern Africa Malawi v. the Attorney General (2009), Constitutional Case No. 3 of 2009

Richard Wilham Sawe v. Woitara Richard Sawe (1992), Civil Appeal No. 38 of 1992, TZCA, 9

Saika Saidy v. Theresa Saide, Albert Shrunsole, and Jukba Saidy (1973), Supreme Court Civil Appeal No.4/73 NS 148

Scholastica Benedict v. Martin Benedict (1993), Court of Appeal of Tanzania at Mwanza, Civil Appeal No. 26 of 1988 (unreported)

Shilubana and Others v. Nwamitwa (2008), (CCT 03/07) (2008) ZACC 9; 2008 (9) BCLR 914 (CC); 2009 (2) SA 66 (CC), June 4

Tabitha Wangechi Nderitu v. Simon Nderitu Kariuki (1997) [1998], eKLR

Uganda Association of Women Lawyers and others v. Attorney General (2002) (Constitutional Petition No. 2 of 2003), (2004) UGCC 1

Wachokire Succession (2002) Cause No. 192 of 2000

White v. White (2001), 1AC 596 (HL)

Notes

1. Additional sources of law, such as executive orders, binding statements of policy, and bylaws, are not reviewed in detail.

2. The Act allowed only the husband to claim damages from the alleged co-adulterer respondent and to assert a claim on the wife's property. The wife could not claim similar damages where the husband committed adultery. Only the wife, however, was allowed to claim alimony if her petition was granted. Both provisions were declared discriminatory.

3. Other countries, including Burkina Faso, Cameroon, Côte d'Ivoire, Ethiopia, Gabon, Malawi, Nigeria, Rwanda, Sierra Leone, and Swaziland, have similar constitutional provisions. Enforcement of the constitutional provisions to override discriminatory legislation varies across countries. Section 211(3) of the South African Constitution makes customary law subject to the Constitution, Section 9 of which establishes the right to equality and nondiscrimination.

4. The declaration of invalidity has to be confirmed by the Constitutional Court under Section 172 of the Constitution.

5. The section is Section 172 of the South African Constitution: "*Powers of courts in constitutional matters* 1. When deciding a constitutional matter within its power, a court (a) must declare that any law or conduct that is inconsistent with the Constitution is invalid to the extent of its inconsistency; and (b) may make any order that is just and equitable, including (i) an order limiting the retrospective effect of the declaration of invalidity; and (ii) an order suspending the declaration of invalidity for any period and on any conditions, to allow the competent authority to correct the defect."

6. Sections 20 and 28 of the Swaziland Constitution set out equality in the eyes of the law.

7. Criteria for a good test law case include the ability to show clear standing to bring the case and a fact pattern that addresses the issues and is compelling, raises the legal issues of interest, and provides a strong case for a favorable ruling.

8. The United Kingdom has reviewed these laws. A landmark House of Lords judgment in the case of *White v. White* in 2001, which overturned decades of legal precedent, provides for the equal splitting of marital property.

9. In both *Malinki v. Malinki* and *Mtegha v. Mtegha*, the magistrates' court held that a spouse wishing to claim a share of property not in his or her name had to show financial contribution. Contributions to maintenance of property items, housekeeping, and child care were not sufficient.

10. In *Adeyemi v. Adeyemi*, the wife failed to tender receipts to show a financial contribution to the property acquired during the marriage. The lack of proof disentitled her from receiving a share of the property.

11. Under section 114 (1) of Tanzania's Law of Marriage Act (1971), "The court shall have power, when granting or subsequent to the grant of a decree of separation or divorce, to order the division between the parties of any assets acquired by them during the marriage by their joint efforts or to order the sale of any such asset and the division between the parties of the proceeds of sale. The court . . . (d) *shall incline towards equality of division*" (emphasis added).

12. Section 56 (1) of Zambia's Matrimonial Causes Act (2007) allows the court to consider several factors when determining financial relief on divorce, including "(f) *the contributions made by each of the parties to the welfare of the family, including any contribution made by looking after the home or caring for the family*" (emphasis added).

13. Marriages are not businesses; this criterion is taken to mean that the participating parties are seeking to maintain themselves financially or acquire assets over time.

14. Assessors are also appointed in common law customary courts.

15. But, as highlighted in the *Akinnubi* case, a widow who is not the head of her household may be regarded as chattel (Nwabueze 2010).

16. Preexisting tenure systems based on usage rights may protect the interests of particularly vulnerable groups, such as indigenous communities, urban slum dwellers, and marginal settlements, better than formal titling processes (Delville 2000; Adler, Porter, and Woolcock 2008).

17. Article 153 of the Inheritance Code of the Comoros sets out the matrilineal Manyahuli custom as follows: "Manyahuli is a custom that is uniquely observed in the Comoros Island. Manyahuli attributes to girls the land or the family house. The following are excluded from the Manyahuli: boys, grandsons, brothers, male cousins, uncles, husband, and wife. Male children cannot dispose Manyahuli property but can only enjoy and administer it." Article 157 mandates that "a woman to whom the title of Manyahuli has been recognized will be able to dispose completely without the intervention of third parties."

18. Under patrilineal customary law in Malawi, the guardian has to repay the bride wealth that was given, which may make him reluctant to support the wife.

19. In *Georgina Mazunyane v. Rodney Chalera (2004)*, the magistrates' court held that matrimonial property should be divided equitably in customary marriages. In this case, matrimonial property was divided equally.

20. It is not clear to what extent the statutory exemption still applies after the Married Women's Property Act came into force. The case law on the issues is conflicting.

21. Educated women in higher income groups and with extensive networks may also be able to forum shop (Griffiths 1998).

References

Adler, Daniel, Doug J. Porter, and Michael Woolcock. 2008. "Legal Pluralism and Equity: Some Reflections on Land Reform in Cambodia." Justice for the Poor Briefing Note. World Bank, Washington, DC.

Ashenafi, Meaza, and Zenebeworke Tadesse. 2005. "Women, HIV/AIDS, Property and Inheritance Rights: The Case of Ethiopia." United Nations Development Programme, New York.

Ayuko, Bonita, and Tanja Chopra. 2008a. "The Illusion of Inclusion: Women's Access to Right in Northern Kenya." Legal Resources Foundation Trust, Nairobi.

———. 2008b. "The Mystery of Capital Formation in Sub-Saharan Africa: Women, Property Rights and Customary Law." *World Development* 36 (7): 1223–46.

Badri, Balghis. 2005. "Feminist Perspectives in the Sudan." Paper presented at the workshop "Feminist Perspectives," Free University of Berlin, May 26–27.

Banda, Fareda. 2003. "Global Standards: Local Values." *International Journal of Law, Policy and the Family* 17 (1): 1.

Baraza, Nancy. 2009. "Family Law Reforms in Kenya: An Overview." Paper presented at the Heinrich Böll Foundation's Gender Forum, Nairobi, April 30.

Center for Reproductive Rights. 2003. "Women of the World: Laws and Policies Affecting their Reproductive Lives—Francophone Africa." Center for Reproductive Rights, New York.

Chopra, Tanja. 2008. "Building Informal Justice in Northern Kenya." Legal Resources Foundation Trust, Nairobi.

Delville, Philippe L. 2000. "Harmonising Formal Law and Customary Land Rights in French-Speaking West Africa." In *Evolving Land Rights, Policy and Tenure in Africa*, ed. Camilla Toulmin and Julian Quan, 97–121. London: Department for International Development.

Diarra, Marthe, and Marie Monimart. 2006. "Landless Women, Hopeless Women: Gender, Land and Decentralisation in Niger." IIED Issues Paper 143, International Institute for Environment and Development, London.

Emery, Vanessa. 2005. "Women's Inheritance Rights in Nigeria: Transformative Practices." University of Toronto, Faculty of Law, Toronto.

FIDH (International Federation for Human Rights). 2008. "The Nigeria NGO Coalition Shadow Report to the CEDAW Committee." FIDH, Paris.

Frémont, Jacques. 2009. "Legal Pluralism, Customary Law and Human Rights in Francophone African Countries." *Victoria University of Wellington Law Review* 40 (1): 149–65.

Government of Zimbabwe. 2009. "Zimbabwe: Combined Report of the Republic of Zimbabwe in Terms of the Convention on the Elimination of all Forms of Discrimination Against Women." Government of Zimbabwe, Harare.

Griffiths, Anne. 1983. "Legal Duality: Conflict or Concord in Botswana?" *Journal of African Law* 27 (2): 150–61.

———. 1998. "Legal Pluralism in Botswana: Women's Access to Law." *Journal of Legal Pluralism and Unofficial Law* 42: 123–39.

IRIN (Integrated Regional Information Networks). 2005. "Zambia: Humanitarian News and Analysis." December 21, 2005. http://www.irinnews.org/country .aspx?country=zm.

Isser, Deborah H., Stephen C. Lubkemann, and Saah N'Tow. 2009. *Looking for Justice: Liberian Experiences with and Perceptions of Local Justice Options*. Washington, DC: United States Institute of Peace.

Kamungi, Prisca Mbura, Johnstone Summit Oketch, and Chris Huggins. 2004. "Land Access and the Return and Resettlement of IDPs and the Refugees in Burundi." In *From the Ground Up: Land Rights, Conflict and Peace in Sub-Saharan Africa*, ed. Chris Huggins and Jenny Glover. 195–267. Pretoria: Institute of Security Studies.

Kane, Minneh, Keith Mackiggan, Chris Mburu, Ibrahim Gassama, Emma Morley, and Christian Eldon. 2004. "Sierra Leone: Legal and Judicial Sector Assessment." World Bank, Legal Vice Presidency, Washington, DC.

Kent, Allison D. 2007. "Custody, Maintenance, and Succession: The Internalization of Women's and Children's Rights under Customary Law in Africa." *Michigan Journal of International Law* 28 (2): 507.

Lambert, Priscilla, and Druscilla Scribner. 2008. "Gender Matters: A Case Study Analysis of Constitutional Provisions." Paper presented at the annual meeting of the American Political Science Association, Boston, August 28.

Legal Assistance Centre and International Women's Human Rights Clinic. 2008. "Supplementary Submission to the Committee on Racial Discrimination: Supplementing Namibia's 2007 Country Report." Georgetown University Law Center, Washington, DC.

Mwambene, Lea. 2005. "Divorce in Matrilineal Customary Law Marriage in Malawi: A Comparative Analysis with the Patrilineal Customary Law Marriage in South Africa." University of the Western Cape, Cape Town, South Africa.

Nwabueze, Remigius N. 2010. "Securing Widows' Sepulchral Rights through the Nigerian Constitution." *Harvard Human Rights Journal* 23 (1): 141–55.

Odinkalu, Chidi A. 2005. "Pluralism and the Fulfillment of Justice Needs in Africa." Africa Governance Monitoring and Advocacy Project, Open Society Institute, New York.

Penal Reform International. 2000. *Access to Justice in Sub-Saharan Africa: The Role of Traditional and Informal Justice Systems.* London: Astron Printers.

Rakotoson, Lalaina R., and Kathryn Tanner. 2006. "Community-Based Governance of Coastal Zone and Marine Resources in Madagascar." *Ocean & Coastal Management* 49 (11): 855–72.

UN (United Nations). 2003. *Benin United Nations Human Development Report 2003.* New York: United Nations.

———. 2005a. *Committee on the Elimination of Discrimination against Women, Observation Finales: Gabon.* CEDAW/C/GAB/CC/2–5, New York.

———. 2005b. *Committee on the Elimination of Discrimination against Women Thirty-Third Session 5–22 July 2005, Concluding Comments: Benin.* CEDAW/C/BEN/CO/1-3, UN, New York.

———. 2007. *Côte d'Ivoire Public Administration Country Profile.* Department of Economic and Social Affairs, Division of Public Administration and Development Management, UN, New York.

UNHCR (United Nations Refugee Agency). 2003. "An Act to Govern the Devolution of Estates and Establish Rights of Inheritance for Spouses of Both Statutory and Customary Marriages." National Legislative Bodies, UNHCR, New York.

Chapter 4

Women's Rights in Practice:
Constraints to Accessing Justice

Enshrining rights in laws and constitutions is an important first step, as chapter 2 showed. But having them on the books is not sufficient to ensure that they are actually enjoyed in practice.

This chapter examines the gaps between de jure and de facto economic rights for women in Sub-Saharan Africa. It focuses on how the judicial and customary legal systems play out in practice and how easy (or hard) it is for women to access justice. At issue is how the formal judicial or customary systems support de jure rights, whether based in statutory or formal customary law. Issues of custom, tradition, and informal dispute resolution mechanisms enter in only insofar as they affect the likely access to formal customary law proceedings or judicial courts.

The plurality of laws offers choice, but in practice nearly all legal systems treat women and men differently, and women's access to equitable justice remains a challenge (box 4.1). Some factors affecting access are gender specific, such as the greater social pressure women face not to bring disputes into the judicial system, differences in access resulting from women having less mobility and time than men, and the discriminatory outcomes and lack of gender sensitization in both formal and customary legal systems. Other factors, such as affordability of justice or lack of awareness of legal rights, are common to men and women from the poorer sectors of society, but they can take longer to rectify for women, who may be marginalized in their own communities.

The chapter begins with formal judicial systems before turning to customary systems of justice. Judicial systems can be undermined through lack of resources, popular concerns about legitimacy, and restriction of access to the urban elite. Customary systems, in theory more accessible, may not offer the same opportunities for justice to women as to men, and they, too, may be captured by the local elite.

BOX 4.1

Shortcomings of the Justice System from the Chief Justice in Ghana

Some people working in the justice system, including officials at the highest levels, are acutely aware of the challenges women face in accessing justice. The Chief Justice of Ghana has called for efforts by stakeholders, including the judiciary, to tackle the biases within the justice sector, noting the following:

> In many countries, and more particularly in Africa, where the illiteracy rate is quite high, the justice system has never been kind to women; it fails them. The obstacles, both formal and informal, that women encounter in their attempt to access justice are quite numerous. Most national constitutions, laws and international conventions, instruments, protocols, etc. seek to promote equality between men and women, but the reality is still a mirage. Although there are constitutional and other statutory provisions that on paper afford women a fair measure of protection, polices, procedures and practices often prevent women from the full and equal enjoyment of these rights and privileges and hinder them from accessing justice.

Source: Wood 2008, 8.

Formal Judicial Systems in Practice

Many formal judicial systems in Sub-Saharan Africa suffer from a severe lack of resources, rendering them unable to enforce the laws on the books. State funding of court systems can represent less than 1 percent of the government budget. The number of judges is often as low as 1 per 100,000 people (by contrast, New Zealand has 250 lawyers per 100,000 people, Spain has 445, and Brazil has almost 500). Kenya has a backlog of about 1 million cases, 300,000 of them before the High Court in Nairobi (Machuhi 2007; Muriuki 2007).

Even if a woman secures a favorable judgment, enforcement mechanisms are often weak, suffer from bureaucratic delays, and are prone to tactical blocking strategies by the opposing party (box 4.2). These problems reinforce a general lack of trust in the system that leaves many women reluctant to start a process that, even if successful, may not deliver practical results. But weak enforcement may also work to women's disadvantage in some cases, as discriminatory laws are similarly undermined if they are not implemented.

Institutional Shortcomings

Too few women and a lack of gender sensitivity.   Africa's legal systems suffer from several shortcomings. One is the challenges women face in accessing the

BOX 4.2

Delaying and Denying Justice in Ghana

Once a case gets to court, the backlog of cases may mean that it takes years to resolve. These backlogs delay—and often deny—justice, as the case of Rita Charlotte Eshon in Ghana reveals.

After her husband died, Eshon applied for a grant of letters of administration, to which the husband's family objected. After seven years in court, she finally obtained a judgment in her favor. In the meantime, however, the family had harvested the coconuts from the farm, which was no longer productive. It had also been collecting rent for the house and defied a court order to pay the rent to the court for Eshon's benefit. The family appealed the decision to the High Court, further delaying the case.

Source: Fenrich and Higgins 2002.

law and legal precedents, without which they may not be aware of their formal economic rights. But in many countries, there is a more fundamental problem: legal professionals, including lawyers and judges themselves, may not be aware of the law or of the rights contained in their country's constitution. There is limited publication and dissemination of laws—evident in the efforts needed to collect the data for Women–LEED–Africa. The availability of case law to the legal profession is also shockingly limited. These problems stem partly from the weak communication infrastructure between provincial courts and courts in urban centers as well as from inadequate training.

Other problems include the dearth of women in the legal system and the lack of gender sensitivity. The number of female judges and other senior legal officers is low nearly everywhere in Sub-Saharan Africa (table 4.1). Female judges are not necessarily more sensitive to gender-based discrimination, though it may be significant that the landmark case of *Mary-Joyce Doo Aphane* in 2010, which overturned decades of barriers to land registration by women married in community of property, was decided by the only appointed female High Court judge in Swaziland. (The case is discussed in chapter 3.)

In many countries, the judiciary is male dominated and patriarchal (box 4.3 illustrates some notable exceptions). Women may be reluctant to access the formal system if they believe that the prospect of an impartial hearing is remote, especially if they regard the system as corrupt and inefficient. Gender insensitivity can extend to court employees such as clerks and ushers, who influence court procedure (table 4.2).

Table 4.1 Number of Male and Female Judges in Kenya, 2009

Court	Total	Male	Female
High Court	51	32	19
Court of Appeal	12	12	0

Source: Kamangu 2010.
Note: Data are as of June 2010. In April 2010, the only female Court of Appeal Judge, Lady Justice Joyce Aluoch, was appointed to the International Criminal Court at The Hague.

Table 4.2 Number of Male and Female Magistrates and Court Officers in Cameroon, 2009

Type of court or judicial officer	Total	Male	Female
Magistrates' court	826	642	184
Bailiffs and process servers	319	257	62

Source: Lobti 2010.

BOX 4.3

Women Are Participating at Senior Levels of the Legal Profession in Several Countries

A significant number of women were heading legal institutions in several countries in Africa in 2009. In Botswana, the Attorney-General, Dr. Athaliah Molokomme, was the founding head of the Gender Unit at the Secretariat of the Southern African Development Community. In Ghana, the Chief Justice, the Acting Inspector General of Police, the Director of Immigration, and the Attorney General/Minister of Justice of Ghana were all women. In Liberia, Professor Christiana Tah was the Minister of Justice and Attorney General.

The Southern African Development Community (SADC) Protocol on Gender and Development set a target of 50 percent representation of women in politics and decision-making positions at all levels by 2015. Statistics from SADC countries show some advancement toward that goal, with more progress at lower levels of courts than at higher levels. In 2009, 67 percent of regional court presidents in Mauritius, 44 percent of regional court judges in South Africa, and 43 percent of judges of industrial courts in Botswana were women. Zimbabwe had achieved gender parity at the level of labor court presidents, and Tanzania and Mauritius had attained parity at the magistrate level, where the share of women was 49 percent in Botswana, 43 percent in Namibia, 42 percent in Lesotho, 41 percent in Zimbabwe, and 30 percent in South Africa. In Tanzania, 56 percent of judges on both the Court of Appeal and the High Court were women.

Source: SADC 2009.

Challenges to Access

A range of constraints limit women's access to the legal system in Africa including lack of affordability, lack of awareness of legal rights, and discouragement by social pressure.

Lack of affordability.   Filing a claim entails many costs, such as court fees, which act as a financial barrier. Some countries charge a range of administrative fees, including charges for investigative work and the paper used for depositions. Bribes may also be needed to have a claim heard (Isser, Lubkemann, and N'Tow 2009).

The ratio of lawyers to the general population is generally low, reflecting capacity constraints and the inadequate system of legal education. Malawi has 77 lawyers for its population of 11 million people (USAID 2009). Sierra Leone has about 100 practicing lawyers for its population of 5.5 million people, and 90 of them are based in Freetown (Maru 2006). Most lawyers are based in cities, and their fees are prohibitive for the rural poor, particularly women. Legal aid schemes are rare. And even where nongovernmental organizations are operating, women's lack of awareness may prevent them from approaching them.

A 2009 study in Ethiopia found that in civil cases in the Federal Courts of First Instance, particularly family law cases, women were more likely than men to file suits (figure 4.1). Women were able to access the legal system because of reforms that improved the efficiency of the court system and dramatically reduced costs by no longer requiring a party to be represented by a lawyer (a reform based partly on the dearth of lawyers) and reducing the costs of filing (Hammergren and Mitiku 2010). The impact of these reforms can be seen in the striking increase in the use of these courts over time. Progress still has to be made in narrowing the gender gaps in non–family law cases, such as commercial and labor law cases, particularly in relation to the low number of cases taken to the higher and superior courts.

The share of female plaintiffs is much lower in higher courts, because on average, women's claims are of lower monetary value and women are less likely than men to appeal (Rodríguez 2000).[1] The lack of legal representation may also affect the quality of legal outcomes for women in some cases. The ability of women to represent themselves effectively will depend on their capacity and the complexity of the legal process.

Magistrates' courts can be more accessible to the general population than higher courts, because they extend outside capital cities. The law usually limits their jurisdiction to a monetary ceiling, however, which land claims can exceed. A plaintiff who initiates a claim in a magistrates' court risks a decision in which the court rules that it has no jurisdiction to hear the claim, which must instead be heard in the High Court. Having already wasted time and money, plaintiffs—particularly women—may find that starting anew in a court that may be far from home is both intimidating and financially onerous.

Figure 4.1 The Number of Female Plaintiffs in Ethiopia Has Been Rising—But Male Plaintiffs Still Dominate in Higher and Superior Courts

(number of individual plaintiffs in civil cases, by gender, 2005/06–2008/09)

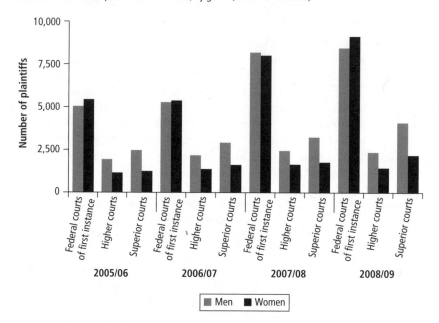

Source: Hammergren and Mitiku 2010.

Lack of awareness of legal rights.   Many women are unaware of statutory rights they may have under divorce, inheritance, or land laws. Especially in rural areas, many women are not educated and have never interacted with any part of the formal legal system. In addition, the language of the statutes and court procedures—English, French, Portuguese, or Spanish—is rarely their mother tongue.

Botswana attempted to rectify this situation by simplifying and translating laws affecting women into local languages and circulating a handbook. Standard court forms in English were translated into Setswana and included in the appendix. The handbook was distributed free to social workers, educators, and women's groups (Molokomme 1990). Distribution of the handbook represents a step in the right direction. It needs to be accompanied by parallel services, such as the provision of legal aid to poor women.

Lack of familiarity with court processes, common to all new court users, is a disadvantage. Women may not know that it can be advantageous to appear in person, for example, rather than submit written depositions.

Social pressure.   Immediate family members, in-laws, and the wider local community often discourage women from pursuing claims in court. As Unity

Dow, who successfully challenged Botswana's discriminatory nationality laws, said, "The Traditionalists charged that I was influenced by foreign ideas and that I was seeking to change their culture. Many women distanced themselves from me" (Dow 2001, 326–27) (see box 3.2 in chapter 3). Women may come under heavy social pressure not to disturb the status quo; if they do, they and their children may be ostracized, harassed, stigmatized, or subjected to violence (Harrington and Chopra 2010).

Customary Systems in Practice

Women in Africa face multiple constraints in accessing justice in customary legal systems. Although customary law may be geographically and culturally more accessible to women, their experience in customary institutions still differs greatly from that of men, in both customary tribunals and informal traditional practices.

Institutional Shortcomings

Customary systems in Africa suffer from many shortcomings. Problems include the small number of women decision makers in customary courts, the weak autonomy of some customary courts, corruption and favoritism, and the fact that some customary courts have failed to keep up with evolving customary practices.

Dearth of women decision makers in customary courts.   Women have traditionally been excluded from adjudicating matters of customary law. They are therefore unable to influence its evolution (Ayuko and Chopra 2008).

A 2007 analysis of Sierra Leone's local court system—an institution that has legal authority to adjudicate cases of customary law—revealed the small number of women working in and using the system (Koroma 2007). Court members were appointed from each chiefdom: of 123 members surveyed, only 7 were women. Of 30 court clerks, only 1 was a woman. And most parties to the cases were men.

Some countries have attempted to redress the imbalance through state legislation, which may set a minimum quota for female representation on bodies such as local council courts (box 4.4).[2] But it is unclear how—or whether—these provisions are enforced in practice or whether women in these bodies can really challenge discriminatory practices.

Some customary systems do involve women as leaders. In the *Shilubana* case in South Africa (2008), the Constitutional Court respected the decision of the traditional authority to break with custom and appoint a female chief for the first time in the history of the traditional Valoyi community in Limpopo. In 2001, Botswana appointed it first female Paramount Chief (box 4.5)

BOX 4.4

The Experience of Women Councillors in Local Customary Courts in Uganda

Local council courts in Uganda are formal state-recognized customary courts. By law, at least 30 percent of councillor judges must be women. The Local Government Act requires that the executive committee of the local council courts include at least one woman.

The effect of this law has reportedly been somewhat muted by discriminatory practices by judges. According to one female court member, woman on these councils are rarely consulted, and their views are not taken seriously when they share them.

Court sessions normally last for several hours and take place outside office hours. These hours make it harder for women to participate, as they are usually burdened with domestic responsibilities. There have been ongoing efforts to address these concerns. Operational guidelines for these courts that cover human rights and gender sensitivity training have been developed and translated into local languages.

Source: Twinomugisha and Kibuka 1997; Penal Reform International 2000; Ellis, Manuel, and Blackden 2006.

Weak autonomy of customary courts.   The village chief who serves as the adjudicator in the customary court is often also in charge of many other administrative functions and economic decisions in village life (Gauri 2009). As well as adjudicating disputes, the village chief may also be responsible for making the rules, collecting taxes, and distributing resources. If he is not directly responsible for these activities, members of his family may be. The village chief is generally physically and socially closer to the claimant than a judge in a state or federal court would be and can generally intervene in her daily life and networks with greater ease. Women may be intimidated in approaching a local leader, who can potentially negatively affect their everyday life, to settle their disputes.

Corruption and favoritism.   When a dispute is unresolved, a claimant may need to access the hierarchy of customary courts or councils. Some claimants have the right to appeal to the formal courts, but the local leader can sometimes block the appeal. In this case, the claimant can do little to force the issue. Women generally have little influence persuading a village chief to submit a dispute to more powerful authorities (box 4.6). And even if a case does go higher, the papers or claim can be fixed (through bribes, for example) to secure the outcome desired by the local chief. In addition, customary law can be applied unfairly, and favoritism or abuse of sanctions, such as excessive use of fines, may be used (Maru 2006).

BOX 4.5

Making History: Botswana's First Female Paramount Chief

Botswana achieved a milestone in 2001 when the elders of the Balete people elected Mosadi Seboko the first female Paramount Chief. She was elected following the death of her father and brother, the preceding chiefs. Initially, the elders resisted her appointment, on the grounds that custom dictated that only men could rule. At a meeting of a *kgotla* (a community council that also functions as a customary law court) attended by hundreds of people, Seboko argued that she should be appointed on the strength of the Botswana constitution, which guarantees freedom from discrimination. Her appointment marked an extraordinary change in a tribe that until relatively recently did not allow women even to attend *kgotla* meetings.

As one of the eight Paramount Chiefs in Botswana, Seboko presides over community disputes in her 30,000 member tribe. Since being elected, she has highlighted women's issues, such as domestic violence (she divorced her husband on this basis) and women's sexual rights.

Three of Botswana's 15 chiefs are now women. As members of the House of Chiefs, which Seboko once headed, they advise the government on custom and tribal property.

Source: Matemba 2005.

BOX 4.6

Nowhere to Turn: Women's Complaints of Harassment in Malawi

Women can be especially vulnerable to pressure from local village chiefs, and they have limited recourse to higher authorities outside the village. They often lack the networks to counter unlawful land-grabbing and other breaches of their rights by local leaders. As one woman commented:

> When my husband chased me [from my land], I knew this was a violation of my rights. Now, the Chief is perpetuating this same violation because he seems to have now grown an interest in my very small piece of land. He is giving me so much pressure that I am now at a loss as to where to take my complaint, since this is the very same Chief who helped me when I complained to him after my husband chased me away.

Source: NIZA 2009, 33.

Failure of customary courts to keep up with evolving customary practices.   Urbanization, the weakened role of communal resources in daily life, and the growth of the market economy are driving change in many villages in Africa. These practices may be evolving more rapidly than customary courts are willing to acknowledge. For example, customary laws in Botswana traditionally excluded women from inheriting property. But a 2009 study of Tlokweng, a peri-urban area adjoining the capital, Gaborone, suggests that married daughters can now claim a share of their parents' estate and that equal sharing of property between siblings of both genders is common. Community elders' view of customary practices has not kept up with these changes. If family members contest an estate, the courts in Tlokweng are likely to apply traditional customary law, which gives the bulk of property to the oldest son (Kalabamu 2009).

Challenges to Access

Women too often on the margins.   Traditional justice mechanisms (including religious courts) can marginalize and exclude the landless and women, especially young, unmarried women. Most customary courts are adjudicated by and tend to favor men in their decision making. Marital disputes, including disputes with implications for control over assets, may be settled in ways that stop husbands from losing face, even when they are obviously in the wrong— an approach that is rarely taken with women. Women may be unable to voice their grievances directly, having to rely instead on the male head of the family to decide whether to bring the grievance to the elders' attention. In addition, a woman may have no right to speak unless directed to do so.[3]

If a woman is from an outside clan or lineage, her standing in the village may well be diminished even further. And as customary courts are by their very nature localized, they are less equipped to resolve disputes in which the parties are from different ethnic backgrounds.

A 2007 analysis of the local courts in Sierra Leone revealed that most of the cases were civil and a significant number involved women. Many cases involved men's failure to pay child support or a man having an affair with another man's wife. In most of these cases, both parties were men, with the affected women not party to the lawsuit.

Most of the female litigants in Botswana who managed to overturn the status quo in customary courts had a wide range of resources, including education, financial stability, social status, and extensive networks (Griffiths 2002). Interviews by anthropologists and sociologists provide evidence from other settings that suggests that these resources are also crucial in gaining acceptance of women as decision makers in traditional communities. Too often women's relative lack of economic power is reinforced by receiving less favorable treatment in traditional forums for dispute resolutions (Schärf and others 2002; Ayuko and Chopra 2008).

Religious courts can expand access—but can be biased.   Religious courts are likely to be gender biased and patriarchal in their decisions, given their all-male composition (there are no female *kadhis* [judges] in Africa).[4] Women's experiences in religious courts vary. In Tanzania, many women are reluctant to take family disputes involving maintenance, custody, or divorce to the BAWAKTA committees, the central arbiters of religious law by the state, which operate as courts of first instance (trial courts).[5] Most women view these committees as resisting reform and generally favoring men. They are also reluctant to pursue claims in the secular magistrates' courts, suggesting that women in Tanzania are marginalized from the justice system (Hirsh 2009).

By contrast, Kenya's *kadhi* court system, which is under the close supervision of secular courts, is used predominately by women, who win most of the cases. Women view these judges as younger and less traditional than the local elders—and more sympathetic to women. The *kadhis* are civil servants and thus accountable to the state; they come from outside the local community, offering a more neutral forum for dispute settlement than local elders, who are more prone to belittle or prejudge women's complaints (Hirsh 2009).

The differences in women's perceptions in Tanzania and Kenya highlight how the application of religious laws varies. It also illustrates the importance of accountability mechanisms. For some women, religious courts may be the sole venue with any legitimacy; any biases in these tribunals may thus completely exclude them from the justice system.

Conclusion

In both formal and customary systems, women face challenges in asserting their claims to household assets and land. In formal systems, statutory codes may be discriminatory; they need to be reformed. In addition, problems of legitimacy persist, because of corruption and the weakness of enforcement mechanisms.

Women often perceive customary systems as having greater legitimacy, but they have traditionally been excluded from exerting influence in these systems, resulting in discriminatory outcomes. These outcomes often come to the fore in inheritance disputes, particularly where land is involved. Customary rules of inheritance that favor male heirs and the husband's family over the wife's often reinforce the dependency of women on the goodwill of male family members.

One way of establishing a framework of accountability is to empower women to assert their claims in both legal frameworks. Building awareness of their rights is essential, as is promoting informal and formal networks, such as women's cooperatives and professional associations. Improved access to justice is possible for women, but it rarely happens without networks, resources, and coordinated advocacy.

Cases Cited

Attorney General of the Republic of Botswana v. Unity Dow (1994), Case Report Court of Appeal (6) BCLR 1, pp. 326–27

Shilubana and Others v. Nwamitwa (2008), (CCT 03/07) (2008) ZACC 9; 2008 (9) BCLR 914 (CC); 2009 (2) SA 66 (CC), June 4

Notes

1. The lower monetary value of claims by women may be explained by women's lack of confidence in pursuing claims other than family law actions such as child support (Rodríguez 2000).
2. Tanzania's 1999 Village Land Act established village land councils, in which three of the seven council members had to be women.
3. Studies that substantiate these points include Ayuko and Chopra 2008; Cotula 2007; Das and Maru 2009, who analyze the *shalish* (informal community justice) system in Bangladesh; and Kane, Oloka-Onyango, and Tejan-Cole 2005.
4. Malaysia's appointment of its first women Sharia court judges in 2010 could pave the way for more women.
5. BAWAKTA was a national Muslim organization that originated in a broad ethnic base in Tanzania.

References

Ayuko, Bonita, and Tanja Chopra. 2008. "The Illusion of Inclusion: Women's Access to Right in Northern Kenya." Legal Resources Foundation Trust, Nairobi.

Cotula, Lorenzo. 2007. *Gender and Law: Women's Rights in Agriculture* (rev. 1). FAO Legislative Study 76, Food and Agriculture Organization of the United Nations, Rome.

Das, Maitreya, and Vivek Maru. 2009. *Framing Local Conflict and Justice in Bangladesh.* Policy Research Working Paper 5781, Sustainable Development Department, World Bank, Washington, DC.

Dow, Justice Unity. 2001. "How the Global Informs the Local: The Botswana Citizenship Case." *Health Care for Women International* 22 (4): 319–31.

Ellis, Amanda, Claire Manuel, and Mark Blackden. 2006. *Gender and Economic Growth in Uganda: Unleashing the Power of Women.* p. 68. Washington, DC: World Bank.

Fenrich, Jeanmarie, and Tracy E. Higgins. 2002. "Promise Unfulfilled: Law, Culture, and Women's Inheritance Rights in Ghana." *Fordham International Law Journal* 25: 259–341.

Gauri, Varun. 2009. "How Do Local-Level Legal Institutions Promote Development?" Justice and Development Working Paper Series 6, World Bank, Washington, DC.

Griffiths, Anne. 2002. "Women's Worlds, Siblings in Dispute over Inheritance: A View from Botswana." *Africa Today* 49 (1): 61–82.

Hammergren, Linn, and Sintayehu Mitiku. 2010. "Uses and Users of Justice in Africa: The Case of Ethiopia's Federal Courts." Report 57988, World Bank, Washington, DC.

Harrington, Andrew, and Tanja Chopra. 2010. "Arguing Traditions: Denying Kenya's Women Access to Land Rights." Justice for the Poor Research Report 2/2010, World Bank, Washington, DC.

Hirsh, Susan. 2009. "State Intervention in Muslim Family Law in Kenya and Tanzania: Applications in the Gender Context." In *Muslim Family Law in Sub-Saharan Africa*, ed. Shamil Jeppie, Ebrahim Moosa, and Richard Roberts, part II, chapter 10, 315–17. Chicago: University of Chicago Press.

Isser, Deborah H., Stephen C. Lubkemann, and Saah N'Tow. 2009. *Looking for Justice: Liberian Experiences with and Perceptions of Local Justice Options*. Washington, DC: United States Institute of Peace.

Kalabamu, Faustin T. 2009. "Towards Egalitarian Inheritance Rights in Botswana: The Case of Tlokweng." *Development Southern Africa* 26 (2): 209–23.

Kamangu, Jane. 2010. "Note on Women's Participation in the Judiciary in Kenya," Background paper prepared for this study.

Kane, Minneh, J. Oloka-Onyango, and Abdul Tejan-Cole. 2005. "Reassessing Customary Law Systems as a Vehicle for Providing Equitable Access to Justice for the Poor." Paper presented at the conference "New Frontiers of Social Policy," Arusha, Tanzania, December 12–15.

Koroma, Braima. 2007. "Local Courts Record Analysis Survey in Sierra Leone." Justice Sector Development Program and Justice for the Poor Program, World Bank, Washington, DC.

Lobti, Emilia. 2010. "Note on Women's Participation in the Judiciary in Cameroon," Background paper prepared for this study.

Machuhi, Eunice. 2007. "Kenya: One Million Cases Pending in Courts—CJ." *All Africa*, August 8. http://allafrica.com/stories/200708071187.html.

Maru, Vivek. 2006. "Between Law and Society: Paralegals and the Provision of Justice Services in Sierra Leone and Worldwide." *Yale Journal of International Law* 31 (2): 426–76.

Matemba, Yonah H. 2005. "A Chief Called 'Woman': Historical Perspectives on the Changing Face of Bogosi (Chieftainship) in Botswana, 1834–2004." *JENdA: A Journal of Culture and African Women Studies* 7: 18–29.

Molokomme, Athaliah. 1991. "Disseminating Family Law Reforms: Some Lessons from Botswana." *Journal of Legal Pluralism and Unofficial Law* 30: 303–29.

Muriuki, Albert. 2007. "Kenya: Slow Judicial System a Major Obstacle to Growth." *All Africa*, October 2. http://allafrica.com/stories/200710021003.html.

NIZA (Netherlands Institute for Southern Africa) and ActionAid International. 2009. *Women's Land Rights in Southern Africa: Consolidated Baseline Findings from Malawi, Mozambique, South Africa, Zambia, and Zimbabwe*. Amsterdam: NIZA and ActionAid.

Penal Reform International. 2000. *Access to Justice in Sub-Saharan Africa: The Role of Traditional and Informal Justice Systems*, 66–67. London: Astron Printers.

Rodríguez, Marcela V. 2000. *Empowering Women: An Assessment of Legal Aid under Ecuador's Judicial Reform Project*. Washington, DC: World Bank.

SADC (Southern African Development Community). 2009. "Towards Gender Parity in 2015 in SADC: Did You Know That...." *Gender News* 1 (9)3.

Schärf, Wilfried, Chikosa Banda, Ricky Röntsch, Desmond Kaunda, and Rosemary Shapiro. 2002. "Access to Justice for the Poor of Malawi? Appraisal of Access to Justice Provided to the Poor of Malawi by the Lower Subordinate Courts and the Customary Justice Forums." Department for International Development, Governance and Social Development Resource Centre, London.

Twinomugisha and Kibuka. 1997. *Good Governance and Easing Social Tensions in Uganda: Studies of Operations and Justice of Local Councils*. New York: United Nations Development Programme.

USAID (U.S. Agency for International Development). 2009. *Africa Regional Rule of Law Status Review*. Washington, DC: USAID.

Women–LEED–Africa (Women's Legal and Economic Empowerment Database), http://documents.worldbank.org/query?title=Women+LEED+Africa+Database developed by Mary Hallward-Driemeier, Tazeen Hasan, Jane Kamangu, Emila Lobti, and Mark Blackden. Development Economics, World Bank.

Wood, Georgina. 2008. "The Role of the Judiciary in Promoting Gender Justice in Africa." Report on the Partners for Gender Justice Conference, Accra, Ghana, November 19–21.

Chapter 5

The Way Forward

The preceding chapters have shown the complexity of the legal framework in Sub-Saharan African countries and how multiple legal systems, combined with de facto practice, can enhance or undermine women's access to and control over property. Ultimately, a woman's potential ability to engage in any form of economic activity derives from a baseline of assets for investments and the capacity to independently determine how to use them. Discriminatory inheritance practices and formal legal restrictions applying only to women's legal capacity, employment outside the home, and administration of personal assets are barriers that the state too often condones. The customary and social norms from which these laws derive represent a still deeper challenge to reform.

This chapter discusses ways to address the many sources of gender gaps in formal legal and economic rights that affect women's ability to access assets. It provides general guidelines and illustrates how particular countries are implementing them. The discussion examines four areas: strengthening the substance of the law, ensuring that existing benefits are accessible and secured, and educating women about their rights and empowering them to exercise them. The set of recommendations focuses on the process and not only the content, as how a reform is handled can be as important as the substantive changes sought in determining the success of the larger process.

Strengthening Legal Substance

Steps to strengthen the substance of the law can be taken at the level of the constitution. Discrimination can also be addressed in formal statutes and customary law.

Changing the Constitution

As constitutions provide the guiding principles for a country and are used to measure the validity of statutes, ensuring the primacy of nondiscrimination based on gender is perhaps the most important single element of reform.

Several constitutions in the region exempt customary and religious laws from the principle of nondiscrimination in family and inheritance law, undermining women's property rights. Women in customary marriages cannot contest discriminatory customary laws on the grounds of unconstitutionality, and even the protection of a repugnancy test is uncertain.

Subjecting all sources of law to the principle of nondiscrimination strengthens women's rights. If protections are important enough to be included as a guiding constitutional principle, they should protect the entire population and cover the important family and financial decisions that affect everyone's lives.

Even with the constitutional provision of nondiscrimination in place, many statutes remain on the books—or are even added—that accord women and men different property rights (box 5.1). Ensuring the primacy of this constitutional provision is thus an important start but not the final step.

Reforming Formal Law

A basic step for improving women's economic rights and access to property is to bring consistency to legal provisions, including by removing contradictory provisions in existing areas of the law. Discriminatory legislation,

---

BOX 5.1

Removing Exemptions to Nondiscrimination Provisions in Kenya

Kenya's new constitution, agreed to by referendum in 2010, removes the exemptions to discrimination granted to customary laws in family and inheritance matters since independence. Although religious laws remain exempt, this move represents a major breakthrough in how women's property rights may be enforced in the future. How constitutional litigation will be used to challenge discriminatory customary practices, and whether it will alter judicial decision making, has yet to be seen.

Cases such as *Otieno v. Ougo* (1987)—in which the claim of the widow and children to determine the burial arrangements for the deceased (with resulting implications for the division of the estate) were set aside in favor of the customary laws of the husband's clan—could be decided differently in the future. But progress will also depend on judicial independence from ethnopolitical pressures.

The new constitution also allows for the direct application of international law in courts without the need for domestic enacting legislation, making Kenya a monist state. This, too, could affect how the courts deal with discriminatory legal provisions from all sources.

Source: Women–LEED–Africa database; Stamp 1991.

including restrictions on women's ability to own, administer, transfer, and bequeath property, should be repealed.

Removing restrictions on married women's legal capacity.   All statutory constraints on women's legal capacity should be removed. These constraints include head-of-household laws and restrictions on women's capacity to work outside the home, file a legal claim, testify in court, and open a bank account. The successful reform of these laws in Ethiopia and Namibia has shown that change is possible without incurring a backlash from society.

Recognizing nonmonetary contributions in separate property regimes.   Where separate property regimes prevail, and no alternatives are available, the passage of legislation specifically recognizing the nonmonetary contribution by a spouse should be a priority. Ultimately, a 50–50 division of marital property on divorce should be the yardstick.

Mandating joint titling of land.   Joint titling of land and the marital home is essential in protecting women's interest in what are usually the most valuable marital assets. One of the main criticisms of formal land-titling reforms is that they have marginalized the poor, particularly women. Joint titling of land is allowed in Kenya, for example, but it is rarely carried out, leaving the vast majority of land owned solely by men.

Mandatory joint titling can ensure that women are included on the title; a legal provision, such as that used in Tanzania, that a spouse is included in the title reduces ambiguity. For joint titling to work, identification or registration processes may have to be reformed (to ensure that women can obtain birth and marriage certificates easily) or alternative methods for proof of identification considered.

In some regions of Ethiopia, photos as well as names are required in the certificate. Photos are a useful form of identification where literacy rates are low. They also make it difficult for the husband to sell or rent the land without the wife's consent. Comparisons across regions in Ethiopia demonstrate that small differences in the titling program can have a strong impact on whether the title includes women's names (box 5.2).

Land administration personnel would benefit from gender sensitization training to ensure that they are aware of women's claims over land. Fees for titling should be kept low to enable the majority of the population to benefit. In more developed economies, incentives such as tax breaks for joint titling should be considered. At a minimum, legal restrictions on women's ability to title land in their own name should be removed (see the discussion of *Aphane* in Swaziland in chapter 3), including the requirement that a male assistant be present at the time of registration.

BOX 5.2

Subtle Differences in Titling Requirements, Important Differences in Outcomes: Lessons from Ethiopia

In 2003, the main regions of Ethiopia began a process of land certification aimed at reducing tenure insecurity and encouraging investment. The process was modeled on the land certification process undertaken several years earlier in the Tigray region.

In Tigray, the land certificate was issued in the name of the household head; the other regions required that the certificate be in joint names (box figure 5.2.1). In Amhara and in the south, space was provided to include the photos of both spouses on the certificate; in Oromia, only the head of household's photo was included.

After several years, land titling by women had risen. But the impact of mandatory joint titling was weaker where only the photo of the household head was required. A simple procedural step such as including space for both names and photos on the land certificate can thus enhance the impact of land reform.

Figure B5.2.1 Different Policies Have a Strong Impact on Whose Name Land Is Titled

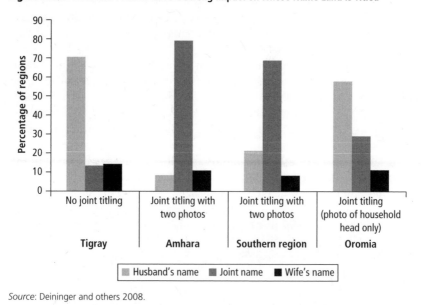

Source: Deininger and others 2008.

Enacting labor laws to promote equality. Many countries have enacted equal right to work and equal pay labor laws, based on International Labour Organization Conventions 100 and 111. Countries that have not need to address the gap. Governments should also consider labor legislation guaranteeing maternity leave and other labor rights relating to pregnant and breastfeeding women, balancing the protection of women against restrictions that may deny them the chance to earn a living.

Governments should also review restrictions on labor such as night work and the type of work women can perform. Laws that may have been passed with the intention of protecting women can restrict their mobility and employment opportunities. In Sudan, an Act applying to the State of Khartoum preventing women from working after 5 p.m. and in certain sectors was met with protest by women's groups and ultimately repealed (Badri 2005).

Reforming Customary Law

Customary law can be strengthened by drawing on the strengths of traditional systems and extending statutory recognition and nondiscrimination to customary rights.

Drawing on the strengths of traditional systems.   Given the centrality of customary law in the lives of many people in Sub-Saharan Africa, policy makers must fully understand customary norms and the incentives to reform discriminatory practices. They must appreciate differences in what constitutes justice—punitive and focused on the individual or restorative and focused on the community—in designing policies to expand the outreach of the legal system.

The formal justice sector can learn from traditional methods of dispute resolution. Toward that end, links between the formal and informal sector should be encouraged. In Ghana, the formal judicial sector is working with the Traditional House of Chiefs to assess traditional dispute mechanisms and develop learning modules on modern dispute resolution practices for both traditional chiefs and staff working in the formal sector (Bhansali 2010).

Engagement with traditional leaders and de facto decision makers is crucial to enhance women's access to traditional forums. Appealing to benign concepts in customary law, such as the protection of women and social justice, can help women reaffirm their access to land and their claims in marital and inheritance disputes (Ayuko and Chopra 2008). Research on the drivers behind changes in customary law should be undertaken.

Extending statutory recognition and nondiscrimination to customary rights. The formal land titling system ignored traditional land tenure systems. Women's access to land under customary tenure systems are often secondary user rights—that is, user access depends on male relatives. But where customary rights are not recognized, women can be left in an even more vulnerable situation, with no rights to land at all.

Some countries have passed laws recognizing communal land rights, and some have attempted to improve the status of women's rights in traditional tenure systems. Because few local communities can afford to register customary land rights, one approach is for the government to recognize customary landholding that has not been formally registered but that has used inexpensive local methods of documentation, with the option to upgrade the documentation. This approach creates enforceable rights for communities without the complexity and expense of a formal titling process (see Deininger and others 2008).[1] For example, Mozambique's land legislation, passed in 1997, allows people to apply for title to land if they have used it for 10 years. Women should be made aware of these rights under the law.

In much of Sub-Saharan Africa, customary marriages and consensual unions, neither of which is protected by formal statutes, are the main form of unions. The formal system can benefit women by legally recognizing these relationships, thereby granting women access to marital property and inheritance rights they may not otherwise have.

Most courts have tried to find creative solutions to providing property rights to women when they do not fall under the statutory umbrella, but they do so in an inconsistent manner. A better solution would be for countries to legislate such rights across all areas that affect access to property for women in customary marriages.

Some countries have enacted laws to safeguard women in customary marriages and consensual unions. Ghana provides for inheritance rights to women in customary marriages but not rights to property in divorce. Mozambique has legislated rights to marital property for women in de facto unions and customary marriages but not on the death of the husband or partner. In its Recognition of Customary Marriages Act of 1998, South Africa extends the community of property regime to all customary marriages.

A range of laws that limit the property a widow can inherit need reform. For example, Zambia's Intestate Succession Act of 1989, which allows the surviving spouse to inherit 20 percent of the deceased's property, does not apply to customary land, which accounts for 81 percent of land in Zambia (Machina 2002; see also Ministry of Lands of the Republic of Zambia 2006).

Securing Existing Benefits

Beyond enhancing the substance of laws, it is important to improve the functioning of the legal system to ensure that existing rights are realized. Countries can do so by strengthening enforcement, expanding access to laws and legal decisions, improving the transparency and accountability of the system, making the system more hospitable to women, and tackling practical constraints to accessing justice.

Strengthening Enforcement
Strengthening the enforcement of existing laws requires both political and financial resources. Political will is required to strengthen the independence of the judiciary and extend the reach of the legal system. Allocating adequate

budgetary resources is also important to strengthen the enforcement capacity of justice sector institutions.

State enforcement capacity varies greatly in the region. Capacity-building efforts are needed in fragile postconflict states, where little enforcement infrastructure exists. In more stable countries, state capacity often fails to extend to rural communities. The budgeting decisions a government makes reflect the priority given to the legal sector and the enforcement of law as a whole.

Strengthening enforcement likely benefits the population as a whole. But to the extent that it improves the enforcement of women's rights, women would benefit disproportionately. For example, countries such as Ghana, Malawi, Zambia, and Zimbabwe impose criminal penalties and fines for grabbing property and evicting widows from the marital home. But the efficacy of these measures depends on how strictly these laws are enforced.

Expanding Access to Laws and Legal Decisions

Judicial decision makers, lawyers, and ordinary citizens cannot refer to laws they are unaware of. In the 1980s and 1990s, law reporting lapsed in many parts of Africa. Many governments gave up publishing statutes; in some instances, magistrates and judges were forced to rely on their old notes from law school. Lack of access to laws and legal decisions has greatly diminished the development of national and regional jurisprudence (Widner 2001; International Crisis Group 2006).

It is essential to make laws available, through paper publication and online posting, where feasible. A copy of the constitution and relevant statutes and treaties should be available in every tribunal, including magistrates' courts and local and village courts. Laws should be translated into local languages and dialects and explained in simplified terms. Case law that promotes women's property rights should be identified and widely circulated.

Recent initiatives to improve court reporting and to publish more cases are gathering support. Between 2001 and 2009, Kenya's National Council of Law Reporting (NCLR) substantially reduced a backlog of 20 years of unreported cases (Walsh 2010). Hard copies of court decisions had been kept in a central office, but they were not easily accessible to legal professionals. NCLR catalogued the cases and organized the files, published bound volumes of cases, and made all records available electronically. The online availability of precedents has dramatically reduced the time judges take to file their opinions. Knowing that others are now far more likely to read their opinions also improved incentives to strengthen the quality of opinion writing. The NCLR substantially increased access to the law in Kenya, establishing a model that could be replicated elsewhere in the region.

The Southern African Legal Information Institute also publishes online court judgments. Its database covers 16 countries in southern and eastern Africa.

Improving Transparency and Accountability

The local community and civil society can boost the transparency and accountability of the justice system through monitoring exercises. Citizens' reporting initiatives, such as judiciary dialogue cards used by magistrates' court users in Kenya, can cheaply provide feedback on how the justice system operates (Walsh 2010). Civil society should be encouraged to monitor public appointments and the implementation of laws and to vocalize concerns though human rights reporting and investigative journalism. Civil society groups should be included in policy initiatives aimed at establishing and monitoring access to justice indicators (UNDP 2004). These steps would improve the operation of the judicial system as a whole, with the more vulnerable likely benefitting disproportionately.

Improving the management of court records and making records available to the public is another tool for improving transparency. The Court Administration Reform Project in Ethiopia improved the management of paper records, recorded court proceedings, and created a case tracking system, improving the capacity to track and analyze gender-sensitive cases (Walsh 2010).

Accountability of local justice mechanisms can be increased by ensuring some measure of external oversight. In addition to establishing ombudsmen, review officers, and oversight mechanisms by judges, policy makers could integrate civil society into the monitoring of traditional justice mechanisms. The resources and capacity to adopt these measures will obviously vary. Local appeals systems should not necessarily be created, as appeals can be blocked. Instead, an aggrieved party who is not satisfied with an outcome should be able to bring the claim into the formal system (Bhansali 2010). Guidelines for formalized or quasi-formal local customary courts could be drawn with clear definitions regarding jurisdiction (box 5.3).

Making the System More Hospitable to Women

Several sets of actions could make the legal system more hospitable to women. One would be to increase women's participation in judicial decision-making bodies. Rwanda, Tanzania, and Uganda use statutory quotas to boost women's participation in land tribunals and other judicial or quasi-judicial bodies, though concerns remain that their voices are not heard (see box 4.4 in chapter 4). Still, meaningful participation can start only once the presence of women is seen as the norm. It is this initial bar to entry that quota systems overturns. Enforcing the rules requires oversight.

A second way to improve women's experience with the legal system would be to expand sensitivity training in statutory and traditional sectors (box 5.4). Legal rights can be undermined by unsupportive implementers of the law, including judges, traditional leaders, land registry officers, land board tribunal members, and schools, which prepare the next generation of practitioners.

BOX 5.3

Guidelines for Strengthening Local Customary Courts

Various guidelines could help strengthen village courts:

- Require that the village court be held in public.
- Establish rules for recusal when a chief has family or business relations with a party in a dispute.
- Allow parties a "preemptory strike"—a chance to reject the chief or tribunal member without showing cause—as is often done in formal arbitration.
- Rotate the chairmanship among the members of the tribunal.
- Maintain records (supported by training and resources).
- Adopt strategies, including quotas, for increasing female membership of village courts.

Source: Das and Maru 2009.

BOX 5.4

Sensitizing Legal Professionals to Gender Issues

The International Association of Women Judges Jurisprudence of Equality Program (JEP) trains judges and legal practitioners in applying international and regional human rights conventions to cases in domestic courts that involve discrimination or gender violence. Its workshops and seminars for judges focus on the concrete meanings of theoretical concepts of equal protection and nondiscrimination. Many JEP-trained judges credit the program with alerting them to their own and other's hidden biases (and to stereotypes that sustain those biases) and to helping them find more effective and sensitive ways to question witnesses.

JEP-trained judges have launched initiatives to improve access to the legal system. The Kenya Women Judges Association, for example, has developed checklists of documents that widows should bring to court when their husband dies. JEP has become an official part of the Judicial Training Institute in Tanzania and has been incorporated into other training courses in Kenya and Uganda.

Source: Wood 2008.

Tackling Practical Constraints to Accessing Justice

The obstacles facing women and their needs should be addressed on their own, rather than as part of measures to increase access by the poor. To encourage compliance and increase access to the formal system, all procedural steps should be simple, inexpensive, and easy to carry out.

Increasing accessibility.   Several measures can help make the legal system more accessible. One measure is reducing court costs, such as fees. Exempting the very poor from paying fees would remove a significant constraint they face in accessing justice. Extrajudicial costs, including bribes, should be addressed through anticorruption strategies, such as monitoring. Delays in the justice system should also be addressed. Delays and adjournments should be tracked and strategies developed to reduce blockages in the system.

Another measure is printing all court forms and laws in local languages, using simplified language. Help desks and information kiosks in courts can help users understand proceedings and their claim's progress.

Facilitating marriage registration and the recognition of customary marriages.   Registry offices are often far from where the parties live, and the decision to register may well rest with the husband. Verifying that a customary marriage took place if it was not registered is often difficult, and husbands or family members often deny that a customary marriage took place when property disputes arise. In Ghana, registration was initially compulsory, but low rates of registration because of lack of awareness of where and how to register, as well as the costs and logistical challenges of traveling to a register's office, resulted in the law being changed to make registration discretionary for a transition period (Fenrich and Higgins 2002).

Registration should not be a barrier for women in customary marriages. The law should be reformed to allow all surrounding circumstances to be considered in establishing the existence of a relationship. One way of facilitating this process is by appointing local registration officers who have a degree of flexibility on standards of proof.

Broadening the scope of legal services.   Restrictions on the provision of legal services can be a barrier to access. If the market for legal services is limited to accredited lawyers, costs can be prohibitive, and the scarcity of lawyers can impede wider community access. In these cases, liberalizing entry barriers— such as restrictions on unauthorized practice—will open provision of legal services to less expensive legal professionals, such as paralegals (box 5.5).

Other methods to broaden the scope of legal services include legal aid clinics and mobile courts, which provide valuable assistance to women (box 5.6) (Manning 1999). About 39,000 women in Kenya received free legal assistance

BOX 5.5

Using Paralegals to Provide Low-Cost Legal Assistance to the Poor

Many of the region's countries have paralegal services. Paralegals are long-established legal service providers in South Africa, where community organizations such as Black Sash set up "advice centers" in the 1960s to help the black community navigate apartheid regulations. Since the end of apartheid, these services have focused on violence against women, employment, and land restitution.

Sierra Leone uses paralegals to bridge the gap between poor communities and the formal legal sector. Paralegals can also straddle overlapping legal systems, because they are often closer to communities. And the training of female paralegals empowers women directly in their communities.

The Timap paralegal program in Sierra Leone employs 67 paralegals in 29 locations. They handle a broad range of cases, including child support, family disputes, inheritance, land disputes, and employment.

Paralegals often use mediation and alternative dispute resolution to resolve disputes. When these mechanisms fail, they can refer clients to two Timap–employed lawyers. In many cases, the mere threat of formal litigation can resolve a dispute. Timap has provided assistance in more than 1,000 cases that would otherwise have fallen outside the scope of the legal system.

Source: www.timapforjustice.org.

BOX 5.6

Equipping Women in Uganda with Knowledge of the Law

In Uganda, women never leave the offices of the Federation of Women Lawyers (FIDA) empty-handed. They leave with either a letter inviting the other party to the dispute to come to mediation or a piece of paper stating the (formal) law. Knowledge of the law may be sufficient to redress the inequality in negotiating strength and allow the parties to settle the dispute without third-party mediation.

Over the long term, organizations like FIDA may help transform social attitudes that adversely affect decisions made by traditional legal systems. Knowledge of equal rights by both men and women will give women greater negotiating power before traditional justice forums.

Source: Penal Reform International 2000.

from Federation of Women Lawyers legal aid clinics between 2004 and 2006 (Chesoni, Muigai, and Kanyinga 2006).

Considering alternative dispute resolution mechanisms.   Mechanisms such as mediation can be an alternative to the formal adversarial system in such areas as family law and property disputes. They may also be more familiar to communities already accustomed to traditional justice forums, such as village courts or councils of chiefs. Mechanisms can be backed by the formal system and employ statutory, customary, or religious law. When following this approach, both formal courts and traditional justice forums should adhere to the principles of human rights for all ethnic groups and nondiscrimination against women.

Small claims courts are a useful fast-track mechanism. They do not require lawyers, and the process is generally less structured than a regular court hearing. More of such courts would help women assert claims to marital assets and help small business owners settle commercial disputes.

Increasing Women's Awareness

Improving substantive protections and access to the legal system will have little impact if women are unaware of the laws protecting them. Disseminating information on existing protections and provisions, particularly in rural areas and among those who are less educated, is thus crucial.

The greatest impact is likely to be on key life decisions: marriage, acquisition of property, and inheritance. Registering a marriage can extend statutory protections to women. Titling marital property jointly ensures greater control over key assets. Writing a will—and having one's husband and parents write wills— to specify that the wife (or daughter) inherits a share of the estate can ensure against other family members, particularly in-laws, disinheriting the woman.

Nongovernmental organizations are developing outreach programs to promote such steps (examples can be found in NIZA 2009). Social media, such as public radio and street theater, are good delivery mechanisms. Existing social networks—such as women's cooperatives or collectives, which are natural venues for disseminating information—should also be used. Men also need to be included, in order to gain wider acceptance of these values.

Choosing a Beneficial Marital Property Regime

Women should be encouraged to choose beneficial marital property regimes. The best regime will often be community of property, particularly if not all assets are jointly titled or the woman's contribution to the family business is unpaid. Where women have their own assets or a separate business in their own name, a separate property regime may better serve their interests.

Titling Marital Property Jointly

To prevent ambiguity regarding the equitable division of marital property, women should take steps to ensure that the marital home is titled jointly. Doing so can protect their share of the marital home even in separate property regimes that do not recognize nonmonetary contributions.

As women are rarely in a position to demand joint titling, statutory provisions requiring it would help them retain a share of the marital home following the end of a marriage, because of divorce or death. Where community of property regimes are available and not subject to the husband's administrative control, women should be made aware of the benefits of selecting this regime.

This approach may not apply to poorer communities, where the value of the traditional dwellings may not make it worthwhile legally delineating ownership. In these cases, rights of occupation or use of land may better serve women's interests.

Using Prenuptial Agreements

Awareness of prenuptial agreements should be increased. For example, in Kenya, which has a separate property regime, the law recognizes prenuptial agreements, although they are rarely used. Beyond building awareness of their existence, a focus should be on the issues prenuptial agreements should cover. Clauses in Muslim marriage contracts should spell out property as being jointly owned and address issues other than property rights, such as polygamy, the right to work outside the home, the right to divorce, and custody of children on divorce. Many women lack the negotiating power to ask for a prenuptial agreement. Templates produced by nongovernmental organizations could increase access to such agreements.[2]

Writing Wills That Ensure Women's Access to a Share of the Estate

Lack of awareness and prevailing social norms in many countries in Sub-Saharan Africa ensure that even in literate, urban communities, few people draw up wills. In some communities in Nigeria, for example, drafting a will implies that a wife is anxious to hasten her husband's death, and a widow can face accusations of murder if her husband does die (Ewelukwa 2002).

Some countries lack legislation that allows for drafting wills. This gap should be closed.

Enforcing wills is also a challenge. In Zambia, written wills that bequeath property to a wife may simply be ignored by the husband's family, and the widow can do little to enforce them (Mwenda, Mumba, and Mvula-Mwenda 2005).

Building awareness, advocating through social media, and strengthening enforcement capacity must be integral to any legislative drive to encourage the writing of wills. In Namibia, where human immunodeficiency virus (HIV) rates are among the highest in the world, local legal clinics, in collaboration with the United Nations Children's Fund, are providing training on will writing. This training provides an opportunity not only to make final arrangements but also to educate people about the importance of explicitly providing for all members of their families (Aids Law Unit Legal Assistance Centers 2001).

Proceeding with Conviction—and Respect

How a reform is handled can be as important as the substantive changes themselves in determining the success of the larger process. Awareness building, learning activities, grassroots advocacy, and lobbying of decision makers are all integral parts of the process, particularly in the overlaps among customary, religious, and statutory laws.

Understanding the Context

Successful reformers need to understand the context and underlying rationale for existing provisions if they are to engage constructively with the people whose support is needed to enact change (box 5.7). Understanding the context increases the likelihood that the strengths of existing systems can be harnessed as changes are made.

Reformers have to consider the types of law to be reformed and the drafting of new laws. Legislation can rarely be imported wholesale from another country, largely because every country is different. Even within countries, the social context and economic conditions can vary greatly. Policy makers can nevertheless look at legislation in other countries to see if it can be adapted domestically, particularly where countries share cultural traits (Bhansali 2010).

In many countries, customary and religious laws applied in tribunals provide the most accessible justice system for most of the population. Learning from what works well in these systems while avoiding their shortcomings can help reformers in their efforts to improve the lives of the most vulnerable and marginalized women of society. Models of mediation used in these systems are increasingly viewed as a low-cost, less adversarial method of resolving disputes, particularly in family law. The focus should be on drawing on the strengths of these models, encouraging their evolution in a less discriminatory and more inclusive direction, and increasing accountability.

Reforming Statutes

Successful legal reform involves multiple stakeholders: government, judiciary, legal personnel and professional associations, religious and traditional authorities, civil society, law enforcement agencies, land boards, social media, and many others. Enacting a law is just the start: acceptance of the law in a community, women's effective access to the law, and enforcement are also needed. Sometimes large shifts in legal frameworks are possible—after historic shifts

BOX 5.7

Conducting a Gender-Disaggregated Assessment of the Legal Landscape before Embarking upon Reform

One of the first steps policy makers and their advisers need to take before attempting to implement reform is to conduct a gender-disaggregated assessment of the legal landscape of the country. This assessment should include focus group discussions that solicit the views of women from different social, economic, and ethnic backgrounds.

The following steps can enhance the understanding of how the law affects women, in theory and in practice:

- Review laws that single out women (or married women) or laws that likely have a differential impact on women, in order to identify discriminatory and beneficial laws.

- Identify contradictory provisions that could undermine women's rights.

- Use country surveys to document de facto practices, including where disputes are handled. Determine why disputes are not taken to dispute-resolution forums.

- Understand the different types of courts, including customary and religious courts, by studying their location relative to the populations they are supposed to serve, their procedures, and their jurisdiction. Identify how the judicial, customary, and religious courts interact with one another.

- Identify barriers to access to different sources of law, in general and for women in particular.

- Conduct court-user studies, tracking case outcomes on a gender-disaggregated basis.

- Research customary and religious laws to identify nondiscriminatory norms or laws that help women access property, discriminatory laws, and channels that can be more favorable to women.

Source: Adapted from Bhansali 2010; Kane, Oloka-Onyango, and Tejan-Cole 2005.

---

in political regimes, for example, or during postconflict reconstruction. More often, changes are incremental.

Progress can take time. But tools are available for effecting change. Reformers can support "impact" litigation, launch domestic and international campaigns, lobby parliament, submit shadow reports to international treaty committees, and use the media to advocate for reform.

Reform agendas are often spearheaded by social movements, including women's groups, civil society organizations, labor unions, legal and judicial associations, and parliamentary support groups, sometimes with the support of international donor agencies or nongovernmental organizations.

One approach to reform is to build capacity and strengthen networks of women's groups, including associations of lawyers and judges, business organizations, and parliamentary groups. Such networks coalesced to mount successful legal challenges such as the *Unity Dow* (2004) citizenship case in Botswana (see box 3.2 in chapter 3) and the *Mary-Joyce Doo Aphane* (2010) property rights case in Swaziland.

A second approach involves lobbying the executive through round-table conferences and discussions with parliamentarians. Where civil society is inexperienced in lobbying, it should seek training, perhaps from donors. Experience with public-private dialogue has been encouraging, but it is important that this process consciously include women and ensure that issues of importance to women are on the table.[4]

Learning from Reforms

Attempts in 2002 and 2009 to reform Mali's Family Code met resistance from religious groups (including some women), who protested the reforms on the grounds that they outlawed polygamy, did not recognize religious or customary marriages, and undermined traditional gender roles. Underlying this opposition was the religious authorities' fear that they would lose their power over legitimizing marriages and adjudicating inheritances (Wing 2009). The new family code was adopted in August 2009, but it had to be approved by the president to become law. The president refused to support the new code, which has therefore not been enacted.

Other Muslim-majority countries have recently reformed family codes, placing limits on polygamy and giving women increased rights to divorce. Their experience—and the unsuccessful experience of Mali—could provide lessons for reformers (box 5.8).

Endorsement from religious and community leaders can smooth the path to reform, underscoring the crucial role of consultations with civil society organizations, women's groups, and religious authorities. The support of strong political leaders can also be important.

Where endorsement by religious groups is not forthcoming domestically, support from other Muslim-majority countries can confer legitimacy on domestic reform efforts. For example, the first female Sharia judges were appointed in Malaysia in 2010, after a *fatwa* (religious edict) declared their appointment permissible. The move could pave the way for greater participation by women in Sharia courts in other countries.

Alliances with government leaders and international pressure can also help support reform, depending on the local political context, as illustrated in the case of Benin described in box 5.8. "Impact litigation" can also have far-reaching effects on reform.

BOX 5.8

Reforming Family Codes: Lessons from Benin, Botswana, and Morocco

Benin

Benin's new family code, adopted in 2004, raised the minimum age of marriage, made monogamy the sole form of civil marriage, and outlawed forced marriages and the practice of *levirate* (wife inheritance). The strong commitment to and leadership of the reform process at the highest political levels illustrate how crucial they can be in spearheading change.

The reform movement was supported by influential political leaders, such as Rosine Vieyra, a former first lady and sitting member of the National Assembly; the president of the National Assembly; and the president of the High Court. The fact that the president of the National Assembly was a strong advocate for reform made it difficult for legislators to vote against the new code. Lobbying by women's organizations, including legal associations such as Women and Law and Development in Africa and the Association des Femmes Juristes du Benin, also played a fundamental role. International institutions—such as the U.S. Agency for International Development, through its Women's Legal Rights Initiatives, and the World Bank (2010), through capacity-building interventions—were an important source of international support and funding.

Botswana

In Botswana, the successful challenge by women's groups against discriminatory citizenship laws in the *Unity Dow* (2004) case, their subsequent lobbying, and international attention ultimately led to the ground-breaking Abolition of Marital Power Act (2004), which abolished head-of-household laws in statutory marriages (Mookodi 2005).

Morocco

In Morocco, women's groups initially pressed for reform in 1993. Eleven years later, in 2004, a new family code, largely meeting their expectations, came into force. The reforms include limits on polygamy, the lifting of divorce restrictions for women, an increase in the minimum age of marriage for both men and women, and enhanced rights of inheritance for women from male relatives.

Religious groups initially challenged the reforms, but they eventually endorsed them as consistent with Islamic values. The reform process was given legitimacy at the highest level by King Hasan II and his successor, King Mohammed. Committees were established comprising religious scholars and representatives from women's groups.

Exogenous factors also contributed to the acceptance of reform. The bombing in Casablanca in 2003 tipped the political balance, turning public opinion against the opposition of Islamic parties, who in turn wanted to distance themselves from extremist actions. Morocco was also bidding to become a member of the European Union. In addition, free trade agreements with the European Union and the United States stepped up the pressure for reform (Arshad 2006).

Conclusion

This chapter provides a menu of options and examples to guide reformers in the region. It argues for including the principle of nondiscrimination based on gender in every country's constitution and applying the principle to all women, regardless of marital, ethnic, or religious status. The principle should also apply to areas of the law that define property rights and legal capacity—rights that are both of intrinsic importance and instrumental in enabling women to pursue economic opportunities.

Short-term wins likely to improve the enforcement and accessibility of legal systems include registration of marriages, joint titling of property, exemption of court fees for poor women, and sensitivity training for legal professionals. Medium- to long-term institutional development and governance improvement measures are needed to strengthen the law and justice institutions in the formal, customary, and religious systems. Successful reforms indicate that reformers have to understand the constraints in society before embarking on reform initiatives, and they need to engage with the actors who can potentially ease or obstruct the reform process.

Reform should be seen as a long-term goal that provides staggered benefits. Changing laws is a necessary part of this process, but it alone cannot close gender gaps in economic rights; education and acceptance are also needed. The experience in Sub-Saharan countries and elsewhere reveals that changing social norms take time—but without targeted reform, it may take even longer.

Cases Cited

Attorney General of the Republic of Botswana v. Unity Dow (1994) Case Report Court of Appeal (6) BCLR 1

Mary Joyce Doo Aphane v. Registrar of Deeds, Minister of Justice and Constitutional Affairs and the Attorney General (2010) Civil case No: 383/2009

Otieno v. Ougo (1987), 1 KLR (G&F)

Notes

1. Examples of codes are the *plans fonciers ruraux* in West Africa.
2. The All India Muslim Personal Law Board, in conjunction with Muslim reform activists, drafted a model marital contract that provides enhanced rights to divorce, restricts polygamy, and increases access to marital property. The model contract was ultimately withdrawn because of resistance from conservative scholars (Subramanian 2008).
3. Chapter 10 in the companion volume (*Enterprising Women: Expanding Opportunities in Africa*) is devoted to strengthening women's voice in the policy process.

References

Aids Law Unit Legal Assistance Centers. 2001. *Training Manual for Trainers on Will Writing and Inheritance in Namibia.* Windhoek, Namibia.

Arshad, Amna. 2006. "Ijtihad as a Tool for Islamic Legal Reform: Advancing Women's Rights in Morocco." *Kansas Journal of Law & Public Policy* 16: 129.

Ayuko, Bonita, and Tanja Chopra. 2008. *The Illusion of Inclusion: Women's Access to Rights in Northern Kenya.* Legal Resources Foundation Trust, Nairobi.

Badri, Balghis. 2005. "Feminist Perspectives in the Sudan." Paper presented at the workshop "Feminist Perspectives," Free University of Berlin, May 26–27.

Bhansali, Lisa. 2010. "Africa Regional Justice Note: A Review and Lessons Learned." World Bank, Africa Public Sector Reform, Washington, DC.

Chesoni, Atsango, Salome Muigai, and Karuti Kanyinga. 2006. *Promoting Women's Human Rights and Enhancing Gender Equality in Kenya.* Stockholm: Swedish International Development Cooperation Agency.

Das, Maitreya, and Vivek Maru. 2009. "Framing Local Conflict and Justice in Bangladesh." Policy Research Working Paper 5781, Sustainable Development Department, World Bank, Washington, DC.

Deininger, Klaus, Daniel A. Ali, Stein Holden, and Jaap Zevenbergen. 2008. "Rural Land Certification in Ethiopia: Process, Initial Impact, and Implications for Other African Countries." *World Development* 36 (10): 1786–812.

Ewelukwa, Uche. 2002. "Post-Colonialism, Gender, Customary Injustice: Widows in African Societies." *Human Rights Quarterly* 24 (2): 424–86.

Fenrich, Jeanmarie, and Tracy E. Higgins. 2002. "Promise Unfulfilled: Law, Culture, and Women's Inheritance Rights in Ghana." *Fordham International Law Journal* 25: 259–341.

International Crisis Group. 2006. "Liberia: Resurrecting the Justice System." Africa Report 107, Washington, DC.

Kane, Minneh, J. Oloka-Onyango, and Abdul Tejan-Cole. 2005. "Reassessing Customary Law Systems as a Vehicle for Providing Equitable Access to Justice for the Poor." Paper presented at the conference "New Frontiers of Social Policy," Arusha, Tanzania, December 12–15.

Machina, Henry. 2002. "Women's Land Rights in Zambia: Policy Provisions, Legal Framework and Constraints." Paper presented at the Regional Conference on Women's Land Rights, Harare, Zimbabwe, May 26–30.

Manning, Daniel. 1999. "The Role of Legal Services Organizations in Attacking Poverty." Background paper for the *World Development Report 2000/01*, World Bank, Washington, DC.

Ministry of Lands of the Republic of Zambia. 2006. "Zambia Draft Land Policy." Republic of Zambia, Lusaka.

Mookodi, Godisang B. 2005. "Situating the Legal Status of Women in Development Processes: The Case of Botswana." Paper presented at the 11th Codesria General Assembly "Rethinking African Development: Beyond Impasse, Towards Alternatives," Maputo, December 6–10.

Mwenda, Kenneth, Florence Mumba, and Judith Mvula-Mwenda. 2005. "Property-Grabbing under African Customary Law: Repugnant to Natural Justice, Equity, and Good Conscience, Yet a Troubling Reality." *George Washington International Law Review* 37: 949.

NIZA (Netherlands Institute for Southern Africa) and ActionAid International 2009. *Women's Land Rights in Southern Africa: Consolidated Baseline Findings from Malawi, Mozambique, South Africa, Zambia, and Zimbabwe*. Amsterdam: NIZA and ActionAid.

Penal Reform International. 2000. *Access to Justice in Sub-Saharan Africa: The Role of Traditional and Informal Justice Systems*, 66–67. London: Astron Printers.

Stamp, Patricia. 1991. "Burying Otieno: The Politics of Gender and Ethnicity in Kenya." *Signs* 16 (4): 808–45.

Subramanian, Narendra. 2008. "Legal Change and Gender Inequality: Changes in Muslim Family Law in India." *Law & Social Inquiry* 33 (3): 631–72.

Udry, Christopher, John Hoddinott, Harold Alderman, and Lawrence Haddad. 2004. "Access to Justice Practice Note." UNDP, New York.

UNDP (United Nations Development Programme). 2004. "Access to Justice Practice Note." UNDP, New York.

Walsh, Barry. 2010. "In Search of Success: Case Studies in Justice Sector Development in Sub-Saharan Africa." Report 57445, World Bank, Washington, DC.

Widner, Jennifer. 2001. "Courts and Democracy in Postconflict Transitions: A Social Scientist's Perspective on the African Case." *American Journal of International Law* 95 (1): 64–75.

Wing, Susanna D. 2009. "Exploring Democracy, Women's Rights, and Legal Reform in Francophone Africa." Paper presented at the conference "Rethinking Development: Societal Transformations and the Challenges of Governance in Africa and the Middle East," Yale University, New Haven, CT, January 30–31.

Wood, Georgina. 2008. "The Role of the Judiciary in Promoting Gender Justice in Africa." Paper presented at the Partners for Gender Justice Conference, Accra, Ghana, November 19–21.

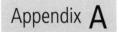
Appendix A

Scoresheets

Indicators Based on Constitutions, International Conventions, and Statutes in Effect as of June 2011

Table A.1 Scoresheet 1: Ratification of international conventions by African countries

	Country characteristics			Convention ratified						Type of state	
Country	Income level (2011)	Legal system	CEDAW	Africa Women's Rights Protocol	ILO Convention 100 (equal pay) for work of equal value)	ILO Convention 111 (non-discrimination in employment)	ILO Conventions 4, 41, 89, 1990 Protocol (night work)	ILO Convention 181 (maternity protections)	Monist	Dualist
Angola	Middle Income	Civil	Yes	Yes	Yes	Yes	Yes	No	No	Yes
Benin	Low Income	Civil	Yes	Yes	Yes	Yes	Yes	No	Yes	No
Botswana	Middle Income	Common	Yes	No	Yes	Yes	No	No	No	Yes
Burkina Faso	Low Income	Civil	Yes	Yes	Yes	Yes	Yes	No	Yes	No
Burundi	Low Income	Civil	Yes	No	Yes	Yes	Yes	No	Yes	No
Cameroon	Middle Income	Civil	Yes	Yes	Yes	Yes	Yes	No	Yes	No
Cape Verde	Middle Income	Civil	Yes	No	Yes	Yes	No	No	Yes	No
Central African Republic	Low Income	Civil	Yes	No	Yes	Yes	Yes	No	Yes	No
Chad	Low Income	Civil	Yes	Yes	Yes	Yes	Yes	No	Yes	No
Comoros	Low Income	Civil	Yes	Yes	Yes	Yes	Yes	No	Yes	No
Congo, Demo. Rep.	Low Income	Civil	Yes	Yes	Yes	Yes	Yes	No	Yes	No
Congo, Rep.	Middle Income	Civil	Yes	No	Yes	Yes	Yes	No	Yes	No
Côte d'Ivoire	Middle Income	Civil	Yes	Yes	Yes	Yes	Yes	No	Yes	No
Equatorial Guinea	Middle Income	Civil	Yes	No	Yes	Yes	No	No	Yes	No
Eritrea	Low Income	Civil	Yes	No	Yes	Yes	No	No	Yes	No
Ethiopia	Low Income	Civil	Yes	No	Yes	Yes	No	Yes	Yes	No
Gabon	Middle Income	Civil	Yes	Yes	Yes	Yes	Yes	No	Yes	No
Gambia, The	Low Income	Common	Yes	Yes	Yes	Yes	No	No	No	Yes
Ghana	Middle Income	Common	Yes	Yes	Yes	Yes	Yes	No	No	Yes
Guinea	Low Income	Civil	Yes	No	Yes	Yes	Yes	No	Yes	No
Guinea-Bissau	Low Income	Civil	Yes	Yes	Yes	Yes	Yes	No	Yes	No

Country	Income	Legal								
Kenya	Low Income	Common	Yes	No	Yes	Yes	Yes	No	No	Yes	No
Lesotho	Middle Income	Common	Yes	Yes	Yes	Yes	No	No	No	No	Yes
Liberia	Low Income	Common	Yes	Yes	No	Yes	No	No	No	No	Yes
Madagascar	Low Income	Civil	Yes	No	Yes	Yes	Yes	No	No	Yes	No
Malawi	Low Income	Common	Yes	Yes	Yes	Yes	Yes	No	No	Yes	No
Mali	Low Income	Civil	Yes	Yes	Yes	Yes	Yes	No	No	Yes	No
Mauritania	Middle Income	Civil	Yes	No	Yes	Yes	Yes	No	No	Yes	No
Mauritius	Middle Income	Civil	Yes	Yes	Yes	Yes	No	No	No	No	Yes
Mozambique	Low Income	Civil	Yes	Yes	Yes	Yes	No	No	No	Yes	No
Namibia	Middle Income	Common	Yes	No	Yes	Yes	Yes	No	No	Yes	No
Niger	Low Income	Civil	Yes	No	Yes	Yes	No	No	No	Yes	No
Nigeria	Middle Income	Common	Yes	Yes	Yes	Yes	Yes	No	No	No	Yes
Rwanda	Low Income	Civil	Yes	Yes	Yes	Yes	No	No	No	Yes	No
São Tomé and Principe	Middle Income	Civil	Yes	No	Yes	Yes	No	No	No	—	—
Senegal	Middle Income	Civil	Yes	Yes	Yes	Yes	Yes	No	No	Yes	No
Seychelles	Middle Income	Common	Yes	Yes	Yes	Yes	No	No	No	No	Yes
Sierra Leone	Low Income	Common	Yes	No	Yes	Yes	No	No	No	No	Yes
Somalia	Low Income	Civil	No	No	No	Yes	No	No	No	—	—
South Africa	Middle Income	Common	Yes	Yes	Yes	Yes	Yes	No	No	Yes	No
Sudan	Middle Income	Common	No	No	Yes	Yes	No	No	No	No	Yes
Swaziland	Middle Income	Common	Yes	Yes	Yes	Yes	No	No	No	No	Yes
Tanzania	Low Income	Common	Yes	Yes	Yes	Yes	Yes	No	No	No	Yes
Togo	Low Income	Civil	Yes	Yes	Yes	Yes	Yes	No	No	Yes	No
Uganda	Low Income	Common	Yes	Yes	Yes	Yes	No	No	No	No	Yes
Zambia	Middle Income	Common	Yes	Yes	Yes	Yes	No	No	No	No	Yes
Zimbabwe	Low Income	Common	Yes	Yes	Yes	Yes	No	No	No	No	Yes

Source: CEDAW, African Union, International Labour Organization, and recent news reports.
Note: CEDAW is the Committee on the Elimination of Discrimination against Women. ILO is the International Labour Organization. — Not available.

Table A.2 Scoresheet 2: Selected features of constitutions of African countries

Country	Income level (2011)	Legal system	Recognizes nondiscrimination based on gender as a guiding principle	Includes specific provision for gender equality	Guarantees private property ownership	Explicitly provides for gender equality in property ownership	Recognizes equal rights to work, right to equal pay for work of equal value, or both	Recognizes customary law as prevailing in certain areas	Grants individuals right to challenge constitutionality of statutes	Grants right to challenge constitutionality of statutes only to executive branch
Angola	Middle Income	Civil	Yes	Yes	Yes	No	No	No	No	Yes
Benin	Low Income	Civil	Yes	Yes	Yes	No	Yes	No	Yes	Yes
Botswana	Middle Income	Common	Yes	No	No	No	No	Yes	Yes	No
Burkina Faso	Low Income	Civil	Yes	Yes	Yes	No	Yes	No	No	Yes
Burundi	Low Income	Civil	Yes	Yes	Yes	No	Yes	No	Yes	No
Cameroon	Middle Income	Civil	Yes	Yes	Yes	No	Yes	No	No	Yes
Cape Verde	Middle Income	Civil	Yes	No	Yes	No	Yes	No	Yes	No
Central African Republic	Low Income	Civil	Yes	Yes	Yes	No	Yes	No	Yes	No
Chad	Low Income	Civil	Yes	Yes	Yes	No	No	Yes	Yes	No
Comoros	Low Income	Civil	Yes	Yes	Yes	No	Yes	No	Yes	Yes
Congo, Demo. Rep.	Low Income	Civil	Yes	Yes	Yes	No	Yes	Yes	Yes	Yes
Congo, Rep.	Middle Income	Civil	Yes	Yes	Yes	No	Yes	Yes	Yes	No
Côte d'Ivoire	Middle Income	Civil	Yes	Yes	Yes	No	No	No	Yes	Yes
Equatorial Guinea	Middle Income	Civil	Yes	Yes	Yes	No	No	No	No	Yes
Eritrea	Low Income	Civil	Yes	Yes	Yes	Yes	No	No	Yes	No
Ethiopia	Low Income	Civil	Yes	Yes	Yes	No	Yes	Yes	Yes	No
Gabon	Middle Income	Civil	Yes	Yes	Yes	Yes	No	No	Yes	Yes
Gambia, The	Low Income	Common	Yes	Yes	No	No	No	Yes	Yes	No
Ghana	Middle Income	Common	Yes	No	Yes	No	No	Yes	Yes	No
Guinea	Low Income	Civil	Yes	Yes	Yes	No	No	No	No	No

Country	Income	Legal system						
Guinea-Bissau	Low Income	Civil	Yes	Yes	No	No	Yes	No
Kenya	Low Income	Common	Yes	Yes	No	Yes	Yes	No
Lesotho	Middle Income	Common	Yes	No	Yes	Yes	Yes	No
Liberia	Low Income	Common	No	Yes	Yes	Yes	Yes	No
Madagascar	Low Income	Civil	Yes	Yes	Yes	No	No	Yes
Malawi	Low Income	Common	Yes	Yes	No	Yes	Yes	No
Mali	Low Income	Civil	Yes	Yes	No	No	No	Yes
Mauritania	Middle Income	Civil	Yes	Yes	No	No	Yes	No
Mauritius	Middle Income	Civil	Yes	No	No	Yes	Yes	No
Mozambique	Low Income	Civil	No	Yes	No	No	Yes	No
Namibia	Middle Income	Common	Yes	Yes	No	Yes	Yes	No
Niger	Low Income	Civil	Yes	Yes	No	Yes	Yes	Yes
Nigeria	Middle Income	Common	Yes	Yes	No	Yes	Yes	No
Rwanda	Low Income	Civil	Yes	Yes	No	Yes	Yes	No
São Tomé and Príncipe	Middle Income	Civil	Yes	Yes	—	—	—	—
Senegal	Middle Income	Civil	Yes	Yes	Yes	No	No^a	Yes
Seychelles	Middle Income	Common	Yes	Yes	Yes	No	Yes	No
Sierra Leone	Low Income	Common	Yes	Yes	Yes	Yes	Yes	No
Somalia	Low Income	Civil	Yes	Yes	Yes	No	Yes	No
South Africa	Middle Income	Common	Yes	Yes	Yes	No	Yes	No
Sudan	Middle Income	Common	Yes	Yes	Yes	No	Yes	No
Swaziland	Middle Income	Common	Yes	Yes	Yes	No	Yes	No
Tanzania	Middle Income	Common	Yes	Yes	Yes	No	Yes	Yes
Togo	Low Income	Civil	Yes	Yes	Yes	Yes	Yes	No
Uganda	Low Income	Common	Yes	Yes	Yes	No	Yes	No
Zambia	Middle Income	Common	Yes	Yes	No	Yes	Yes	No
Zimbabwe	Low Income	Common	Yes	No	Yes	Yes	Yes	No

Source: National constitution of each country.

Note: — Not available.

a. By statute, citizens can bring constitutional challenges in the high or ordinary courts.

Table A.3 Scoresheet 3: Legal recognition of and limitations on customary and religious law in African countries

Country	Income level (2011)	Legal system	Constitution recognizes customary law and prohibits discrimination with a clear test (such as a bill of rights)	Constitution recognizes customary law and explicitly exempts it from nondiscrimination provisions	Constitution is silent about customary law	Constitution formally recognizes religious law	Constitution explicitly limits ability of religious law to discriminate based on gender	Customary law is granted statutory recognition as source of law	Explicit statutory recognition limits customary law based on nondiscrimination (such as a bill of rights or repugnancy test)	Religious law has statutory recognition as source of law	Statutes limit ability of religious law to discriminate based on gender	Establishment of formal customary courts	Recognition of informal customary courts	State formally recognizes religious courts
			Constitutional recognition					**Statutory recognition**						
Angola	Middle Income	Civil	No	No	Yes	No	n.a.	No	n.a.	No	n.a.	No	No	No
Benin	Low Income	Civil	No	No	Yes	No	n.a.	No	n.a.	No	n.a.	No	No	No
Botswana	Middle Income	Common	No	Yes	No	No	n.a.	Yes	Yes	Yes	Yes	Yes	Yes	No
Burkina Faso	Low Income	Civil	No	No	Yes	No	n.a.	No	n.a.	No	n.a.	No	No	No
Burundi	Low Income	Civil	No	No	Yes	No	n.a.	No	n.a.	No	n.a.	Yes	No	No
Cameroon	Middle Income	Civil	No	No	Yes	No	n.a.	Yes	Yes	Yes	Yes	Yes	No	Yes
Cape Verde	Middle Income	Civil	No	No	Yes	No	n.a.	No	n.a.	No	n.a.	No	No	No
Central African Republic	Low Income	Civil	No	No	Yes	No	n.a.	—	—	—	n.a.	No	No	No
Chad	Low Income	Civil	Yes	No	No	No	n.a.	Yes	Yes	Yes	—	—	Yes	No
Comoros	Low Income	Civil	No	No	Yes	Yes	No	—	—	No	No	No	No	No
Congo, Demo. Rep.	Low Income	Civil	Yes	No	No	No	n.a.	No	—	No	n.a.	Yes	No	No
Congo, Rep.	Middle Income	Civil	No	No	Yes	No	n.a.	No	n.a.	No	n.a.	No	—	No
Côte d'Ivoire	Middle Income	Civil	No	No	No	No	n.a.	Yes	Yes	No	n.a.	No	No	No
Equatorial Guinea	Middle Income	Civil	Yes	No	No	No	n.a.	No	n.a.	No	n.a.	No	No	No
Eritrea	Low Income	Civil	No	No	Yes	No	n.a.	Yes	n.a.	Yes	No	Yes	No	Yes
Ethiopia	Low Income	Civil	Yes	No	No	Yes	Yes	Yes	Yes	Yes	Yes	Yes	Yes	Yes

Country	Income	Legal System	1	2	3	4	5	6	7	8	9	10	11	12
Gabon	Middle Income	Civil	No	No	Yes	No	n.a.	No	n.a.	No	n.a.	No	No	No
Gambia, The	Low Income	Common	No	Yes	No	Yes	Yes	Yes	Yes	Yes	No	Yes	Yes	Yes
Ghana	Middle Income	Common	No	Yes	No	Yes	No	Yes	Yes	Yes	Yes	No	No	No
Guinea	Low Income	Civil	No	No	Yes	No	n.a.	No	n.a.	No	n.a.	No	Yes	No
Guinea-Bissau	Low Income	Civil	No	No	Yes	No	n.a.	No	n.a.	No	Yes	No	—	No
Kenya	Low Income	Common	Yes	No	No	Yes	Yes	Yes	Yes	Yes	Yes	Yes	No	Yes
Lesotho	Middle Income	Common	No	Yes	No	Yes	No	Yes	Yes	Yes	Yes	Yes	Yes	No
Liberia	Low Income	Common	Yes	No	No	No	n.a.	Yes	Yes	Yes	n.a.	Yes	No	No
Madagascar	Low Income	Civil	No	No	Yes	No	n.a.	—	—	—	n.a.	—	Yes	No
Malawi	Low Income	Common	Yes	No	No	No	n.a.	Yes	Yes	Yes	Yes	No	No	No
Mali	Low Income	Civil	No	No	Yes	No	n.a.	No	Yes	No	No	No	No	No
Mauritania	Middle Income	Civil	Yes	No	No	Yes	No	No	n.a.	No	n.a.	No	No	No
Mauritius	Middle Income	Civil	No	Yes	No	Yes	No	No	n.a.	Yes	Yes	No	No	No
Mozambique	Low Income	Civil	Yes	No	No	No	n.a.	Yes	Yes	Yes	n.a.	Yes	Yes	No
Namibia	Middle Income	Common	Yes	No	No	No	n.a.	Yes	Yes	Yes	Yes	Yes	No	No
Niger	Low Income	Civil	Yes	No	No	No	n.a.	Yes	Yes	Yes	Yes	Yes	Yes	No
Nigeria	Middle Income	Common	Yes	No	No	Yes	No	Yes	Yes	Yes	Yes	Yes	No	Yes
Rwanda	Low Income	Civil	Yes	No	No	No	n.a.	Yes	Yes	Yes	n.a.	Yes	No	No
São Tomé and Principe	Middle Income	Civil	No	No	Yes	No	n.a.	No	n.a.	No	n.a.	—	—	No
Senegal	Middle Income	Civil	No	No	Yes	No	n.a.	Yes	No	Yes	No	No	No	No
Seychelles	Middle Income	Common	No	No	Yes	No	n.a.	No	n.a.	No	n.a.	No	No	No
Sierra Leone	Low Income	Common	No	Yes	No	Yes	No	Yes	Yes	Yes	Yes	No	No	No
Somalia	Low Income	Civil	Yes	No	No	Yes	No	No	No	—	No	Yes	No	Yes
South Africa	Middle Income	Common	Yes	No	No	Yes	Yes	Yes	Yes	Yes	n.a.	Yes	No	No
Sudan	Middle Income	Common	Yes	No	No	Yes	No	No	No	No	No	Yes	Yes	Yes
Swaziland	Middle Income	Common	Yes	No	No	No	n.a.	Yes	Yes	Yes	n.a.	Yes	No	No
Tanzania	Low Income	Common	No	No	Yes	No	n.a.	Yes	Yes	Yes	n.a.	No	No	No
Togo	Low Income	Civil	Yes	No	No	No	n.a.	Yes	Yes	Yes	n.a.	No	Yes	No
Uganda	Low Income	Common	Yes	No	No	Yes	Yes	Yes	Yes	Yes	Yes	Yes	—	Yes
Zambia	Middle Income	Common	No	Yes	No	No	n.a.	Yes	Yes	Yes	n.a.	Yes	No	No
Zimbabwe	Low Income	Common	No	Yes	No	No	n.a.	Yes	Yes	Yes	n.a.	Yes	No	No

Source: National constitutions, codes, and statutues.
Note: n.a. = not applicable.

Table A.4 Scoresheet 4: Legal capacity of men and women in African countries

Country	Income level (2011)	Legal system	Husband is formally recognized as head of household	Husband is given right to choose location of marital domicile	Wife requires husband's permission to open bank account	Husband can deny wife permission to pursue trade or profession or to work outside the home
Angola	Middle Income	Civil	No	No	No	No
Benin	Low Income	Civil	No	Yes	No	No
Botswana	Middle Income	Common	Yes	Yes	Yes	No
Burkina Faso	Low Income	Civil	No	Yes	No	No
Burundi	Low Income	Civil	Yes	No	No	No
Cameroon	Middle Income	Civil	Yes	Yes	Yes	Yes
Cape Verde	Middle Income	Civil	No	No	Yes	No
Central African Republic	Low Income	Civil	Yes	Yes	No	No
Chad	Low Income	Civil	Yes	Yes	—	—
Comoros	Low Income	Civil	Yes	No	No	No
Congo, Demo. Rep.	Low Income	Civil	Yes	Yes	Yes	Yes
Congo, Rep.	Middle Income	Civil	Yes	Yes	No	Yes
Cite d'Ivoire	Middle Income	Civil	Yes	Yes	No	Yes
Equatorial Guinea	Middle Income	Civil	No	—	No	No
Eritrea	Low Income	Civil	No	No	No	No
Ethiopia	Low Income	Civil	No	No	No	No
Gabon	Middle Income	Civil	Yes	Yes	No	Yes
Gambia, The	Low Income	Common	No	No	No	No
Ghana	Middle Income	Common	No	No	No	No

Country	Income	Legal System				
Guinea	Low Income	Civil	Yes	Yes	No	Yes
Guinea-Bissau	Low Income	Civil	Yes	Yes	Yes	Yes
Kenya	Low Income	Common	No	No	No	No
Lesotho	Middle Income	Common	No	No	No	Yes
Liberia	Low Income	Common	Yes	No	No	No
Madagascar	Low Income	Civil	No	No	No	No
Malawi	Low Income	Common	Yes	No	No	No
Mali	Low Income	Civil	Yes	Yes	Yes	Yes
Mauritania	Middle Income	Civil	No	No	No	No
Mauritius	Middle Income	Civil	No	No	No	No
Mozambique	Low Income	Civil	No	No	No	No
Namibia	Middle Income	Common	No	No	No	Yes
Niger	Low Income	Civil	Yes	Yes	No	No
Nigeria	Middle Income	Common	No	No	No	No
Rwanda	Low Income	Civil	Yes	Yes	No	No
São Tomé and Principe	Middle Income	Civil	No	No	—	No
Senegal	Middle Income	Civil	Yes	Yes	No	No
Seychelles	Middle Income	Common	No	No	No	No
Sierra Leone	Low Income	Common	No	No	No	No
Somalia	Low Income	Civil	Yes	Yes	—	—
South Africa	Middle Income	Common	No	No	No	No
Sudan	Middle Income	Common	Yes	Yes	No	Yes
Swaziland	Middle Income	Common	Yes	Yes	Yes	Yes
Tanzania	Low Income	Common	No	No	No	No
Togo	Low Income	Civil	Yes	Yes	Yes	Yes
Uganda	Low Income	Common	No	No	No	No
Zambia	Middle Income	Common	No	No	No	No
Zimbabwe	Low Income	Common	No	No	No	No

Source: National family codes and statutes.
Note: — Not available.

Table A.5 Scoresheet 5: Marital property regimes in African countries

Country	Income level (2011)	Legal system	Default marital property regime	"Community of property" is allowed	Marriage statutes recognize customary marriages	Polygamy is formally allowed	Husband is recognized as head of household and allowed to administer or manage community of property alone	Husband must gain wife's consent in managing marital property	Husband has power to administer personal property of wife	Husband can pay community debts from personal property of wife	Husband can use community property to pay own personal debts
Angola	Middle Income	Civil	Community	Yes	No	No	No	No	No	No	No
Benin	Low Income	Civil	Separate	Yes	No	No	No	No	No	No	No
Botswana	Middle Income	Common	Customary	Yes	Yes	No	No	No	No	No	No
Burkina Faso	Low Income	Civil	Community	Yes	No	Yes	No	Yes	No	No	No
Burundi	Low Income	Civil	Customary	Yes	No	No	No	Yes	No	No	No
Cameroon	Middle Income	Civil	Community	Yes	Yes	Yes	Yes	No	Yes	Yes	Yes
Cape Verde	Middle Income	Civil	Community	Yes	No	No	No	No	No	No	No
Central African Republic	Low Income	Civil	Separate	Yes	No	Yes	No	Yes	No	No	No
Chad	Low Income	Civil	Community	Yes	Yes	Yes	—	—	—	—	—
Comoros	Low Income	Civil	Community	Yes	No	Yes	No	No	No	No	No
Congo, Demo. Rep.	Low Income	Civil	Community	Yes	No	No	No	Yes	No	No	No
Congo, Rep.	Middle Income	Civil	Community	Yes	No	Yes	No	Yes	No	No	No
Côte d'Ivoire	Middle Income	Civil	Community	Yes	No	No	No	Yes	No	No	No
Equatorial Guinea	Middle Income	Civil	—	—	Yes	Yes	—	—	—	—	—
Eritrea	Low Income	Civil	Community	Yes	Yes	No	No	No	No	No	No
Ethiopia	Low Income	Civil	Community	Yes	Yes	No	No	No	No	No	No
Gabon	Middle Income	Civil	Separate	Yes	No	Yes	No	Yes	No	No	No
Gambia, The	Low Income	Common	Separate	No	Yes	Yes	No	No	No	No	No
Ghana	Middle Income	Common	Separate	No	Yes	Yes	No	No	No	No	No
Guinea	Low Income	Civil	No provision	Yes	No	No	No	No	No	No	No
Guinea-Bissau	Low Income	Civil	Community	Yes	No	No	Yes	No	No	No	No
Kenya	Low Income	Common	Separate	No	Yes	Yes	No	No	No	No	No
Lesotho	Middle Income	Common	Community	Yes	Yes	Yes	No	No	No	No	No
Liberia	Low Income	Common	Separate	Yes	Yes	Yes	No	No	No	No	No
Madagascar	Low Income	Civil	Community	Yes	Yes	No	Yes	No	No	No	No

Dowry legally required (goes straight to wife)	Bride price to her family/wealth legally required	Dowry/bride price legally recognised	Bride price/dowry customarily required	Symbolic/fixed sum (where legally required; amt in statute)	Dowry or bride price are banned	Women in statutory marriages are entitled to some of the marital property upon divorce	Women in customary marriages are entitled to some of the marital property upon divorce	Women in consensual unions are entitled to some of the marital property upon divorce	Marital property is divided equally upon divorce	Wife's nonmonetary contribution is recognized in determining share of property she receives in countries with separate property regimes	Right of women married under statutory law to inherit is recognized	Right of women married under customary law to inherit is recognized	Woman's ability to inherit in a consensual union is recognized	Statutory recognition is granted to customary law in property inheritance (through succession acts, for example)	Nonmonetary contributions to matrimonial property are recognized in determining inheritance	Wife's portion of joint property is recognized in cases of intestate inheritance	Widow has right to remain in and use house and land of husband upon his death, at least until she remarries	Right of maintenance from deceased's estate	Childless women have right to inherit if husband dies intestate
No	No	No	Yes	No	No	Yes	No	Yes	Yes	Yes	Yes	No	Yes	No	Yes	Yes	Yes	Yes	Yes
No	No	Yes	Yes	Yes	No	Yes	No	No	No	No	Yes	No	No	No	No	Yes	Yes	Yes	Yes
—	—	—	Yes	—	—	No	No	No	No	No	No	No	No	Yes	No	No	No	No	No
No	No	No	Yes	No	Yes	Yes	No	No	Yes	Yes	Yes	No	No	No	No	Yes	Yes	Yes	Yes
No	No	yes	Yes	No	No	No	No	No	No	No	No	No	No	No	No	No	No	No	No
No	No	no	Yes	No	Yes	No	No	No	No	Yes	Yes	No	Yes	No	No	Yes	Yes	Yes	No
—	—	—	—	—	—	Yes	No	Yes	Yes	Yes	Yes	No	Yes	No	Yes	Yes	Yes	No	Yes
No	Yes	Yes	Yes	No	No	—	No	—	—	—	Yes	No	No	No	No	—	—	—	Yes
Yes	Yes	Yes	Yes	No	No	Yes	—	—	Yes	Yes	Yes	—	—	—	Yes	Yes	—	—	Yes
Yes	No	Yes	Yes	No	No	Yes	Yes	No	No	No	Yes	No	Yes	No	Yes	Yes	Yes	Yes	Yes
—	Yes	Yes	Yes	Yes	No	Yes	No	No	Yes	No	Yes	No	No	No	No	Yes	Yes	Yes	Yes
—	Yes	Yes	—	Yes	—	Yes	No	No	Yes	Yes	Yes	No	No	No	No	Yes	Yes	Yes	Yes
No	No	No	—	No	Yes	Yes	No	No	Yes	Yes	Yes	No	No	No	Yes	Yes	No	No	Yes
No	No	—	Yes	No	Nob	—	No	No	No	—	No	No	No	No	No	No	No	No	No
No	No	—	Yes	No	Yes	Yes	—	—	Yes	Yes	Yes	No	—	No	Yes	Yes	—	—	Yes
No	No	—	Yes	No	No	Yes	Yes	Yes	Yes	Yes	Yes	No	Yes	No	Yes	Yes	No	Yes	Yes
No	No	—	Yes	No	Yes	Yes	No	No	No	No	Yes	No	No	No	Yes	Yes	Yes	Yes	Yes
—	—	—	Yes	No	No	No	No	No	No	No	Yes	No	No	Yes	No	No	Yes	No	Yes
No	No	No	Yes	No	No	Yes	No	No	No	No	Yes	Yes	No	Yes	Yes	Yes	Yes	Yes	Yes
Yes	Yes	Yes	—	Yes	No	Yes	No	No	Yes	No	Yes	No	No	No	No	Yes	Yes	Yes	Yes
—	—	—	Yes	—	—	Yes	No	Yes	Yes	Yes	Yes	No	Yes	No	Yes	—	—	—	Yes
Yes	Yes	Yes	Yes	No	No	No	No	No	Yes	No	Yes	No	Yes	No	No	Yes	Yes	Yes	Yes
—	—	—	yes	No	No	Yes	No	No	Yes	No	Yes	No	Yes	Yes	Yes	Yes	Yes	—	Yes
—	—	Yes	Yes	No	No	Yes	Yes	No	No	—	Yes	Yes	No	Yes	—	Yes	Yes	—	Yes
—	Yes	yes	Yes	—	—	Yes	No	No	No	Yes	Yes	Yes	No	Yes	Yes	Yes	Yes	Yes	Yes

continued

Table A.5 Scoresheet 5: Marital property regimes in African countries　*continued*

Country	Income level (2011)	Legal system	Default marital property regime	"Community of property" is allowed	Marriage statutes recognize customary marriages	Polygamy is formally allowed	Husband is recognized as head of household and allowed to administer or manage community of property alone	Husband must gain wife's consent in managing marital property	Husband has power to administer personal property of wife	Husband can pay community debts from personal property of wife	Husband can use community property to pay own personal debts
Malawi	Low Income	Common	Separate	No	Yes	No	No	No	No	No	No
Mali	Low Income	Civil	Separate	Yes	No	Yes	No	Yes	No	Yes	Yes
Mauritania	Middle Income	Civil	Separate	No	No	Yes	No	No	No	No	No
Mauritius	Middle Income	Civil	Community	Yes	No	No	No	Yes	No	No	Yes
Mozambique	Low Income	Civil	Community	Yes	Yes	No	No	No	No	No	No
Namibia	Middle Income	Common	Community	Yes	Yes	No	No	Yes	No	No	No
Niger	Low Income	Civil	Separate	Yes	Yes	Yes	Yes	No	No	No	No
Nigeria	Middle Income	Common	Separate	No	Yes	Yes	No	No	No	No	—
Rwanda	Low Income	Civil	Community	Yes	No	No	No	Yes	No	No	No
São Tomé and Principe	Middle Income	Civil	Community	Yes	No	No	No	No	No	No	No
Senegal	Middle Income	Civil	Separate	Yes	Yes	Yes	No	No	No	No	No
Seychelles	Middle Income	Common	Separate	No	No	No	No	No	No	No	No
Sierra Leone	Low Income	Common	Separate	Yes	Yes	Yes	No	No	No	No	No
Somalia	Low Income	Civil	Separate	—	—	Yes	—	—	—	—	—
South Africa	Middle Income	Common	Community	Yes	Yes	Yes	No	Yes	No	No	No
Sudan	Middle Income	Common	Separate	—	Yes	Yes	No	No	No	No	No
Swaziland	Middle Income	Common	Customary	Yes	Yes	Yes	Yes	No	Yes	Yes	Yes
Tanzania	Low Income	Common	Separate	No	Yes	Yes	No	No	No	No	No
Togo	Low Income	Civil	Separate	Yes	Yes	Yes	No	Yes	No	Yes	Yes
Uganda	Low Income	Common	Separate	No	Yes	Yes	No	No	No	No	No
Zambia	Middle Income	Common	Separate	No	Yes	Yes	No	No	No	No	No
Zimbabwe	Low Income	Common	Separate	Yes	Yes	Yes	No	Yes	No	No	No

Source: National family and inheritance codes and statutes.
Note: — Not available.

Dowry and bride price						Division of property upon divorce					Inheritance of property								
Dowry legally required (goes straight to wife)	Bride price to her family/wealth legally required	Dowry/bride price legally recognised	Bride price/dowry customarily required	Symbolic/fixed sum (where legally required; amt in statute)	Dowry or bride price are banned	Women in statutory marriages are entitled to some of the marital property upon divorce	Women in customary marriages are entitled to some of the marital property upon divorce	Women in consensual unions are entitled to some of the marital property upon divorce	Marital property is divided equally upon divorce	Wife's nonmonetary contribution is recognized in determining share of property she receives in countries with separate property regimes	Right of women married under statuatory law to inherit is recognized	Right of women married under customary law to inherit is recognized	Woman's ability to inherit in a consensual union is recognized	Statutory recognition is granted to customary law in property inheritance (through succession acts, for example)	Statutory recognition of a minimum share that a wife inherits on the death of her husband	Wife's portion of joint property is recognized in cases of intestate inheritance	Widow has right to remain in and use house and land of husband upon his death, at least until she remarries	Right of maintenance from deceased's estate	Childless women have right to inherit if husband dies intestate
—	—	—	Yes	—	—	No	Yes	No	No	No	Yes	Yes	No	Yes	Yes	Yes	Yes	Yes	Yes
Yes	—	Yes	Yes	Yes	No	Yes	No	No	No	No	Yes	No	No	Yes	No	Yes	Yes	Yes	Yes
Yes	—	Yes	Yes	No	No	Yes	No	No	No	No	Yes	No	No	No	No	Yes	Yes	No	Yes
—	—	—	—	—	—	Yes	No	No	Yes	Yes	Yes	No	No	No	No	Yes	Yes	Yes	Yes
No	No	—	Yes	No	No	Yes	Yes	Yes	Yes	Yes	Yes	Yes	No	Yes	No	Yes	No	No	Yes
—	—	—	Yes	—	—	Yes	No	No	Yes	Yes	Yes	Yes	No	Yes	Yes	Yes	Yes	No	Yes
—	—	—	Yes	No	No	Yes	No	No	No	No	Yes	No	No	Yes	No	Yes	Yes	Yes	Yes
—	—	Yes	Yes	—	—	No	No	No	No	No	Yes	No	No	Yes	No	Yes	Yes	Yes	Yes
Yes	—	Yes	Yes	No	No	Yes	No	No	Yes	No	Yes	No	No	No	Yes	Yes	Yes	Yes	Yes
—	—	—	—	—	—	Yes	Yes	Yes	Yes	Yes	Yes	Yes	Yes	No	—	—	—	—	—
Yes	—	Yes	Yes	No	No	Yes	No	No	No	No	Yes	No	No	No	No	Yes	Yes	No	Yes
No	No	—	—	No	No	Yes	No	No	No	No	Yes	No	No	No	No	Yes	No	—	Yes
—	Yes	Yes	Yes	No	No	Yes	No	No	No	No	Yes	Yes	Yes	Yes	Yes	Yes	Yes	Yes	Yes
—	—	—	Yes	—	—	—	—	—	—	—	Yes	—	—	—	—	Yes	—	—	Yes
No	No	Yes	Yes	No	No	Yes	Yes	No	Yes	Yes	Yes	Yes	No	Yes	Yes	Yes	No	Yes	Yes
Yes	—	Yes	yes	No	No	No	No	No	No	No	Yes	No	No	Yes	No	No	Yes	—	Yes
—	—	—	Yes	No	No	No	No	No	No	No	No	No	No	Yes	No	No	No	No	No
—	No	Yes	Yes	No	No	Yes	Yes	No	No	Yes	No	No	No	Yes	No	No	Yes	No	No
—	Yes	Yes	—	No	No	Yes	No	No	No	No	Yes	No	No	Yes	No	No	Yes	Yes	Yes
—	Yes	Yes	—	—	—	Yes	No	No	No	No	Yes	No	No	Yes	No	Yes	Yes	Yes	Yes
No	No	No	Yes	No	No	Yes	No	No	No	Yes	Yes	No	No	Yes	Yes	No	Yes	Yes	Yes
—	Yes	Yes	Yes	No	No	Yes	Yes	No	No	Yes	Yes	Yes	No	Yes	Yes	No	Yes	Yes	Yes

Table A.6 Scoresheet 6: Land Rights in African Countries

Country	Income level (2011)	Legal system	Women's land rights are granted statutory protection under land laws	Statutory recognition is granted to customary law governing ownership or distribution of land	Customary land is exempt from succession	Women are entitled to co-ownership through marriage
Angola	Middle Income	Civil	No	Yes	No	Yes
Benin	Low Income	Civil	Yes	Yes	No	No
Botswana	Middle Income	Common	Yes	Yes	Yes	No
Burkina Faso	Low Income	Civil	Yes	No	No	No
Burundi	Low Income	Civil	No	Yes	Yes	No
Cameroon	Middle Income	Civil	Yes	Yes	No	No
Cape Verde	Middle Income	Civil	—	No	No	No
Central African Republic	Low Income	Civil	Yes	Yes	No	No
Chad	Low Income	Civil	No	No	—	No
Comoros	Low Income	Civil	No	Yes	—	No
Congo, Demo. Rep.	Low Income	Civil	No	No	No	No
Congo, Rep.	Middle Income	Civil	Yes	Yes	No	No
Côte d'Ivoire	Middle Income	Civil	No	No	No	No
Equatorial Guinea	Middle Income	Civil	Yes	No	No	No
Eritrea	Low Income	Civil	Yes	No	No	No
Ethiopia	Low Income	Civil	No	No	No	No
Gabon	Middle Income	Civil	No	Yes	No	No
Gambia, The	Low Income	Common	Yes	Yes	Yes	No
Ghana	Middle Income	Common				

Country	Income	Legal				
Guinea	Low Income	Civil	No	No	No	No
Guinea-Bissau	Low Income	Civil	No	Yes	—	No
Kenya	Low Income	Common	Yes	Yes	Yes	No
Lesotho	Middle Income	Common	No	Yes	Yes	No
Liberia	Low Income	Common	No	Yes	No	No
Madagascar	Low Income	Civil	No	Yes	Yes	No
Malawi	Low Income	Common	No	Yes	No	No
Mali	Low Income	Civil	No	Yes	No	No
Mauritania	Middle Income	Civil	No	No	No	No
Mauritius	Middle Income	Civil	Yes	No	No	Yes
Mozambique	Low Income	Civil	Yes	Yes	No	No
Namibia	Middle Income	Common	Yes	Yes	Yes	Yes
Niger	Low Income	Civil	Yes	Yes	Yes	No
Nigeria	Middle Income	Common	No	No	Yes	No
Rwanda	Low Income	Civil	No	Yes	Yes	No
São Tomé and Principe	Middle Income	Civil	—	—	No	No
Senegal	Middle Income	Civil	No	No	No	No
Seychelles	Middle Income	Common	No	No	No	No
Sierra Leone	Low Income	Common	No	Yes	Yes	No
Somalia	Low Income	Civil	No	No	No	No
South Africa	Middle Income	Common	Yes	Yes	No	Yes
Sudan	Middle Income	Common	No	Yes	Yes	No
Swaziland	Middle Income	Common	No	Yes	Yes	No
Tanzania	Low Income	Common	Yes	Yes	Yes	Yes
Togo	Low Income	Civil	No	No	Yes	No
Uganda	Low Income	Common	Yes	Yes	Yes	No
Zambia	Middle Income	Common	Yes	Yes	Yes	No
Zimbabwe	Low Income	Common	Yes	Yes	No	No

Source: National family, inheritance, and land codes and statutes.
Note: — Not available.

Table A.7 Scoresheet 7: Restrictions on and Protection of Women's Labor Rights in African Countries

Country	Income level (2011)	Legal system	Statutory protection for nondiscrimination in the workplace	Statutory protection is granted to equal pay for work of equal value	Women face statutory restrictions on industries in which they may work	Pregnant women face statutory restrictions on industries in which they may work	Women face statutory restrictions on hours they may work	Pregnant women face statutory restrictions on hours they may work	Statutory requirements exist providing maternity leave, mandating duration of maternity leave, and way in which it is funded	Mandated minimum duration of paid maternity leave	Mandated percentage of salary to be paid by employer during maternity leave
Angola	Middle Income	Civil	Yes	Yes	No	Yes	No	Yes	Yes	56 days	100
Benin	Low Income	Civil	Yes	Yes	Yes	Yes	No	Yes	Yes	14 weeks	100
Botswana	Middle Income	Common	No	No	No	No	No	No	Yes	12 weeks	25
Burkina Faso	Low Income	Civil	Yes	Yes	Yes	Yes	Yes	Yes	Yes	14 weeks	100
Burundi	Low Income	Civil	Yes	Yes	Yes	Yes	Yes	Yes	Yes	12 weeks	50
Cameroon	Middle Income	Civil	Yes	Yes	Yes	Yes	Yes	Yes	Yes	14 weeks	100
Cape Verde	Middle Income	Civil	Yes	Yes	No	Yes	No	Yes	Yes	45 days	Variable formula
Central African Republic	Low Income	Civil	Yes	Yes	Yes	Yes	Yes	Yes	Yes	14 weeks	50
Chad	Low Income	Civil	Yes	Yes	Yes	Yes	Yes	Yes	Yes	14 weeks	50
Comoros	Low Income	Civil	Yes	Yes	Yes	Yes	Yes	Yes	Yes	14 weeks	100
Congo, Demo. Rep.	Low Income	Civil	Yes	Yes	Yes	Yes	Yes	Yes	Yes	14 weeks	67
Congo, Rep.	Middle Income	Civil	Yes	Yes	Yes	Yes	Yes	Yes	Yes	15 weeks	50
Côte d'Ivoire	Middle Income	Civil	Yes	Yes	Yes	Yes	Yes	Yes	Yes	14 weeks	100
Equatorial Guinea	Middle Income	Civil	Yes	Yes	No	Yes	No	Yes	Yes	12 weeks	75
Eritrea	Low Income	Civil	Yes	No	Yes	Yes	No	Yes	Yes	60 days	100
Ethiopia	Low Income	Civil	Yes	Yes	Yes	Yes	No	Yes	Yes	90 days	100
Gabon	Middle Income	Civil	Yes	Yes	Yes	Yes	Yes	Yes	Yes	14 weeks	100
Gambia, The	Low Income	Common	No	No	No	No	No	No	Yes	12 weeks	100

Country	Income	Legal							Duration	Benefit (%)
Ghana	Middle Income	Common	Yes	No	No	No	Yes	Yes	12 qeeks	100
Guinea	Low Income	Civil	Yes	Yes	Yes	No	Yes	Yes	14 weeks	100
Guinea-Bissau	Low Income	Civil	Yes	Yes	Yes	No	No	Yes	60 days	100
Kenya	Low Income	Common	Yes	No	No	No	No	Yes	3 months	100
Lesotho	Middle Income	Common	Yes	Yes	Yes	No	Yes	Yes	12 weeks	0
Liberia	Low Income	Common	No	No	Yes	No	No	No	n.a.	n.a.
Madagascar	Low Income	Civil	Yes	Yes	Yes	Yes	Yes	Yes	14 weeks	100
Malawi	Low Income	Common	Yes	No	No	No	No	Yes	8 weeks	100
Mali	Low Income	Civil	Yes	Yes	Yes	Yes	Yes	Yes	14 weeks	100
Mauritania	Middle Income	Civil	Yes	Yes	Yes	Yes	Yes	Yes	14 weeks	100
Mauritius	Middle Income	Civil	No	Yes	Yes	Yes	Yes	Yes	12 weeks	100
Mozambique	Low Income	Civil	Yes	No	No	No	Yes	Yes	60 days	100
Namibia	Middle Income	Common	Yes	No	No	No	Yes	Yes	12 weeks	80
Niger	Low Income	Civil	Yes	Yes	Yes	No	Yes	Yes	14 weeks	50
Nigeria	Middle Income	Common	Yes	Yes	No	Yes	No	Yes	12 weeks	50
Rwanda	Low Income	Civil	Yes	No	Yes	No	Yes	Yes	12 weeks	67
São Tomé and Principe	Middle Income	Civil	Yes	Yes	Yes	Yes	Yes	Yes	60 days	100
Senegal	Middle Income	Civil	Yes	Yes	Yes	Yes	Yes	Yes	14 weeks	100
Seychelles	Middle Income	Common	Yes	No	No	No	Yes	Yes	10 weeks	Flat rate for 10 weeks
Sierra Leone	Low Income	Common	—	Yes	—	Yes	—	—	—	—
Somalia	Low Income	Civil	—	—	—	—	—	Yes	14 weeks	50
South Africa	Middle Income	Common	Yes	No	No	No	Yes	Yes	4 months	45
Sudan	Middle Income	Common	No	Yes	Yes	Yes	No	Yes	8 weeks	100
Swaziland	Middle Income	Common	Yes	Yes	No	No	No	Yes	12 weeks	0
Tanzania	Low Income	Common	Yes	No	Yes	Yes	Yes	Yes	84—100 days	100
Togo	Low Income	Civil	Yes	No	Yes	Yes	Yes	Yes	14 weeks	100
Uganda	Low Income	Common	Yes	Yes	Yes	No	No	Yes	60 days	100
Zambia	Middle Income	Common	No	No	No	No	No	Yes	12 weeks	100
Zimbabwe	Low Income	Common	Yes	No	No	No	No	Yes	98 days	100

Source: National labor codes and statutes.
Note: — Not available.

Appendix B

Comparison of Databases on Women and the Law

Table B.1 Comparison of databases on women and the law

Indicator	Women–LEED–Africa (47 countries)	Women, Business, and the Law 2010 (28 countries)	Food and Agriculture Organization Land Rights Database (28 countries)
Sources of law	Constitutions, international conventions, and statutes, each reported separately	Constitutions, international conventions, and statutes, but database does not identify source of law determining each indicator	Constitutions, international conventions, and statutes, each reported separately
Treatment of customary law	Recognition in constitution, statutes, or both; extent of limitations on gender-based nondiscrimination protections	Not included	Recognition in constitution, statutes, or both
Property and land rights	Property rights in marriage, divorce, and inheritance; land rights	Gender equality in movable and immovable property	Land rights
Legal capacity	Statutes and recognition of customary and religious law; equality in conducting economic transactions independently (for example, opening a bank account or working outside the home)	Indicator shows whether legal capacity is "equal" or "unequal" but does not identify which transactions trip the indicator (future editions may provide this information)	Not included
Labor	Provisions based on International Labour Organization (ILO) conventions, national constitutions, and statutes, each reported separately	Provisions based on ILO conventions, national constitutions, and statutes; includes parental leave	Not included
Database of laws	Yes	Yes	Yes
Additional material	Examples from case law where conflicting or overlapping sources of law apply to illustrate how women's economic rights are interpreted in practice	Information on credit bureaus and small claims courts	Statistics on land ownership

Database of Court Cases

Table C.1 Database of court cases

Country/case	Date	Court	Citation	Source	Ruling
Botswana					
Molomo v. Molomo	1979	High Court	[1979–80] B.L.R. 250	Griffiths (1983)	Litigants were sophisticated people with business acumen (school teachers who traveled and lived in the capital). The court awarded the wife half the value of the cattle, a house, and custody of the couple's young children, rejecting the application of customary life on the basis of the mode of life exemption.
Moisakamo v. Moisakamo	1980	High Court	MC 106	Griffiths (1983)	The court ruled that there is no automatic right to equal division of property and looked instead at the sources of the couple's assets. Because their income was produced by the wife's efforts, she was theoretically entitled to more than half of their assets, but pleadings stated that both parties contributed equally. The mode of life provision was not applied, because the marriage took place after passage of the Married Women's Property Act.
Busang v. Busang	1982	Customary Court, Chief's court	MO 378/82	Griffiths (1983)	The chief's court made no award to the wife, on the grounds that she had practiced witchcraft and deserted her husband. It accepted the earlier decree of divorce from the High Court based on these allegations.
Seitshiro v. Seitshiro	1982	Customary Court, Tswana Chief	—	Griffiths (1983)	The court awarded the wife four head of cattle plus the cattle jointly acquired. She was not awarded estate cattle. Customary law allows a wife to acquire property on divorce, but customary property is excluded.
Rabantheng v. Rabentheng	1988	High Court	[1988] B.L.R. 260	Quansah (2009)	The court awarded the wife one-third of the value of the marital home, which was in the sole name of the husband, because she had made a direct financial contribution. The court did not recognize the wife's nonmonetary contributions.
AG of the Republic of Botswana v. Unity Dow	1995	Court of Appeal	[1994] (6) BCLR 1	Lambert and Scribner (2008)	The court ruled that the citizenship laws, which did not allow women married to nonnationals to pass their nationality on to their children, was discriminatory and unconstitutional. Although discrimination on the grounds of gender was not specifically addressed in the Constitution, the court held that such a provision could be implied in order to give effect to the objectives of the Constitution. The court's interpretation thereby expanded the ambit of the constitutional clause on nondiscrimination.

Case	Year	Court	Citation	Source	Summary
Mbenge v. Mbenge	1997	Court of Appeal	[1997] B.L.R.142	Quansah (2009)	The court ruled that the principle of universal partnership created a right of the cohabiting woman to 50 percent of the couple's assets upon divorce. The ruling affirmed the common law right to property for women in consensual unions or quasi-customary marriages.
Bodutu v. Motsamai	2006	High Court	[2006] 2 B.L.R. 252	Quansah (2009)	The court affirmed the common law right to property for women in consensual union or quasi-customary marriages, indicating that universal partnership can arise through a tacit agreement.
Mogorosi v. Mogorosi	2008	Court of Appeal	[2008] BWCA 18	Hubbard (2010)	The court applied the principle of universal partnership in recognizing the woman's nonmonetary contribution to the business run by the man with whom she had cohabited for 15 years. The case originated in the customary courts. The woman had worked for the business and performed household duties, including caring for the couple's children. The court awarded her a 20 percent share of the man's estate, valued at the date on which the cohabitation broke down. The ruling affirmed the common law right to property for women in consensual unions or quasi-customary marriages.
Cameroon					
Alice Fodje v. Nadans Kette	1986	Court of Appeal	[1986] BCA/45/86	Ebi (2008)	The court recognized the property rights of a wife in a customary marriage on divorce. Judge Florence Arrey held that the wife had the right to occupy the marital home and to collect rent from two other houses.
Ashu v. Ashu	1986	High Court	BCA/62/86	Ngwafor (1999)	The court ruled that a wife is not entitled to a share of the marital estate because she herself is property according to customary law.
Affaire Succession Lonla Kuete	1991	Court of Appeal West Province	Arret No. 2/ Coutume of 24 October 1991	Ebi (2008)	The court rejected primogeniture in favor of male heirs.
Chibikom v. Zamcho Florence	1993	Supreme Court	No. 14/L of 4 February 1993	Ebi (2008)	The court ruled that any custom that deprives women of succession rights to their parents' estate is unconstitutional and contrary to public order. The custom that a married woman did not have the capacity to administer her father's estate was overruled.

continued

Table C.1 Database of court cases *continued*

Country/case	Date	Court	Citation	Source	Ruling
Gboron Yaccoumba v. Anemena Suzanne v. Mbombo Asang and Ndam Emile	1997	Court of Appeal Bafoussam	Arret No. 002/c 23 October 1997	Ebi (2008)	The court rejected a widow's claim to entitlement from her deceased husband's estate under Islamic law on the grounds that under local customary law, a wife does not inherit.
Baba Iyayi v. Hadija Aninatoou	2000	Supreme Court	Arret No. 083 of 32 March 2000	Ebi (2008)	The court ruled that French law supersedes Muslim law if the deceased contracted a civil marriage. If he did not, Islamic law applies.
Ethiopia					
Ms. Kedija Bashir	Constitutional Court	House of Federation	Cassation Division Case No. 12400	Ashenafi (2005)	The court ruled that under the Constitution, the party had the right to choose between a civil court and sharia court. Sharia courts have jurisdiction only when all the parties consent. Article 34(5) of the Constitution states: "This Constitution shall not preclude the right of parties to voluntarily submit their dispute for adjudication in accordance with religious or customary laws. Particulars should be determined by law."
Gabon					
P.E.N. and F.E.O. v. D.N.B.	1996	Court of Cassation (highest Court)	Case no.13/95-96 La revue de CERDIP, 131 (2002)	Odinkalu (2005)	The court ruled that the Nkodje clan's custom known as Ntoumou precludes civic intermarriage among clan members whether or not consanguinity or affinity between them is established.
The Gambia					
Saika Saidy v. Theresa Saide, Albert Henry Shrubsole and Jukba Saidy	1973	Supreme Court	Civil Suits 1972-A-147 NS 148	Journal of African Law (1974)	The court restricted tesamentary discretion in a case involving a Gambian Muslim who willed all his property to his wife. His brother challenged the will. The court ruled that the deceased could not dispose of his property under the Wills Act 1837, that sharia law governed his estate. The repugnancy test applied only to customary law, not sharia.
Ghana					
Quartey v. Martey and Anor	1959	High Court	Ghana L. Rep. 377	Fenrich and Higgins (2002)	The court ruled that assets acquired through the joint effort of a man, his wife, and their children and any property the man acquired as a result are, by customary law, the individual property of the man. The wife's nonmonetary contribution is not recognized under customary law. A different decision would have been reached if there had been a direct financial contribution by the wife.

Gyamaah v. Buor	1962	High Court	[1962] 1 G.L.R 196	Kuenyehia (2008)	A widow who assisted her husband in developing and cultivating 11 cocoa farms sought a court order declaring that she was entitled to a share of the farms following his death. Ownership of the farms had passed to the heirs based on Akan customary laws of inheritance. The lower court held in favor of the widow's right to a share of the property on the grounds that she had assisted in cultivating the farms. On appeal, the High Court overturned the lower court order, holding that the widow had no right to the property and could receive a share of the property only because the heir had previously agreed to share an unspecified portion of the property with her. The court held that, based on the custom of the parties, the wife was not entitled to any specific share of the property but would receive whatever the defendant heir chose to give her. Significantly, the High Court stated that had the widow's assistance been in the form of a substantial financial contribution, she would have been "entitled as of right to a share in the properties acquired by her husband."'
Esselfie v. Quarcoo	1992	Court of Appeal	[1992] 2 Ghana L. Rep. 180	Fenrich and Higgins (2002)	Chief Justice Georgina Wood held that a marriage can be recognized even if customary rites and ceremonies were not fully performed if (a) the parties agreed to live together as man and wife and they did in fact so live; and (b) they obtained the consent of their two families to the marriage. Consent, the court rule, can be implied by conduct.
Kenya					
I v I	1971	High Court	[1971] EA 278	Baraza (2009)	The court held that the Married Women's Property Act applied to marriages solemnized in Kenya.
Karanja v. Karanja	1976	High Court	(2008) 1 KLR (G&F) 171; [1976-80] 1 KLR 389	Baraza (2009)	The court rejected the argument that under Kikuyu customary law women do not own property because they are under their husbands. It rejected discriminatory customary law regarding division of property on divorce, applying statutory law (the Married Women's Property Act) to award the wife one-third of the couple's property.
Otieno v. Ougo	1987	Court of Appeal	(2008) 1 KLR (G&F)	Stamp (1991)	The claim of the widow and children to determine the burial arrangements for the deceased (with resulting implications for the division of the estate) were set aside in favour of the customary laws of the husband's clan.

continued

Table C.1 Database of court cases *continued*

Country/case	Date	Court	Citation	Source	Ruling
Kivuitu v. Kivuitu	1991	Court of Appeal	1991 2 KAR 241	Baraza (2009)	The court applied the principle of nondiscrimination and equal protection of the law in recognizing the wife's nonmonetary contribution in the form of domestic chores and labor on their subsistence farm.
Essa v. Essa	1996	High Court	(1996) EA 53	Baraza (2009)	The court relied on the Married Women's Property Act to award property to a divorced woman who had married under Islamic law. The court reiterated the holding in I v. I that the Married Women's Property Act applies equally to Muslims and non-Muslims.
Omar Said Jaiz v. Naame Ali	—	—	—	Baraza (2009)	The court took *Kivuitu* one step farther to rule that, even without clear evidence of the extent of the actual contribution made by both spouses, the property is considered joint property because it was acquired through a joint venture. The ruling thus recognized the nonmonetary contribution of the wife.
Estate of Lerionka Ole Ntutu	2000	High Court	[2008]eKLR	Killlander (2010)	The court overruled the application of the Maasai custom that disentitles daughters from claiming their father's inheritance in ruling that the daughters of a Maasai man who died intestate had a legitimate claim to inherit his property. The court overruled the application of customary law in inheritance of agricultural land in certain areas to the extent that it discriminated against the daughters. The judge noted that it would violate human dignity and gender equality to construe the Constitution as allowing discrimination against women.
In re Wachokire	2002	Chief Magistrates Court Thika	Succession Cause No. 192 of 2000	Partners for Gender Justice Report of the Accra Conference (2008)	Magistrate H. A. Omondi ruled that under Kikuyu customary law, an unmarried woman lacked equal inheritance rights because of the expectation that she would marry. The court held that this customary provision discriminates against women, in violation of Section 82(1) of the Kenyan Constitution. It also violates Article 18(3) of the Banjul Charter and Article 15(1)–(3) of the Convention on the Elimination of All Forms of Discrimination against Women (CEDAW), which provide for legal equality for men and women.
Andrew Manunzyu Musyoka (Deceased)	2005	High Court	eKLR 1, 7 (High Court] at Machakos)	Ndulo (2011)	The court relied on the principles of equality and nondiscrimination in CEDAW to safeguard women's property rights against discriminatory Kamba customs that held that a daughter is not supposed to inherit from her father's estate. Justice Lenaola used CEDAW to declare the custom repugnant to natural justice and the doctrines of equity.

Case	Year	Court	Citation	Source	Holding
Mary Rono v. Jane Rono and another	2005	Court of Appeal	(2008) 1 KLR (G&F)	Ndulo (2011)	The deceased died intestate, leaving behind a vast tract of land and other properties. The court held that there was no reasonable basis for drawing a distinction between sons and daughters in determining inheritance, that the principles of equality and nondiscrimination prevailed over customary law, which disinherits women. The court applied international law directly to Kenya, a dualist state, basing its action on contemporary thinking on common law theory, which allows application of international and treaty law even where they are not domesticated where there is no conflict. Constitutional principles of equality and nondiscrimination trumped customary law.
Echaria v. Echaria	2007	Court of Appeal	[2007] Eklr; [2007] KECA 1 (2 February 2007) [	Federation of Women Lawyer's Kenya (FIDA) and Georgetown University Law Center (2008)	A five-judge bench overturned earlier decisions of the High Court and Court of Appeal on the recognition of nonmonetary contribution, holding that division of property in marriage is determined by the general laws of contract in Kenya and that a woman must demonstrate having made a monetary contribution. The court rejected the principle of nonmonetary contribution. This decision applies to all similar cases in the future, unless they can be distinguished on the facts or overturned by a full bench of the Court of Appeal.
Lesotho					
Shuping v. Motsoahae	1977	High Court	[1977] LLR p.174	Cotula (2006)	The court held that family property is administered exclusively by the husband, upholding the alienation of a joint estate without the wife's consent. This decision may be affected by the Legal Capacity of Married Persons Act 9 of 2006, which applies to civil but not customary marriages.
Malawi					
Poya v. Poya	1979	High Court	Civil Appeal No. 38 of 1979 N.T.A.C.	Mwambene (2005) a	The court ruled that the marital home built by the husband in the wife's village belongs to the wife. Customary law benefited women in this instance.
Malinki v. Malinki, Mtegha v. Mtegha	1994	Magistrates Court	MC 9MLR 441	Women and Law Southern Africa (2009)	The court ruled that a spouse wishing to claim a share of property not in his or her name must demonstrate having made a financial contribution to its acquisition. Contributions to maintenance of property items, housekeeping, and child care are not sufficient.
Sinalo v Sinapyanga and others	1995	High Court	Civil Cause No. 544/1995	Women and Law Southern Africa (2009)	The court awarded a widow 20 percent of the business that formed part of the estate of her deceased husband based on evidence of the financial contribution she had made to it but rejected her claim to a proprietary interest in her deceased husband's house after refusing to recognized her nonmonetary contribution without evidence of domestic labor.

continued

Table C.1 Database of court cases *continued*

Country/case	Date	Court	Citation	Source	Ruling
Georgina Mazunyane v. Rodney Chalera	2004	Magistrates Court	Civil Case No. 75 of 2004, Mulunguzu Magistrate Court (unreported)	Mwambene (2005)	The court divided marital property equitably on customary divorce.
Nyangulu v. Nyangulu	—	High Court	10 Malawi Law Reports 435	Women and Law Southern Africa (2009)	The court did not recognize the wife's nonmonetary contribution, ruling that "inference of joint ownership of property is not to be made from a mere fact of marriage."
Barnet Phiri v. Fanny Phiri	2006	High Court	Civil Appeal Cause No. 15 2006	Women and Law Southern Africa (2009)	The court held that on dissolution of a customary marriage, all marital property, not just property officially held jointly, must be divided equitably.
Mauritius					
Bhewa v. Government of Mauritius	1990	Supreme Court	[1991] LRC (Const)	http://www.endawnow.org/en/articles/764-family-law-and-marriage-laws.html	The court ruled that a Muslim couple's right to apply certain Islamic laws on marriage, divorce, devolution of property, and polygamy is not guaranteed by the Constitution, because these practices violate civil laws that protect the common good and prevent discrimination against women. The appeal by the petitioners from the lower court was dismissed. The ruling established that civil law principles prevail over parties in a religious marriage.
Namibia					
Myburg v. Commercial Bank of Namibia	2000	Supreme Court	NR255 (SC)	Hubbard (2005)	The court ruled that unconstitutional common laws are automatically invalidated by the provisions of the Constitution. It indicated that customary law in force at the time of independence would survive only if it were not in conflict with the Constitution.
Mofuka v. Mofuka	2001	High Court	2001 NR 318 (HC)	Hubbard (2005)	The court ruled that an unregistered oral prenuptial agreement, express or implied, was valid. Such an agreement binds only the husband and wife, however, not a third party.
Berendt v. Stuurman	2003	High Court	Unreported Judgment Case No (P) 105/2003	Hubbard (2005)	The court declared several sections of Native Proclamation 15 of 1928 unconstitutional and gave the legislature a deadline for replacing the offensive sections. Reform of the offending provision has not yet been carried out. Provisions relating to the administration of estates were changed to give a choice to the indigenous population.

Nigeria

Case	Year	Court	Citation	Source	Description
Nezianya v. Nezianya	1963	—	1963 NLR 352	Women Aid Collective (2008)	The court held that under the native law and custom of the Onitsha, a widow's possession of her deceased husband's property is not that of a stranger, is not adverse to her husband's family, and does not make her the owner, however long she holds the property.
Adesubokan v. Yinusa	1971	Supreme Court	[1971] N.N.L.R. 77	Oba (2011)	The court upheld the right of a Muslim man to write an English statutory will.
Egunjobi v. Egunjobi	1976	Western State Court of Appeal	[1976] 2 F.N.R. 78	Women in Law and Development Africa—Nigeria (2002)	The court awarded the wife a third of the marital property after she provided evidence of her actual contribution, including receipts for the construction of the building acquired during the marriage. The case recognized the wife's nonmonetary contribution but required proof of contribution to establish the share to which she was entitled.
Adeyemi v. Adeyemi	1985	—	[1985] Suit No CB/354D/85	Women in Law and Development Africa—Nigeria (2002)	The court held that the failure of the wife to provide receipts in evidence of her monetary contribution to the property acquired during the marriage disentitled her to the property upon divorce. Her nonmonetary contribution was not recognized.
Kaffi v. Kaffi	1986	Court of Appeal	[1986] 3 Nigeria Weekly Law Report (NWLR); part 2; p. 175.	Women in Law and Development Africa—Nigeria (2002); IFHR (2008)	The court held that the wife's contribution need not be financial in nature. The fact that the wife took care of her husband and family and that the husband had the peace of mind to acquire the property gave the wife an interest in such property. It recognized her nonmonetary contribution under the just and equitable provision in the Matrimonial Causes Act 1970.
Amadi v. Nwosu	1989	Supreme Court	[1992] LPELR-SC.14/1989	IFHR (2008)	The Supreme Court upheld the High Court's decision that in a customary law marriage, where a wife does not have a right to property ownership, she must prove her monetary contribution to family property before she can invoke other laws to claim joint ownership of property. Under customary law, nonmonetary contribution is not recognized.
Nzekwu v. Nzekwu	1989	Supreme Court	[1989] 2 NWLR P.373	IFHR (2008)	The court held that a widow's dealings with her husband's property must receive the consent of his family, that she cannot claim the property as her own. It ruled that she cannot administer her husband's estate on her own and has no ownership rights to that estate.

continued

Table C.1 Database of court cases *continued*

Country/case	Date	Court	Citation	Source	Ruling
Onwchekwe v. Onwuchekwe	1991	Court of Appeal	(1991) 5 NWLR (pt. 197) 739	IFHR (2008)	The court held that the wife did not make a direct financial contribution to the marital home and that her labor was not sufficient to entitle her to a share of the martial assets. It also upheld that the Isikwuato custom in which a wife is owned with her properties by her husband as chattel is not repugnant. According to the ruling, "Because the court is dealing with a customary law, which is peculiar to the people, the determining factor or factors should not be the English Common Law but must be Nigerian Law. It is good law that customary law cannot be said to be repugnant to natural justice, equity and good conscience merely because it is inconsistent with or contrary to English law, as the test of the validity of customary law is never English law."
Nkeaka v. Nkeaka	1994	Court of Appeal	5 NWLR (Part 346) 599	IFHR (2008)	The court ruled that daughters cannot inherit land under customary law but can inherit money.
Akinnubu v. Akinnnubi	1997	Supreme Court	(1997) 2 NLWR 144	Nwabueze (2010)	The court confirmed the legal legitimacy of the Yoruba practice in which daughters but not widows can inherit from men who die intestate, ruling that "under Yoruba customary law, a widow under intestacy is regarded as part of the estate of her deceased husband to be administered or inherited by the deceased family. She could neither be entitled to apply for a grant of letters of administration nor appointed as co-administratrix."
Mojekwu v. Mojekwu	1997	Court of Appeal	(1997) 7 NWLR; Pt 512; 283	International Federation of Human Rights Nigeria NGO Coalition Shadow Report (2008)	The court set aside the Oliekpe custom that disentitles a daughter from inheriting the property of her father where no son survives him.
Mojekwu and others v. Ejikeme and others	1999	Court of Appeal	5 NWLR 402,	Women in Law and Development Africa—Nigeria (2002)	The two great-grandsons and the granddaughter of a man who died intestate appealed the ruling of a lower court in favor of five male members of the family of his brother. The case involved the practice of Nnewi, which pertains when a man leaves behind daughters but no sons. Under these circumstances, the daughter must remain unmarried and bear children who effectively become her dead father's heirs to inherit and carry on the male lineage. The appellants claimed that Nnewi had been performed for the deceased's daughter (the appellants' mother and grandmother),

which entitled her and her children to inherit the property. The respondents claimed that the custom of Nnewi had been performed for the deceased's other daughter, Comfort, entitling her and any of her children to inherit the property. Because Comfort had died childless, however, under customary law, the deceased died without a surviving male heir, thereby causing the property to pass to the deceased's brother or the brother's male issue. On appeal, the court found that these customs discriminated against women and were "repugnant to the principles of natural justice, equity and good sense." The court concluded that the appellants, as blood relations, were entitled to inherit the estate of the deceased and that it would be inequitable to throw them out of their home. Although not explicitly stated, the court based its ruling on the fundamental rights guaranteed to women under Nigeria's constitution and an international convention to which Nigeria was a party.

Case	Year	Court	Citation	Source	Summary
Mojekwu v. Iwuchukwu (appeal of Mojekwu v. Mojekwu)	2004	Supreme Court	(2004) NWLR Pt 883 pg. 196	Nwabueze (2010)	The Supreme Court overturned the earlier decision of the Court of Appeal that there was no justification for the lower court to have pronounced the Ibo custom of Nnewsi repugnant to natural justice, equity, and good conscience, as its repugnancy was not part of the issues joined by the parties. Justice Uwaifo ruled that the language used in the lower court made the pronouncement so general and far-reaching that it seemed to undermine, and was capable of causing strong feelings against, all customs that failed to recognize a role for women. The undermining of customary law in this way was not justifiable.
Obusez v. Obusez	2001	Court of Appeal	[2001] 15 N.W.L.R. 377	Nwabueze (2010)	The brothers of the deceased argued that they—and not the man's widow and infant children—were entitled to administer his estate. They based their argument on Agbor customary law 25, which deems a widow to be chattel to be inherited and therefore, they claimed, unqualified for letters of administration. They invoked the fact that the widow had been married under Marriage Act 27 rather than customary law. The trial court held that a widow who had been married under statute is not a chattel and is entitled to letters of administration. In affirming this decision, the Court of Appeal suggested that the opposite would be true of a widow in the same position who had been married under customary law, in which case Agbor customary law would apply.

continued

Table C.1 Database of court cases   *continued*

Country/case	Date	Court	Citation	Source	Ruling
Uke v. Iro	2001	Court of Appeal	11 NWLR 196	International Federation of Human Rights Nigeria NGO Coalition Shadow Report (2008)	The court overruled on constitutional grounds discriminatory customary law relating to inheritance, ruling that any law or custom that seeks to relegate women to the status of second-class citizens, depriving them of their invaluable and constitutionally guaranteed rights, is unconstitutional and should be consigned to history.
Ukeje v. Ukeje	2001	Court of Appeal	11 NWLR 196	International Federation of Human Rights Nigeria NGO Coalition Shadow Report (2008)	The court voided the Igbo law and custom disentitling a daughter from sharing in her father's estate on the grounds that it violates the provisions of Section 42 (2) of the 1999 Constitution.
Amusan v. Olawumi	2002	Court of Appeal	FWLR 1385	International Federation of Human Rights Nigeria NGO Coalition Shadow Report (2008)	The court held that under Yoruba customary law, both sons and daughters are entitled to inherit their parents' land.
Hon. Emokpae and Three Others. v. Mrs. Nekpen Idubor	2003	—	12 NWLR Part 849	IFHR (2008)	The court ruled that the widow of an intestate man who had been married under Bini native law and custom and who was therefore not entitled to inherit can commence an action against the administration of the estate to protect the interest of her children, who are beneficiaries of the estate, and her personal interest, where it is affected by the administration of the estate.
Muhammadu v. Muhammadu	2003	—	[2003] 6 WRN 36	IFHR (2008)	The court ruled that female heirs are allowed to share in an inheritance like male heirs, in a modified manner. Inheritance is determined by Sharia law.
Mgbemere v. Mgbemere and Oyigboku Suit	2004	—	No/WD/143/04	International Federation of Human Rights Nigeria NGO Coalition Shadow Report (2008)	In divorce proceedings, the court granted the wife ownership of one of the properties acquired during the marriage.

South Africa

Case	Year	Court	Citation	Reference	Description
Mabuza v. Mbatha	2003	High Court	[2003] (4) SA 218	Lambert and Scribner (2008)	The court ruled that customary law can regulate marriage, as long as it does not contravene the equality clause in the Constitution.
Nonkululeko Letta Bhe and Others v. Magistrate Khayelitsha	2003	Constitutional Court	Case CCT 49/2003	Fenrich, Higgins, and Tanzer (2007)	The court invalidated a codified customary law of succession as unconstitutional. Bhe, who had been cohabiting with the deceased, and her two daughters were declared the only heirs. The court claimed that the ruling was just and equitable based on the provisions of the South African Intestate Succession Act.
Elizabeth Gumede v. President of the Republic of South Africa	2008	Constitutional Court	Case CCT 50/08 [2008] ZACC 23	Hirschl and Shachar (2009)	The court declared unconstitutional the customary law in which the husband is the family head and owner of all family property, which he may use in exclusive discretion. It held that customary law that implied that women were not fit or competent to own and administer property violated their right to dignity and equality under the constitution.
Hassam v. Jacobs	2008	High Court	Case No. 5704/20045	Osman-Hyder (2011)	The court ruled that a polygamous widow in an Islamic marriage could inherit under the Intestate Succession Act, that there was no justification to exclude her.
Shilubana and Others v. Nwamitwa	2008	Constitutional Court	http://www.constitutionalcourt.org.za/uhtbin/cgisirsi/nMq9DS8Vwd/MAIN/0/57/518/0/J-CCT3-07C	Lambert and Scribner (2008)	The Constitutional Court upheld the decision of the traditional court to allow the daughter of the deceased chief to succeed to his title. The traditional court's decision represented a break with earlier rulings, which restricted succession to male heirs. The Constitutional Court upheld the jurisdiction of traditional courts to evolve customary law in line with contemporary social values.

Swaziland

Case	Year	Court	Citation	Reference	Description
Mary-Joyce Doo Aphane v. Registrar of Deeds, Minister of Justice and Constitutional Affairs and the Attorney General	2010	High Court	Civil case No. 383/2009	IRIN (2010a)	The attempt by a woman, who was married under a community of property regime, to register property jointly in her name and the name of her spouse was not allowed under a provision of the Deeds Registry Act. The court upheld her claim that the provision was discriminatory and therefore unconstitutional. Significantly, the judge (the first woman appointed to the High Court) used her powers under the Constitution to change the wording of the offending provision so that it would allow registration of community property by women. Under Section 151 (2) of the Constitution, the High Court has jurisdiction to enforce fundamental human rights and freedoms guaranteed by the Constitution, including the right to equality, which is guaranteed by the Constitution.

continued

Table C.1 Database of court cases *continued*

Country/case	Date	Court	Citation	Source	Ruling
Attorney General v. Aphane	2010	Supreme Court	[2010] SZSC 32	IRIN (2010b)	The Attorney General appealed the *Mary-Joyce Doo Aphane* case to the Supreme Court. The Supreme Court in May 2010 upheld the unconstitutionality of the discriminatory provision, but overturned the High Court Judge's decision to "severe" and "read in" the Act on this occasion. It suspended the declaration of illegality for a year, allowing married women to register property in the interim, and allowing for Parliament to amend the legislation in the meantime. However, two years later, Parliament has not amended the legislation.
Tanzania					
Bi Hawa Mohamed v. Ally Sefu	1983	Court of Appeal	(9 of 1983) [1983] TZCA 1	Ellis (2007)	The court recognized the domestic role of a housewife as a legitimate contribution to marital welfare entitling her to part of that property on the dissolution of the marriage.
Mohamed Abdallah v. Halima Lisangwe	1988	High Court	TLR 197 Tanzania	Rwebangira (1996)	The court recognized the clearing of the site by the wife where a house was built as nonmonetary contribution. It also observed that during the course of the (Islamic) marriage, during which the house was built, the wife bore children, reared them, and took care of the marital home, freeing her husband to engage in economic activities. She was therefore entitled to the fruits of her efforts on the dissolution of her marriage.
Keticia Bgumba v. Thadeo Maguma and another	1989	High Court	High Court, Mwanza, Mwalusanya J., Civil App. No. 8/89 (July 18 1989)	Rwezaura (1991)	The court recognized the nonmonetary contribution of a woman during the two years she had cohabited in a consensual union with her husband. The court held that the woman had established the existence of a marriage by cohabitation and repute and that she could therefore claim a share or interest in a house in dispute by virtue of section 160(2) of the Law of Marriage Act.
Richard Wilham Sawe v. Woitara Richard Sawe	1992	Court of Appeal	Civil Appeal No. 38 of 1992, TZCA, 9 June 1994	Peter (2007)	The court held that division of marital property at divorce should be done on a 50:50 basis regardless of the mode of acquisition.

Case	Year	Court	Citation	Source	Description
Scholastica Benedict v. Martin Benedict	1993	Court of Appeal	Mwanza Court of Appeal Cil. App. No. 26/88	Rwezaura (1991)	The court upheld discriminatory customary law relating to supremacy of rights of the male heir. The second (junior) wife, who had one daughter by the deceased, had appealed the decision of the lower court upholding the application of customary law in favor of the inheritance rights of a male heir, the eldest son of nine children by the first (senior) wife, over the second wife's rights to reside with her unmarried daughter in the home in which they had lived with the deceased for more than 15 years. The court held that any marital right the second wife had to reside in the house in which she had lived with the deceased was contingent on whether her daughter had a right to the property that was superior to the male heir's right. Because the male heir's right took precedence, even though he, the first wife, and eight other children resided in another house, the court upheld the lower court decision evicting the second wife and her daughter from the home.
Pulcheria Pundugu v. Samuel Huma Pundugu	1995	High Court	TLR 7	Quansah [2004]	The court disregarded Sukuma customary law and awarded the wife part of the marital property based on her nonmonetary contribution on dissolution of the marriage.
Bernado Ephraim v. Holaria Pastory and Another	2001	High Court	(2001) AHRLR 236	Ellis (2007)	The court set aside Haya customary law in favor of the principle of nondiscrimination, ruling that women can inherit land, including clan land under Haya customary law, and are capable of disposing of such land.
Ndossi v. Ndossi	2001	High Court	Civil Appeal No. 13 of 2001	Global Justice Center (n.d.)	Judge E. Munuo, a woman, held that the widow was entitled to administer the estate on behalf of her children under the Constitution, which provides that "every person is entitled to own property and has a right to the protection of that property held in accordance of the law." She further held that Article 9(a) and (f) of the Constitution recognize human rights by requiring "that human dignity is preserved and upheld in accordance with the spirit of the Universal Declaration of Human Rights," explaining that this clause generally domesticates human rights instruments ratified by Tanzania, including the antidiscrimination principles of CEDAW, Articles 2(b) and (f), and the best interest of the child principle found in Article 3 of the Convention on the Rights of the Child.

continued

Table C.1 Database of court cases *continued*

Country/case	Date	Court	Citation	Source	Ruling
Uganda					
Muwanga v. Kintu	1997	High Court	Divorce Appeal No. 135	Ministry of Justice and Constitutional Affairs of Uganda (2008)	The court ruled that a wife in a customary marriage was entitled to marital property, which she had earned through her nonmonetary contributions.
Uganda Association of Women Lawyers v. AG Constitutional Petition No.2 of 2002	2002	Constitutional Court	Constitutional Court, 10 March 2002	Ellis (2006)	The court repealed sections of the Divorce Act that discriminated against women. When a woman sought a divorce, she had to prove adultery and show that her husband had deserted her, been cruel to her, or failed to maintain her. In contrast, a man had to prove only adultery to obtain a divorce. The Strategic Litigation Coalition brought the case. The court declared the discriminatory provisions unconstitutional.
Zambia					
Chibwe v. Chibwe	2000	Supreme Court	Appeal No. 38/2000 SCZ (Zambia)	UN-Habitat (2005)	The court ruled that the wife, who had been married under Ushi customary law, was entitled to property following her divorce. It awarded her the house built by her husband on a plot registered in her name, and ordered the husband to pay her damages for having attempted to defraud her of the house.
Zimbabwe					
Khoza v. Khoza	1997	High Court	HH 106	UN-Habitat (2005)	The couple had been married under customary law for 23 years, during which time the wife had built and maintained the matrimonial homestead, which was on communal land. Upon dissolution of marriage, the court denied her any right to the matrimonial home and residence on the grounds that the marriage was patrilocal. She was awarded the family's town house in Bulawayo, even though her means of subsistence was farming.
Chapeyama v. Matende and Another	2000	High Court	(2) 356 (s)	Government of Zimbabwe (2009)	The spouses were married in 1990 under customary law. During their marriage, they had two children and acquired several properties jointly, including a house registered in both their names. Upon the breakdown of the marriage, the husband made an application to the court to have the wife's name removed from the deed of assignment. The wife counterclaimed for a fair distribution of all asserts in the house. The High Court decided in favor of the wife, holding that the application of the concept of a tacit universal partnership was fully justified. In dismissing the husband's appeal, the Supreme Court recommended a review of marriage laws to specifically recognize unregistered customary law marriages, as was done under the Administration of Estates Act.

Note: — Not available.

References

Ashenafi, Meaza, and Zenebeworke Tadesse. 2005. "Women, HIV/AIDS, Property and Inheritance Rights: The Case of Ethiopia." UNDP New York: UNDP.

Baraza, Nancy. 2009. "Family Law Reforms in Kenya: An Overview." Paper presented at the Heinrich Böll Foundation's Gender Forum, Nairobi, April 30.

Cotula, Lorenzo. 2006. *Gender and Law, Women's Rights in Agriculture.* FAO Legislative Study 76 Rev. 1, Food and Agricultural Organization, Rome.

Ebi, Joseph Nzalie. 2008. "The Structure of Succession Law in Cameroon: Finding a Balance between the Needs and Interests of Different Family Members." Ph.D. thesis, University of Birmingham, Department of Law, United Kingdom.

Ellis, Amanda, Claire Manuel, and Mark Blackden. 2005. *Gender and Economic Growth In Uganda: Unleashing the Power of Women.* World Bank Directions in Development Series, Washington, DC.

Ellis, Amanda, Mark Blackden, Jozefina Cutura, Fiona MacCulloch, and Holger Seebens. 2007. *Gender and Economic Growth in Tanzania.* World Bank FIAS-GEM Series, Washington, DC.

Federation of Women Lawyers–Kenya, and the International Women's Human Rights Clinic, Georgetown University Law Center. 2008. "Kenyan Laws and Harmful Customs Curtail Women's Equal Enjoyment of ICESCR Rights: A Supplementary Submission to the Kenyan Government's Initial Report under the ICESCR," scheduled for review by the Committee on Economic, Social, and Cultural Rights during its 41st session, November 3–21.

Fenrich, Jeanmarie, and Tracy E. Higgins. 2002. "Promise Unfulfilled: Law, Culture, and Women's Inheritance Rights in Ghana." *Fordham International Law Journal* 25: 259–341.

Fenrich, Jeanmarie, Tracy E. Higgins, and Ziona Tanzer. 2007. "Gender Equality and Customary Marriage: Bargaining in the Shadow of Post-Apartheid Pluralism." *Fordham International Law Journal* 30: 1653–708.

Global Justice Center. n.d. "Legal Tools. CEDAW Case Bank." http://www.globaljustice center.net/casebank/bycountry/tanzania.html.

Government of Zimbabwe. 2009. *Zimbabwe CEDAW Report* . Harare.

Griffiths, Anne. 1983. "Legal Duality: Conflict or Concord in Botswana?" *Journal of African Law* 27 (2): 150–61.

Hirschl, Ran, and Ayelet Shachar. 2009. "The New Wall of Separation: Permitting Diversity, Restricting Competition." *Cardozo Law Review* 30: 2535–59.

Hubbard, Dianne, and Beth Terry 2005. *Marital Property in Civil and Customary Marriages: Proposals for Law Reform.* Gender Research and Advocacy Project: Legal Assistance Center, Namibia.

IFHR (International Federation of Human Rights). 2008. *Nigeria NGO Coalition Shadow Report to the CEDAW Committee.* Paris.

IRIN. 2010a. "Swaziland: Some Women Can Now Own Property." February 25. http://www .irinnews.org/Report/88230/SWAZILAND-Some-women-can-now-own-property.

———. 2010b. "Women's Rights Take One Step Forward, Two Steps Back." June 16. http://www.irinnews.org/printreport.aspx?reportid=89510

Journal of African Law. 1974. Editorial on "Cases Supreme Court of the Gambia, Saika Saidy v Theresa Saidie, Albert Henry Shrubsole and Jibaka Saidy." 18: 183–9.

Killander, Magnus, ed. 2010. *International Law and Domestic Human Rights Litigation in Africa.* Pretoria University Law Press, Pretoria.

Kuenyehia, Akua. 2008. "Women, Marriage and Intestate Succession in the Context of Legal Pluralism in Africa." *JENda: A Journal of Cultural and African Women's Studies.* http://www.africaknowledgeproject.org/index.php/jenda/article/view/569.

Lambert, Priscilla, and Druscilla Scribner. 2008. "Gender Matters: A Case Study Analysis of Constitutional Provisions." Paper presented at the annual meeting of the American Political Science Association, Boston, August 28.

Ministry of Justice and Constitutional Affairs of Uganda. 2008. *Final Report on the Integrated Study on Land and Justice.* Kampala.

Mwambene, Lea. 2005. "Divorce in Matrilineal Customary Law Marriage in Malawi: A Comparative Analysis with the Patrilineal Customary Law Marriage in South Africa." University of the Western Cape, Cape Town, South Africa.

Ndulo, Muna. 2011. "African Customary Law, Customs, and Women's Rights." *Cornell Law Faculty Publications* 187, Ithaca, NY. http://scholarship.law.cornell.edu/facpub/187.

Ngwafor, Ephraim. 1991. "Cameroon: Property Rights for Women: A Bold Step in the Wrong Direction." *Journal of Family Law* 29 (2): 297–302.

Nwabueze, Remigius N. 2010. "Securing Widows' Sepulchral Rights Through the Nigerian Constitution." *Harvard Human Rights Journal* 23: 141–55.

Oba, Abdulmumini A.2011. "Religious and Customary Laws in Nigeria." *Emory International Law Review* 25: 881–95.

Osman-Hyder, Munirah. 2011. "The Impact and Consequences of Hassam and Jacobs on Polygamous Marriages." *Stellenbosch Law Review* 22 (2): 233–46.

Partners for Gender Justice. 2008. *The Role of the Judiciary in Promoting Gender Justice in Africa.* Report of the Accra Conference. Accra.

Peter, Chris Maina, and Helen Kijo-Bisimba. 2007. *Justice in Tanzania: Quarter of a Century of the Court of Appeal.* Legal and Human Rights Center. Mkuki Na Nyoka Publishers, Dar Es Salaam.

Quansah, E. K. 2004. "Recent Developments: Determining Matrimonial Residence of Non-Domiciled Spouses: The Applicable Law in Botswana." *Journal of African Law* 48: 104–10.

———. 2009. "Some Contemporary Challenges Facing Family Law in Botswana." *University of Botswana Law Journal* 9 (June): 25–48

Odinkalu, Chidi A. 2005. *Pluralism and the Fulfillment of Justice Needs in Africa.* Open Society Institute, Africa Governance Monitoring and Advocacy Project, New York.

Rwebangira, Magdelena K. 1996. *The Legal Status of Women and Poverty in Tanzania.* Nordika Afrikain Institutet, Uppsala, Sweden

Rwezaura, B.A. 1990–91. "Tanzania: Family Law and the New Bill of Rights." *Journal of Family Law* 29: 453–61.

Stamp, Patricia. 1991. "Burying Otieno: The Politics of Gender and Ethnicity in Kenya." *Signs* 16 (4): 808–45.

UN-Habitat. 2005. *Land Tenure and Housing Review Zambia*. Nairobi.

WACOL (Women's Aid Collective). 2008. *CEDAW and Accountability to Gender Equality in Nigeria Shadow Report*. Lagos.

Women and Law Southern Africa. 2009. *Malawi CEDAW Shadow Report*. December, Limbe.

Women in Law and Development Africa–Nigeria. 2002 *Advocacy for Better Implementation of Women's Rights in Africa*. July, Lagos.

Index

Boxes, figures, notes, and tables are indicated by b, f, n, and t following the page number.